THE PEACEFUL SLEEPER

Praise for Chrissy Lawler and
The Peaceful Sleeper

"Finally, a book that successfully tames the Wild West of sleep training! Chrissy Lawler acknowledges and explains the complexity of baby sleep while providing clear, accessible steps to make restful nights a reality in your home. And if that isn't enough, she'll have you laughing the whole way through."

—Larry J. Nelson, Ph.D., Professor at
Brigham Young University, School of Family Life

"*The Peaceful Sleeper* offers exhausted parents a calm, evidence-based path through one of the most polarizing topics in modern parenting. With deep clinical expertise and real-life experience, Chrissy Lawler empowers families to build healthy sleep in a way that supports secure attachment, parental well-being, and the entire family system. This book replaces fear and confusion with clarity, confidence, and compassion."

—Dr. Morgan Cutlip, Author and
Relationship Expert

"Sleep is the thing that drives new parents crazy—and it's also the most important thing for your baby's growth and development. In *The Peaceful Sleeper*, therapist and sleep expert Chrissy Lawler gives straightforward, real-world guidance to teach your baby how to sleep soundly and independently. Good sleep isn't luck—it's a skill your baby can learn."

—Sharon Mazel, Parenting Expert and Author of
Bite-Sized Parenting: Your Baby's First Year

THE PEACEFUL SLEEPER

An Intuitive Approach
to Baby Sleep

Chrissy Lawler,
LMFT

JB JOSSEY-BASS™

A Wiley Brand

For general information on our other products and services or for technical support, please contact our Customer Care Department within the United States at (800) 762-2974, outside the United States at (317) 572-3993 or fax (317) 572-4002.

Wiley also publishes its books in a variety of electronic formats. Some content that appears in print may not be available in electronic formats. For more information about Wiley products, visit our web site at www.wiley.com.

Library of Congress Control Number is Available

Cover Design: Paul McCarthy
Cover Art: © Lawler Professional Services, LLC.

Printed and bound by CPI Group (UK) Ltd, Croydon, CR0 4YY

C9781394328864_060226

To Tom—my very best friend and partner in love, laughter,
and all the chaos
And to Maddie, Paisley, London, and Nolan—my favorite girl gang

Contents

Acknowledgments   *xi*

About the Author   *xiii*

Introduction   *xv*

PART I   PARENTING IN THE MODERN AGE   **1**

1   What Exactly Is Sleep Training?   **3**

**2   Everyone Is an Expert
(and Everything Is on Fire!)**   **9**

3   Debunking the Myths   **17**

PART II   SLEEP IS LIFE   **29**

4   Why Quality Sleep Matters for Baby   **31**

5   Why Quality Sleep Matters for Parents   **41**

**6   Why Quality Baby Sleep Matters
for the Rest of the Family**   **51**

**PART III   SLEEP TRAINING IN THE OVERALL
PARENTING PICTURE**   **55**

7   Secure Attachment   **57**

**8   The Gifts of Independence, Resilience,
and Self-Soothing**   **69**

9   The Zone of Proximal Development   **77**

PART IV   ESTABLISHING A STRONG SLEEP FOUNDATION (0–4 MONTHS)   83

10   Understanding Newborn Sleep   85

11   Feeding and Timing   93

12   Calming Strategies and Treating Discomfort   109

PART V   SLEEP TRAINING   125

13   The Importance of Four Months and Teaching Independent Sleep   127

14   The 10-Minute Method   135

15   Naps   153

16   Sleeping Through the Night   163

17   The Other Three Methods and Special Considerations   175

PART VI   LIFE AFTER SLEEP TRAINING   191

18   Scheduling   193

19   Sleep After Sleep Training   201

20   Nap Trapped: When Sacrifice Backfires   207

Conclusion   *221*
Appendix 1: How to Choose Your Approach to Sleep Training   *223*
Appendix 2: Creating a Sleep Log   *227*
Appendix 3: Sleep Training Twins   *235*
Notes   *241*
Index   *263*

Acknowledgments

Writing this book has been the fulfillment of a lifelong dream, and it would not have been possible without so many people who believed in me and cheered me on.

First, thank you to Tom—the most incredible husband and the kind of father I always hoped my children would have. Thank you for always supporting my goals and dreams and running back up to make them happen.

To my girls, the inspiration behind every page:

- Maddie—who first made me a mom and taught me how to love in an entirely new way
- Paisley—endlessly creative, funny, and full of life
- London—pure sweetness, the gentlest soul
- Nolan—fire and passion wrapped in the sweetest silliness

You girls will move mountains. I'm honored to be yours.

To my Mom, who taught me to be confident, brave, and independent, and who always celebrated my love of learning.

To my Dad, who made my education and life experiences possible and instilled the confidence that has carried me through.

To Ashley, the greatest sister and friend a girl could ask for, and to my brothers Ben, Matt, and Dave, who led by example, offered wise advice, and gave me big shoes to fill.

A special thanks to Sam Ofman, who first convinced me to write a book, and to the entire Jossey-Bass team and my editors, who have worked tirelessly to bring it to life.

To my favorite professors Larry Nelson, Laura Walker, and Roy Bean—thank you for shaping me into a critical thinker, for teaching me to love research, and for showing me how to use knowledge to make a difference.

To Lara, Anna, Franzi and Linnea—thank you for being an extension of me, loving my girls so purely, supporting me every step of the way and being such a wonderful part of our family.

And finally, to my Peaceful Sleeper team—Ashley, Susannah, April, Sof, Devin, Danny, Allison, and Whitney. You have laughed with me, cried with me, and built something beautiful alongside me. This book truly would not exist without you. You have changed so many lives. Thank you.

About the Author

Chrissy Lawler, LMFT, is a licensed therapist with more than 15 years of experience. As the founder of *The Peaceful Sleeper*, she has guided more than 400,000 families worldwide to better rest and stronger mental health through her evidence-based, research-backed approach to infant sleep. Featured on *Good Morning America, Newsweek,* and *Better Homes & Gardens,* Chrissy has worked with corporations, executives, professional athletes, and celebrities. A mom of four, she combines clinical expertise with real-life parenting experience, offering parents practical, compassionate tools that deliver proven results in helping babies (and their families) sleep soundly.

Introduction

There's nothing that will stretch you like becoming a parent. If you're reading this book, chances are you're either about to welcome a new baby (yay!) or already in the thick of it. By now, you've probably realized the rumors are true: baby sleep is no joke. It's tricky, nuanced, exhausting, and, for some reason, endlessly controversial. But there *is* a way to get sleep for you and your family in a way that works for you!

You can thrive in the transition to parenthood and reclaim the joy that comes from great sleep. This book will teach you *why* sleep is central to your family's well-being and *how* to get there.

If sleep is what you're here for, I've got you. I'm a licensed marriage and family therapist with more than 15 years of experience. I have four kids of my own, and I've helped thousands of babies learn how to sleep well with a 97% success rate. My life's work is helping families get the sleep they deserve, and I'd love to help you too.

I'm sure you've realized that the world of parenting advice can be daunting and overwhelming. The world of baby sleep can be overwhelming too. You wouldn't be taking time out of your busy life to read a book about baby sleep if you weren't invested in the best possible outcomes for your little one. The problem is, too many parenting experts are schlepping one-size-fits-all approaches, and they establish their dominance by criticizing a different expert with different advice. The result? The parent, the person they're trying to help, ends up feeling discouraged, confused, and like they're failing no matter what they do.

This book is different. I acknowledge that there is no perfect approach for anything in life. Human beings are dynamic creatures with different circumstances and needs, diverse biology, and different families with unique environmental factors. Just as there is no one right way to exercise, no one right way to get optimal nutrition, and no single religion or political party that resonates with everyone, I appreciate that there is not one "right" way to parent or an exact "right" formula to help your baby get great sleep.

What I will do is teach you the fundamental principles at the core of achieving optimal baby sleep and how to apply those to your family. You will be educated, you will be empowered, and you will learn to become the expert on your baby. You will learn how to confidently discern their cues, you will learn how to meet their needs, and you will learn how to get them to sleep well as quickly and efficiently as possible.

This book is an assimilation of what we know about sleep, infants, attachment, parenting in the modern age, and scientific research. You'll learn how to hone your gut instinct and how to weed through loud, contradictory advice and opinions so you can feel like the great parent you've always hoped to be.

This book is also about much more than a sleep training approach. It's really about a parenting approach, combining high warmth and responsiveness with structure, limits and expectations. Researchers call this *authoritative parenting*, and it's widely regarded as the most effective parenting style to raise happy, thriving, well-adjusted children.[1,2,3] Sleep is our case study, but the principles you'll learn can impact every aspect of your parenting journey. When you believe deeply in your children's capabilities, they will believe in themselves. It's our job to cheer them on through manageable struggles so they can build resilience and mastery, not to take struggle away.

When I had my first baby, I should have felt totally prepared. I had degrees in human development and marriage and family therapy, had written theses on attachment and child outcomes, had conducted original research, and had even spent months working in an orphanage in Romania. I'd led parenting groups, taught seminars, and consumed countless research articles and books on babies and parenting. Add to that a supportive husband, loving parents, close friends, and a stable home—I had more resources and education than most new moms.

Yet, I was completely and utterly terrified. I remember the moment we left the hospital like it was yesterday. I held my beautiful baby girl in my arms as a kind nurse popped in and out, finishing our checkout. While she went to get a wheelchair and my husband grabbed the car, I found myself completely alone with my newborn for the first time.

I started crying. *I cannot believe they're just going to send me home with her. I don't know what I'm doing! She's so small and perfect and helpless, and I don't know how to do this! What if I mess it up?* Nothing I'd ever done felt this important, and I had no idea what I was doing.

If you're in that place and you've questioned how you're going to do this parenting thing, whether you feel anxious, unprepared, or overwhelmed, this book is for you.

Yes, this book is about teaching you how to get great sleep for you and your whole family. It's also more than that. You'll learn how to help your baby sleep but also how to build a parenting framework that nurtures their health, confidence, and resilience, while also protecting your own well-being and the strength of your family. **At the heart of everything you'll read, there are two simple principles I want to share:**

1. Getting good sleep is important. How you get there doesn't matter as long as you get there.

2. Being a parent is a beautiful, sacred, tender, and vulnerable experience. We're all trying our best. Let's be nice to each other.

So buckle up, grab a cup of coffee, and let's dive into the wonderful world of babies and baby sleep.

Part I

Parenting in the Modern Age

Chapter 1

What Exactly Is Sleep Training?

"Sleep training" has turned into the Internet's hottest parenting debate. Misunderstandings abound, leaving many well-meaning parents confused about whether it would help or harm their baby. Rest assured, sleep training doesn't just mean crying it out until your baby gives up and falls asleep. It simply means **teaching an infant to fall asleep and stay asleep independently.**

In this book, you will learn a systematic framework to get great sleep for your baby, and how to tune in to understand them on a deep level and meet their needs. Following principles of developmental psychology, you'll learn how to lay a foundation for quality sleep and then give them an opportunity to learn independence. The result is your baby efficiently learning how to fall asleep on their own. This leads to streamlined bedtime and naptime, predictable long naps, and sleeping through the night.

Imagine teaching a child to ride a bike. While there may be a few concentrated days spent in active training and learning, certainly it's more involved than just handing a child a two-wheeler and saying "good luck." The days, weeks, and months of mastering balance and coordination generally culminate into one weekend of practice, with support. The process may look slightly different from child to child, but the principles stay the same. First, help them establish a good foundation to start from. Then, give them space and opportunity when they can handle it; give them assistance when they need it.

Similarly, for the first four months of your baby's life you're fully supporting them to get great sleep. As their brain and their sleep system are developing, you'll work together to lay the groundwork for an optimal sleep foundation. Then, once they're developmentally ready, you step back and see what they can do on their own.

Sleep training is about so much more than the few days that you might allow for protest while they learn. It's about diligently building a strong sleep foundation and then taking the next step to teach your baby independent sleep skills in a way that feels aligned for you and works best for them. You'll learn a tried and true approach that works best for most babies, but you'll also learn how to adapt those principles to your baby and make modifications as needed.

Getting great sleep is one of the best gifts you can give your children to set them up for success mentally, emotionally, and developmentally. The better babies are sleeping, the better parents can be sleeping. And when parents are sleeping well, family systems can thrive.

We know how important sleep is, and that sleep training is an effective way to establish healthy sleep habits. But how and why does it work?

Sleep Architecture

Sleep happens in waves, called *sleep cycles*. We have periods of sleep that are deeper and more restorative, and periods of sleep that are more shallow and active. If babies can learn to fall asleep independently, they can use that same skillset to sleep cycle transition in the middle of the night or naps, leading to less sleep disturbance.

To illustrate this point, let's think of a child swimming. If a child has the skills to go from the surface of the pool and swim 5 feet down on their own to grab a dive toy, we can assume that even after they float back to the surface to take a breath, they'll be able to swim back down to the bottom again. They'll do this over and over again for the course of their time at the pool.

If, however, every time they wanted to get to the bottom of the pool they needed you to give them a push to get them on the trajectory of going down deep, then every time they came back to the surface they'd need that boost again.

It is the same with sleep cycles. If a baby relies on support to get into deep sleep initially, they'll likely need support to get *back* to deep sleep again. When their sleep gets shallow and they're ready for the next sleep cycle, they'll wake all the way up and call for you to help give them that boost again.

BABY SLEEP CYCLES

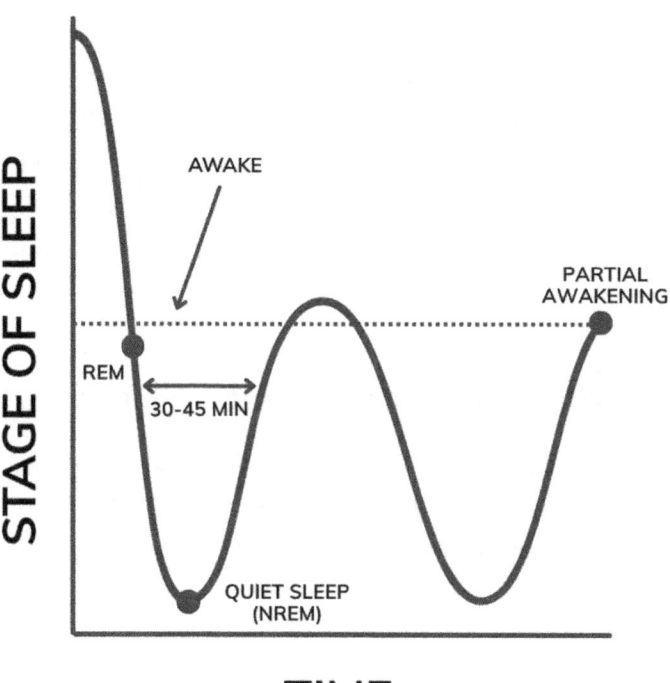

Just as you and I (hopefully) transition through cycles smoothly all night long, our babies too can navigate that shallow sleep period without fully waking. If they do, it's a brief period of readjustment and resettling that they can do on their own without support, just like

What Exactly Is Sleep Training?

you or I might scratch our nose, readjust the pillow, roll over and fall back to sleep without much fuss.

Many well-meaning parents are more than willing to sacrifice their own sleep to give their babies this boost through sleep cycle transitions. Sometimes because they don't think that Baby is capable of this on their own, or sometimes because the temporary drama of teaching this skill feels daunting and overwhelming. Worse, sometimes because they've been exposed to the false narrative that it's unloving, or even *damaging* to facilitate this independent learning process.

On the contrary, there is protest in all aspects of development, and it's our job as parents to lovingly guide our children to independence and resilience so that one day they might be self-assured, confident, capable children and adults. Sometimes this is uncomfortable for them and for us, but it's an important part of their growth, development, and self-esteem. It's not something we do *to* our children; it's something we do *for* them.

Sleep as the Cornerstone of Well-Being

In the chapters to come, I'll make a case for quality sleep and why prioritizing it is the most efficient way to increase your baseline of family happiness and well-being. Mental health is the biggest reason I'm so passionate about sleep. A well-rested family system can be a thriving family system.

I grew up with a mom who struggled deeply with mental health and sleep. As a kid, it was heartbreaking and confusing to watch her struggle. I wanted to help, but I couldn't fix it. Of course now I know it wasn't mine to fix, but that experience planted a seed. Years later, I became a therapist drawn to helping people untangle the pain I had seen up close.

As a professional, I started noticing a pattern: my clients who felt the most "stuck" in depression, anxiety, resentment, or strained relationships almost always struggled with sleep. No matter how much progress we made in therapy, if they weren't sleeping well, everything else seemed to stall. So I got additional training in Advanced Behavioral Sleep Medicine and learned that 80% of people with a mental health diagnosis have co-occurring sleep issues.[1]

When I had my first baby, the overwhelm of feeling out of my depth, sleep deprivation, and hormone disruption led to postpartum depression and anxiety hitting me like a truck. I'm typically extroverted, energetic, and optimistic, but I remember wishing everyone would just take the baby and leave so I could cry by myself. When passive darker thoughts crept in and I started doubting myself, wondering if I was cut out for this, I knew I needed help.

I was *devastated.*

I felt like I was failing as a mom and failing as a therapist because "I have all the skills and tools so I shouldn't be depressed." On a deeper level, I felt like I had failed my own mom. She'd spent her entire life trying to tee me up to be happier than she was, and here I was struggling in the same ways that scared me so much to witness as a child. I felt like I was failing everything and everyone, and I was crushed.

I knew in my soul that I just needed more sleep. If I could get my baby to sleep better, I could sleep better and would begin to thrive. And of course, I knew that therapy and medication are valuable tools too, if needed.

I wish I could tell you it was all rainbows and butterflies after that. Helping my baby sleep well was a way more complicated puzzle than I realized it would be, made worse by all of the "parenting experts" out there fighting over best-practices.

So I went straight to the data and found that:

1. Infant sleep is critical for their optimal development, their positive temperament, and my mental health, which in turn positively boosts mother-child attachment.[2,3,4,5,6]

2. Cry-it-out methods are safe and effective.[7,8,9,10]

To be clear, "cry it out" is not the only way to sleep train your baby, and I will teach you other methods later, but I learned that it is a viable option.[11]

Armed with those two indisputable truths, I went back to the dozens of parenting books and blogs to try to piece together a path that would work for me and my baby. I realized I could take what worked and leave what didn't and weighed advice with my own best judgment.

Eventually, I figured out a path to get fantastic sleep for my baby. I got my own sleep back on track, and I started thriving as a mom. Then I did it three more times and along the way created a sleep training method that has helped hundreds of thousands of families worldwide with a 97% success rate.

I can confidently say that I've cracked the code on optimizing baby sleep, helping parents to customize a plan to work for their family and their baby's nuances.

When your baby is sleeping better, you can sleep better. And when you get better sleep, you will thrive. A thriving parent(s) means thriving children. It's a beautiful upward cycle of positive outcomes.

Chapter 2

Everyone Is an Expert
(and Everything Is on Fire!)

Parenting in the modern age is a whole new beast. While it is true that we have so many advantages that our parents and grandparents didn't have, we have a whole host of stressors they didn't have either.

Take baby gadgets, for example: bottle warmers and sterilizers, baby wipe warmers, video monitors, and even machines to rock the baby or whip up a bottle of formula like an espresso maker. There are so many things that can make our lives "easier" while we're caring for a new baby. In addition to being financially costly, these often unnecessary gadgets can damage more than just our wallets.

Buy Now, Do This

Parents spend months researching, getting advice from friends and family, and weighing which items they have to get. The marketers of each item are inundating new and expecting parents with bold claims promising unrealistic benefits (a diaper that helps your baby sleep through the night) or instilling fear (a baby monitor that could get hacked by a pedophile) in order for you to buy their product instead. Worse, every few years "must-have" baby products get recalled or labeled as dangerous. Everywhere you look, companies are playing on the emotions of new parents. Every baby product seems to come attached with the marketing message "If you really love your baby and want what's best for them, you'll buy *this*." This ends up leaving parents constantly second-guessing themselves and feeling inadequate.

Another parenting concern that has emerged in the last few decades is the intense polarizing *moralization* in the parenting sphere. Unfortunately, it is robbing the joy of parents, adding stress and pressure, and ultimately negatively impacting our children. Instead of getting curious about various parenting choices and neutrally exploring the pros and cons, parents and educators are adding moral value where it does not belong. The result is that every choice seems to come attached with "good parent" or "bad parent" significance.

Let's not forget the most unsettling of all. Each baby that is born is now the lucky recipient of a new bonus parent: the Internet. Conversations about how we birth our babies, what we feed our children, when and whether to vaccinate, sleep training, childhood independence, and dozens of other online parenting conversations can get *incredibly* heated. In nearly every post about any parenting issue, you'll see comments directly or indirectly accusing others of "bad parenting" instead of simply having a difference of opinion or a child with a different need. Comments like "I feel sorry for your children" can be found on posts as innocuous as "sample nap schedule for a nine-month-old."

Everything feels dire, and when the potential cost of doing something (i.e., everything) "wrong" is the safety and well-being of your precious child, the stakes feel higher than ever. The result is that parental anxiety is skyrocketing. This pressure, noise, misinformation, and polarization are making the already difficult task of parenting even more physically and mentally challenging.

In fact, in 2024, the United States Surgeon General issued an advisory stating that parental stress is a significant national health issue.[1] Societal pressures, concerns about children's well-being, and unrealistic parenting ideals are leaving "many families feeling exhausted, burned out, and perpetually behind."

Before we get to the how-tos of optimizing infant sleep, I just want to slow down and highlight a few things:

- You will come across contradicting opinions and advice in your quest for optimal infant sleep and parenting.
- You can learn to be empowered to be the expert on your child.
- It's not that deep. Not everything is on fire, and as long as you're diligently trying your best, you're probably doing a good enough job.

Social media doesn't provide the full picture. What is required of you, dear reader, is to be a critical consumer of information. I'm sure you know by now that not everything you read or see online is true, or is true for you. Yes, even with this book I want you to take what works and leave what doesn't. Filter all of this information through your own experiences, your own truths, and do what you feel is best for your baby and your family. Check my sources, identify my biases (I've got them), and feel free to choose your own path.

Fortunately, across thousands of peer-reviewed studies, one thing we can all agree on is this: good sleep is important and has trickle-down benefits to almost every aspect of life and well-being.[2] However, how you get there will look different from family to family.

When the stakes are high, like the well-being of a child is on the line or there's money to be made, voices can get loud and opinions can get intense. Nowhere is this more true than in the health and wellness space and the parenting space. Unfortunately, baby sleep falls into this crossover, which means you might be exposed to very loud, very contradictory advice telling you that you have to do it this way "or else."

My aim in this book is to give overarching truths as well as nuanced approaches to get optimal baby sleep the "right way" for your family.

Parenting with Social Media

Sorting through contradictory information has always been a challenge we have faced and will continue to face as human beings. Nothing is black and white. People are simply different, our environments are different, and there is a great deal of nuance. For some, almonds are a superfood. For others, almonds are an allergen that can lead to anaphylaxis and death. One cannot make a definitive statement on the benefits of almonds for everyone in the world.

Unfortunately, most of us do not get our information straight from peer-reviewed research. Instead, we read news articles, gather information from self-proclaimed "experts," learn from social media, and get advice from people in our inner circle, like friends and family. Rarely do these sources acknowledge their biases, cite their sources, or highlight their limitations in providing their information. Worse, they often miss the point, cherry-pick details from research to support their claims, or make inferences that don't make sense. All too often you'll find well-intentioned articles or posts touting "research shows" only to go back to the data and find that's not quite what they said.

One frustrating reality is that there are no credentials required to post advice on social media, and frankly some advice is downright dangerous. Additionally, sometimes the most divisive, misinformed content gets the most traction. A blatant untruth might get millions more views or likes than a fact, and we tend to weigh information as more credible if it has more traction on social media. In fact, a study from MIT in 2018 found that true stories take six times longer to reach 1,500 people on X than false ones.[3] This is because misinformation seems to be more novel, exciting, or cutting edge, and people desire to be seen as "in the know."

Because of the way the algorithms work, social media users tend to get similar content served up to them as what they've previously engaged with. I once inadvertently flooded my feed with dog videos because I sent a few to my sister. It took weeks to recover from. When we're scrolling for entertainment purposes, a carefully crafted algorithm isn't a problem. However, when we get the majority of our news and information from a skewed algorithm, this can cause trouble. If you're unintentionally consuming content that has an undercurrent of fear about "bad parenting" and poor child outcomes, you'll take on an unnecessary amount of stress to be perfect.

You can also end up in an echo-chamber of information (or misinformation). If one line of thinking is repeatedly presented, we stop challenging it and accept it as good and true information even if it's not. In a phenomenon called *conformity bias*, people tend to align their attitudes, beliefs, and behaviors with those of a group. This can be seen in nearly every one of my fashion choices. "You think this is cool? Okay, so do I!"

If lots of people seem to think the same thing, we assume they've done the thinking for us and we don't need to dig deeper. This happens because of social pressure, the desire to fit in, or the assumption that the group must be right. This kind of herd mentality can be fine when we're talking about unimportant things like fashion or product choices, but when we're talking about choices that impact our health, well-being, belief systems, or parenting philosophies, it's really important to have multiple viewpoints expressed so we can make more informed, well-rounded decisions. Questioning is good. It's how we learn, grow, deepen our understanding, and gain more compassion for other viewpoints.

Everyone Is an Expert (and Everything Is on Fire!)

The Wild West of Experts

Unfortunately, anyone can say anything online, and many people do. Even likes, comments, reviews, and followers can be bought or are bots. We've all fallen for the gimmicks: the wellness drink with the "proprietary recipe" that ends up being full of sugar and void of vitamins. Or the magnetic eyelashes that were supposed to be *SO easy* but look ridiculous and are impossible to apply. Those missteps are annoying but harmless. The danger comes when misinformation spreads to important matters like health or parenting.

Years ago, a mother in our community tragically died during childbirth with her fourth baby. Instead of following the advice of her doctors, she turned to unlicensed influencers without information about her specific medical history. After her death, reports confirmed that her complications were avoidable and treatable had she been in a hospital. This heartbreaking example shows what can happen when "advice" replaces expertise.

Many well-meaning "functional health coaches," "postpartum fitness trainers," and even "baby sleep consultants" fall under the umbrella of unregulated industries. They may believe they're helping, but their advice can carry unknown risks. Just because advice is true for some doesn't mean it's true for everyone. Sure, cold plunges, celery juice, high-protein meals, or supplements can have health benefits for some, but they may also disrupt hormone regulation or strain kidneys for others. A thin influencer might create a diet or exercise plan without formal training and may leave out the weight loss medication, eating disorder, or plastic surgery that is also part of the equation.

Parenting is no exception. All over the Internet, people with opinions and children call themselves "parenting experts," often with no real education or training.

Perhaps most notable is the parenting influencer Ruby Franke, imprisoned for child abuse and neglect in 2023 after one of her children escaped to a neighbor's house for help. She had millions of subscribers on YouTube and was running a parenting coaching program, yet her own children were bound with duct tape in the basement and emaciated![4]

In your search for guidance, you must be a critical consumer of information. When you weigh advice you're exposed to, ask yourself a few key questions:

- What are their credentials?
- What sources do they cite? Are these their personal ideas or is this substantiated in peer-reviewed research?
- What is their success rate or their reach?
- How do the ideas presented make me feel? Do I leave feeling uplifted, motivated, and inspired or stressed out and inadequate?
- Do the ideas presented make sense to me and fit into my worldview?
- Based on their tone, would I want to be friends with this person, or do I feel judged by them?

You and your family have nuances and individual needs, so you get the final say. Learn what you can, expose yourself to a multitude of ideas, and confidently move forward doing your best. Pivot if and when it's no longer working.

Chapter 3

Debunking the Myths

Over the years, voices against sleep training have gotten incredibly loud. One issue is that "sleep training" can mean many different things to different people, which adds further confusion, guilt, and shame. Additionally, these arguments are rarely addressing family system dynamics as a whole or acknowledging the fundamental importance of quality sleep. When they look only at their perceived harm of "leaving an infant to cry" and neglect the importance of quality sleep, sleep training appears to be detrimental to the infant and selfish of the parent. This could not be further from the truth.

Why Has Sleep Training Gotten Such a Bad Rap?

First, the sleep training of the past was far more intense than it needed to be. Focusing only on the goal of sleeping all night long, the recommendation was to just close the nursery door at 7 p.m., come back at 7 a.m., and whatever happens happens. One popular book I read when I had my first baby in 2013 shared a success story where the baby cried and screamed for four hours the first night but only two hours the second night. By the third night, she didn't fuss at all! It is great that the method worked in three days, I suppose, but I was never going to feel okay letting my precious little babe cry for four hours without me.

What I will propose in the sections to come is a plan to first teach babies a foundational structure of good sleep with support.

Then after four months of age, to teach them to fall asleep and stay asleep independently through a series of 10-minute controlled intervals where they may protest. There may be circumstances where this 10-minute method isn't the right fit for every family, so I'll teach you modifications to tailor to your unique situation. This notion of teaching your baby to sleep independently is what I mean by "sleep training" or what our program sometimes calls "sleep learning."

Fortunately, our method also works in as little as three days, and we're looking at 10 minutes of protest at a time. Where earlier approaches had a laissez faire "Meh, they'll figure it out," approach, my approach to sleep training is far more intentional. Remember you don't *have* to cry it out (CIO) if you don't want to. But I digress . . . more on this later!

Second, as discussed in Chapter 2, there's a ton of misinformation out there, and lots of inferences made that are then stated as facts when they shouldn't be. In fact, even though peer-reviewed research favors sleep training, the social media landscape *appears* to be highly opposed. Interestingly, most parents in Western cultures sleep train their babies. Even though sleep training is a widely practiced, safe, and effective parenting intervention, it has become vilified and, as a result, somewhat censored. Those who oppose sleep training seem to feel a moral obligation to save babies from perceived maltreatment, and as such, they can get intense and mean.

Over the years we've worked with hundreds of influencers who can't or won't post about sleep training even though they share everything else. Of course, they don't want the backlash. I can tell you from personal experience, online bullying and criticism hit deep when you're postpartum and people attack you as a parent when you're trying your best. The result, however, is that the anti-sleep training voices get louder, drowning out the pro-sleep training voices. We then have parents who are suffering, but they feel they have no other choice but to grin and bear it if they want to be good and loving.

Even true experts aren't shielded from backlash because of sleep training misinformation. I recently saw a post featuring a comment on a pediatric neurologist's page when he posted about sleep training. She said, "A child neurologist who hasn't kept up with pediatric sleep research. Big yikes! Sleep training methods don't work and cause long-term harm." His video response simply and gently reminded, "Not only do I keep up with the research, I *am* the research" followed by images of dozens of published scientific journals in which he's the first author.[1]

Frankly, it's a wild phenomenon that random people on the Internet have the audacity to go toe to toe with published researchers, dismissing decades of data, because they read some stuff online that fits their ideas. Unfortunately, this is the world parents are navigating.

Scientific Consensus, Algorithmic Division

An analysis conducted by Tom Valliant in 2024 beautifully portrays the science versus social media opinions around sleep training.[2] He found that of the top 20 baby sleep Instagram accounts, more than half are opposed to sleep training. If these influencers and "coaches" are reaching millions of parents daily and those parents are sharing information with friends and posting on other platforms like Reddit, it's no wonder that misinformation and fear are becoming mainstream beliefs.

He goes on to say:

> *"If we look at 75 clinical trials, over 30,000 babies participated between 1980 and 2022. **The clinical consensus isn't divided: to date, no published research points to sleep training causing harm, and the majority of published pediatric sleep researchers advocate sleep training.**"*[3,4]

As sleep training information gets repeated, the message often drifts far from what the science actually shows. That's why it's worth slowing down to cut through the noise and look directly at the evidence.

So, let's get into the myths about sleep training.

Myth #1: Crying and/or Stress Is Harmful to Babies

One prominent voice referenced often in the anti-sleep training space is the work from Dr. Sears. In one of his articles "The Effects of Excessive Crying" he says:

> *"When trying to understand if excessive crying is harmful for babies, think about the fact that their bodies and brains are flooded with adrenaline and cortisol stress hormones and when developing brain tissue is exposed to these hormones for prolonged periods, these nerves won't form connections to other nerves and will degenerate."*
>
> *"Is it therefore possible that infants who endure many nights or weeks of crying-it-out alone are actually suffering harmful neurological effects that may have permanent implications on the development of sections of their brain?"*[5]

First, this all sounds very intense and scary, but let's dig deeper. He refers to "excessive crying" but he doesn't define what that is. Certainly "excessive crying" doesn't mean "any amount of" crying. Of course, some crying is inevitable on a daily basis, so there must be some mechanisms in baby brains and bodies to tolerate crying without neurological damage, say on a car ride across town. Does 10 minutes of crying inherently count as "excessive"? I don't think so.

Next, he references exposure to stress hormones for "prolonged periods," which, again, does not mean that any amount of exposure is bad. In fact, *some* exposure to stress hormones is inevitable. It's actually good for the brain to encounter some stress and learn how to deal with it. In a 2010 study, Dr. Mark Seery and colleagues found that stressful experiences actually foster resilience, resulting in advantages for mental health and well-being. Their study concluded that "people with a history of some lifetime adversity reported better mental health and well-being outcomes than people with a high history of adversity AND no history of adversity."[6]

Taking a baby out of a warm bath into the cold air will temporarily make them uncomfortable and cry. Buckling them into a car seat, tummy time, cutting a toddler's apple wrong, sharing, or giving a blue plate instead of a pink one will temporarily cause stress that they can learn to work through. Of course, there is a balance. Witnessing domestic violence, for example, is bad stress.

Therefore, we must view stress on a spectrum. There is a difference between productive stress and nonproductive stress. Think of anything in your life that you're proud of. There was surely some stress along the way. Some stress and discomfort are *inevitable* in all aspects of development. What matters is that there is comfort, reassurance, and mastery along the way. Productive stress is beneficial.

He continues:

> *"Researchers at Yale University and Harvard Medical School found that intense stress early in life* can alter the brain's neurotransmitter systems and cause structural and functional changes in regions of the brain similar to those seen in adults with depression."[7]

Again, "intense stress early in life" is not defined, nor does it logically follow that sleep training would fit into this definition at all. These studies cited looked at the effects of child maltreatment and abuse and do not mention sleep training in any way.[8,9,10,11] In fact, the author of this study responded to Dr. Sears' claims and argued that it was unfair to use her work as evidence against sleep training. She said, "Our paper is not referring to routine, brief stressful experiences, but to abuse and neglect. It is a mis-citation of our work to support a non-scientifically justified idea."[12]

Another author whose work was cited responded similarly: "is not relevant to the argument he makes because my work involves babies and young children whose parents are in the pathological range of neglect and maltreatment . . . not children with normative, 'good-enough' parenting."[13]

It's concerning that so many parents are led to believe sleep training is harmful based on these claims when the authors of the studies cited seem to be saying, "Wait, wait, wait, that's not what I said!"

Somehow the idea that sleep training damages baby brains because chronic stress and abuse are harmful to developing baby brains has become a mainstream idea among parents. But sleep training is not chronic stress, nor is it abuse. So we can't take findings about the implications of abuse and neglect and infer that 10-minute controlled crying intervals also elicit the same outcomes.

Myth #2: Separation from Parents Is Harmful

Another myth around sleep training is that "separating" or leaving your baby alone is harmful. In the same article Sears states:

> *"Research has shown that infants who are routinely separated from parents in a stressful way have abnormally* high levels of the stress hormone cortisol, *as well as lower growth hormone levels. These imbalances inhibit the development of nerve tissue in the brain, suppress growth, and depress the immune system."*[14]

I pay particular attention to the words "routinely separated from parents in a stressful way," which *does* feel fundamentally different than sleep training with 10-minute intervals between check-ins. What exactly does "routinely separated from parents in a stressful way" mean? What if they cry every day they're dropped off at daycare? Or they get upset every time you lay them down so you can change the laundry or take a shower? Will that lead to permanent neurological damage? Surely all infants are "routinely separated from their parents" because you're not holding them every second. There *must* be some mechanism in the brain that can tolerate separation, right?

Additionally (and frustratingly), the research cited here was from an experiment where rat pups were taken from their mothers and placed in an incubator.[15] Though we can learn a lot from animal studies, I don't think it's reasonable to then infer that controlled crying episodes while sleep training will lead to the same harm. And what about babies in the NICU? They are separated from their mothers—are we to also assume that those life-saving interventions might lead to permanent neurological damage? Of course not.

Myth #3: Sleep Training Causes Emotional Damage

Unfortunately, the claims made by Dr. Sears and others misconstrue or dramatize the science, leaving parents feeling like they must accept poor sleep and its consequences until it one day gets better on its own, otherwise they're selfishly choosing something harmful for their babies.

Regarding the "emotional implications of excessive crying," Sears goes on to say that outcomes like antisocial behavior, poor school performance, and a tenfold increase in the risk of ADHD are possible.[16] However, the studies he references to support this examine a *condition* researchers called "persistent crying."[17,18] In these studies, it was the very inconsolability of the crying that they were studying. These were infants who "remained distressed and crying despite parental soothing, feeding, rocking, singing, pacing, changing, and pleading" beyond the 12 weeks that colic usually lasts. In fact, these studies went out of their way to make clear that these infants were crying **despite** their parent's best efforts and to absolve them of any blame for the crying episodes.

Instead, the researchers argued that the crying is a symptom of an underlying condition—perhaps neurological—that also causes later cognitive or behavioral issues.[19] Therefore, we can't attribute cognitive impairment to the effects of CIO sleep training. It's not what they were studying, and it's not what they found.

Myth #4: Sleep Training Is a Form of Neglect

Another popular argument against sleep training is that infants, when left to cry, are simply learning that no one will respond to their needs so they give up.[20] They argue that babies are not capable of self-soothing and this "giving up" phenomenon results in later emotional disturbance because they learn that they can't expect to be taken care of.

First, babies *can* and *do* self-soothe. To suggest that they can't calm down on their own is incorrect and is not substantiated by any empirical data. Not only do we see repeated self-soothing while sleep training, we also see infants calm themselves down after countless moments of distress like being put in a car seat, getting a finger stuck, or being put down while a parent uses the bathroom. It is necessary for our babies to have mechanisms in place to regulate themselves to some degree.

Nevertheless, the more daunting message is that when left to "cry it out" our babies give up on warmth, love, and the promise of safety. Some anti-CIO voices say that crying it out leads to the brain becoming so flooded with cortisol it just shuts down in survival mode. When that happens, they postulate that babies stop calling out because they've learned that no one will come for them and their needs cannot be met. They aren't learning to self-soothe; they're experiencing the trauma of abandonment.[21]

Yeesh—that sounds heavy, doesn't it?

This line of thinking is based on research about infant neglect, the development of attachment disorder, and largely comes from Romanian orphanage studies.[22,23,24] I spent four months working in a Romanian orphanage during a college internship. I can *confidently* say that sleep training doesn't compare to the circumstances that lead to infants giving up on love and responsiveness. The method we propose has small bursts of allowing room for protest while carefully watching to make sure we're not pushing them past their window of tolerance. This is extremely different from the neglect and resulting trauma the babies in Romanian orphanages experienced.

In the 1990s, the conditions in the orphanages were horrific. Thousands of children were found tied to their beds and confined in their cribs for years. They were left in soiled clothing, malnourished, neglected, and physically and sexually abused.

Many of these children had developmental delays, attachment disorders, emotional disturbances, and autism-like symptoms. These discoveries led to worldwide humanitarian efforts, and, yes, research about the physical, mental, and emotional effects of neglect and abuse on child development.[25,26]

To suggest that allowing a well-loved and cared for infant to cry before they fall asleep is anything like what these children went through invalidates and minimizes the very real and horrific trauma these orphans experienced.

The orphanage I worked in was considered one of the "good ones." Conditions were drastically improved compared to 20 years prior, and yet, it was still heartbreaking. The room we worked in had 21 babies under 12 months old, with 1–2 staff members. It was almost always silent. The babies were not allowed out of their cribs, even for diaper changes, sponge baths, and feedings. Though they had shelves full of toys that were donated, they never actually got them.

Debunking the Myths

They were taken care of, but there was very little warmth or love. We were constantly scolded for holding them and playing with them. "When you girls are here you hold them too much and love on them too much. That makes them cry more when you aren't here. You make it worse for them," we were told.

So yes, it *is* biologically possible for infants whose needs for warmth and love aren't met to shut off and stop expecting responsiveness. While that is a heartbreaking phenomenon, it is not at all what sleep training does. When you are consistently loving, responsive, and nurturing, their attachment security can absolutely manage instances and intervals of time where they are calling and you aren't available.

Jodi Mindell, PhD, a prominent child psychologist, infant sleep specialist, and associate director of the sleep center at the Children's Hospital of Philadelphia (CHOP), has led multiple literature reviews about sleep training. When asked about the research cited by Dr. Sears and Dr. Narvaez, another opposing voice in the sleep training space, she said:

> *"I am very concerned about the science that is presented. Every article that we looked at, and we looked at every reference that was included in those articles, had basically nothing to do with sleep training."* [27]

Dr. Mindell's research assessed two primary criteria: relevance and grounding.

Relevance: Is it a theoretical article (opinion) or a research study?
Grounding: Is it sleep- or sleep-training specific?

She goes on to say,

> *"many of them were animal studies that were looking at putting animals in poor situations.* [28] *Or they were not related*

to sleep training at all, they were related to some other realm. The studies that have been done—and there are many, many, many studies looking at the outcomes of sleep training, have found, without a doubt, improvements in babies. Improvements in baby's sleep, improvements in baby's mood, improvements in parent well-being, and improvements in long term outcome."[29]

Dr. Mindell offers this caution:

"We need to be very careful about what science we look at and whether or not we can make conclusions from it. Literally ALL of the science we have been presented about this intense damage to babies brains has nothing to do with sleep training. These are studies that are looking at babies who have been severely neglected or abused, or babies who have been in incredibly stressful situations."[30,31,32,33]

The larger issue we have today is that most parents don't dig deep into the data to understand how experts have arrived at the opinions they have to see if we agree with those takeaways. Worse, some take those heated opinions to the Internet and tear well-meaning parents down, adding fear and anxiety when parenting is hard and overwhelming enough as it is.

In dozens of sleep training studies, researchers have found no evidence of harm, even when the methodology includes more CIO than my approach recommends.[34,35] Though yes, cortisol (stress) levels are temporarily increased while infants are crying, they return to baseline. This is a good thing! One study found that cortisol levels were increased in babies during CIO, but when measured again later, their cortisol levels were the same as their counterparts who did not sleep train. Yet the sleep trained babies were sleeping better.[36] Also

Debunking the Myths

noteworthy is the fact that the elevated cortisol levels were still within a normal and healthy range. What the researchers concluded from that study is that sleep training is a short-term intervention that temporarily increases stress a moderate amount but does no long-term damage and works to improve sleep.

Another study addressed the long-term implications of sleep training on childhood outcomes like child mental health, psychosocial functioning, and stress regulation. They also looked at child-parent relationships, maternal mental health, and parenting styles. They concluded that "behavioral sleep techniques have no marked long-lasting effects" and that "parents and health professionals can confidently use these techniques to reduce the short-to medium-term burden of infant sleep problems and maternal depression."[37]

Most confusing of all, many of these "gentle" sleep training books and accounts seem to vilify CIO methods, only to acknowledge at the end that if their approach doesn't work, it's also perfectly fine to let Baby cry for a few minutes while they learn to fall asleep.

The research shows that sleep training does not harm your baby and is a safe and effective way to improve their sleep.[38] That being said, the choice about how to teach your baby this skill remains entirely up to you.

Being a parent is the toughest and most rewarding job you will ever have. Above all, remember that humans are incredibly resilient. If you're consciously doing your best, your kids are going to turn out fine. Far more important than whether you let your baby cry before they fall asleep is the love you pour into them all day long. Make eye contact, smile, laugh together, and offer plenty of hugs, kisses, and "I love yous." Tune into their needs and do your best to support them. That's what matters most. And as you care for your children, remember to be kind to yourself and to other parents. We're all in this together.

Part II

Sleep Is Life

Chapter 4

Why Quality Sleep Matters for Baby

Meeting your baby's sleep needs is one of the most important gifts you can give them. Sleep promotes physical, emotional, social, and intellectual development.

Throughout pregnancy, you likely made many changes in your day-to-day life to optimize your growing baby's development, including changing medications, quitting smoking, abstaining from alcohol, taking vitamins, and even avoiding certain foods and household cleaners so your baby would have the best chance at optimal development in the womb. Getting Baby here safe and healthy was top of mind. Now that they're here, figuring out how to help them develop and thrive is your ultimate goal.

Quality sleep is a crucial part of your baby's development—it supports their physical growth, emotional regulation, cognitive development, and social functioning.[1,2] I sat down with Dr. Sujay Kansagra, director of the Pediatric Neurology Sleep Medicine Program at Duke University. He explained,

> *"Sleep is the foundation of all good health. If you're not getting the sleep you need, everything else crumbles. **There's not a single medical or psychiatric disorder that I know of that doesn't get worse when sleep worsens.** Kids' brains are essentially drinking from a firehose. Sleep is what helps make all those connections—to restore and*

recuperate, both their brains and their bodies. It's abso-
lutely vital for emotional regulation and all aspects of
development."

Physical Development

While babies are sleeping, their brains are growing tremendously.[3] In just a few short months and years they will go from small helpless creatures who can't even control their arms to walking, jumping, and running little humans who can do somersaults.

They sleep most of the time because their brains still have so much growth and development left.[4,5] Think of how incredibly quickly a fetus develops. In just nine months a cluster of cells turned into a living, breathing human with organs. They're ready enough to sustain life outside the womb, but they're far from developed. Our bodies can't physically handle keeping them in the womb any longer, so they have to finish growing in the outside world. This brain and body growth and development happens primarily during sleep.[6] This is why small babies need so much of it. For newborns, they need up to 18 hours a day![7]

This is because during sleep the brain releases growth hormone.[8] If you haven't experienced it yet, there will be times that you see your baby in the morning and you *know* they're bigger than the day before or they have a new skill like smiling or rolling over.

Physical Health and Immune Function

In addition to physical growth, sleep is also essential for the body's repair and recovery processes. During deep sleep, the released growth hormones aid in tissue growth and muscle repair. There is a direct link between sleep and immune function.[9,10,11] This is why almost anytime you're sick, you sleep more. During sleep the body is able to support immune system functioning, fight off infection, and create new antibodies.

Metabolic Health and Weight Management

Sleep affects the hormones that regulate hunger and satiety. Lack of sleep can disrupt these hormones, leading to increased appetite and weight gain. Sleep deprivation leads to decreased levels of leptin, a hormone that suppresses appetite, and increased levels of ghrelin, a hormone that stimulates appetite. Thus, we see a direct link to poor sleep and childhood obesity.[12,13] With our small infants, poor sleep actually leads to more frequent night awakenings and feedings that aren't directly related to their need for caloric intake. They're waking more often and eating more, but not growing better. In fact, one study found that **babies with better sleep habits have less night awakenings and night feedings but are actually growing at a stronger rate.**[14]

Emotional Development

I don't know about you, but I'm super grumpy when I'm sleep-deprived. If I'm well-rested, or maybe by some miracle I've had the chance to sleep in, I wake up feeling like a million bucks. Likewise, well-rested babies wake up cooing and smiling in the morning, ready to start a glorious and happy day. This is because the brain's emotion centers develop during sleep.[15,16,17] This is even true for children with "spirited" (i.e., "difficult") temperaments. Sleep helps us regulate our moods and emotions. Adequate sleep is crucial for emotional stability and mental health.

During sleep, the brain's emotion systems develop and regulate. Sleep deprivation in children and adults can lead to mood swings, increased stress, depression, and anxiety. In our small babies, poor sleep leads to irritability, fussiness, higher reactivity, more sensitivity, and more difficulty soothing. Think of how as an adult, if you're super tired, every little thing bothers you. It's the same phenomenon with our small babies, but worse.

Did you know that 80% of individuals with a mental-health diagnosis have a co-occurring sleep problem?[18] Setting up our children with a good sleep foundation gives them a better chance of lifelong improved mental health.

If we want to set our children up for the best chances of success to be high functioning, happy people (which we do!), we will make sure they get the sleep they need for these areas of the brain to develop optimally. Poor sleep is directly linked to depression, anxiety, mood disorders, as well as ADHD and learning disabilities, which are also linked to further emotional disturbance.[19,20]

While quality sleep is tied to a host of positive mental health outcomes with an upward cycle of benefit, poor sleep quality is linked to a host of negative, compounding mental health outcomes.

Let's think of five-month-old baby James. He seems to have woken up "on the wrong side of the bed." Last night he slept fitfully, waking up multiple times. His parents are exhausted but are powering through. All morning long, he's had one meltdown after another. When his ball rolled out of reach and he couldn't get to it, he started screaming. He wanted to be held all morning. Anytime his parents tried to put him down so they could load the dishwasher or go to the bathroom, he cried. His parents are counting down the minutes until it's naptime because they just need a break and to be hands-free for a minute.

Fortunately, he takes a great nap! When he wakes up two hours later, they seemingly have a brand new baby! He coos and smiles; he laughs and babbles. Mom sets him down on his playmat with some toys where he plays contentedly while she folds some laundry. He's so sweet and happy, she's drawn to come sit on the floor with him as soon as she finishes. She makes eye contact and smiles and tries to get him to laugh. The more he laughs, the more she laughs. The more they're laughing and interacting, the more she's smiling and expressing love. She's hugging him more, kissing him more, and nuzzling into him more. All of this perpetuates his happy feelings.

Good, restorative sleep perpetuates positive interactions and outcomes and poor sleep triggers a downward cycle, even if subtle.

If you already have a baby or toddler, these scenarios probably sound incredibly familiar. Even with all the right sleep tools, you'll inevitably have rough moments occasionally, but when you have a pattern of great sleep, the majority of your interactions can feel more positive. Sleep resets the emotion centers in our brains allowing for optimal emotion regulation and joy. Your baby thrives and is tangibly happier when they get better sleep.

Social Development

Happier babies have happier caregivers. Well-rested kids tend to develop faster socially with coos, smiles, laughs, and other engaging behaviors.[21] Because the emotion centers in the brain have been able to optimally regulate, well-rested babies are happier and more playful.[22] This in turn elicits more social engagement from their caregivers, who aren't as stressed out and overwhelmed. This creates an upward cycle of good relationships. One good thing leads to another good thing. Great sleep kicks off this cascade of positive outcomes.

As human beings, we tend to feed off of and co-regulate each other's emotions. The parent-child bond is particularly susceptible to this co-regulation. Parents and babies can either stress each other out or calm each other down. Interestingly, mothers with postpartum depression report much fussier babies.[23,24] It's unclear in the data how much this is *perceived* infant fussiness because mothers with depression are in a heightened state of overwhelm or if the infants are more agitated and trigger maternal overwhelm and depression. It is likely a combination of both. Of course, in this scenario, both mother and baby need support. We'll address this more in the next section, but mom's sleep deprivation is often a major contributing factor to postpartum depression and anxiety.[25,26,27] If we can get Mom the support she needs to feel good and get Baby the support they need to be content, the relationship will thrive.

This emotional co-regulation plays out in our baby and toddler's social worlds as well. Babies feed off of each other's energy in a phenomenon researchers call *empathetic responding*. When one baby in the vicinity begins to cry, other babies will join in and start crying too. If a particularly fussy baby has a tendency to be upset and stress out their baby friends, they will start to associate a stress response with him.

In other words, it's a lot easier to make friends when you're not always grumpy and sleep-deprived. As babies become toddlers, they tend to gravitate toward people who they like and who put them at ease.[28]

Years ago during my university studies, we had an on-campus preschool with one-way mirrors to conduct observational research. One particular study we were part of looked at toddlers' social relations and empathy. Of course, in a preschool setting there were many times young toddlers cried for a variety of reasons. Though the other kids noticed when anyone cried, their responses weren't the same.[29] When Charley, who usually has a sweet disposition, got her finger stuck and cried, other kids looked on with compassion and empathy or even came to help. When Maverick got mad that someone took his fire truck and cried in protest and anger, the kids noticed and paid attention but distanced themselves, almost as if to say, "This guy again?"

We draw toward people whose energy calms and uplifts us, and we draw away from people who stress us out. Well-rested babies and toddlers have better social relating skills.[30,31]

Intellectual Development

Well-rested kids are smarter, learn faster, and have lower rates of ADHD and learning difficulties.[32,33] This finding is all over the research.

Likely, none of this will surprise you; you've probably spent your whole life realizing that you function better with better sleep. You've heard from parents and teachers that the key to academic performance is a good night's rest. You've felt brain fog and cognitive decline when you're sleep deprived. But just for kicks, let's highlight how and why good sleep impacts our babies cognitive development:

- **Brain maturation and plasticity:** During sleep, the brain reorganizes neural connections, strengthens important pathways, and eliminates unnecessary ones. While development of the central nervous system continues into adulthood, the most dramatic changes occur during the first two years of life. This process is vital for learning, memory, and cognitive development.[34,35]

- **Memory consolidation:** Sleep helps babies consolidate memories and solidify learning. Studies have shown that infants who nap after learning new information demonstrate better recall and retention than those who don't nap. Additionally, quality naps are shown to contribute to the consolidation of declarative, emotional, and procedural memories.[36]

- **Language development:** Good sleep promotes language development, because while babies are sleeping new language is being integrated into existing knowledge. In fact, one study found that infants who were exposed to new words before a nap showed better recognition of those words later compared to infants who didn't nap.[37]

- **Executive function development:** Sleep is vital for the development of executive functions. These are the brain's higher-level cognitive processes that control attention, working memory, inhibitory control (controlling the impulse to hit or snatch a toy), and cognitive flexibility (transitioning to a new activity without melting down). Sleep is critical for developing and strengthening these abilities, particularly during early childhood when the brain is still maturing. Disrupted or insufficient sleep can interfere with these brain processes, making it harder for children to manage impulses, adapt to change, and succeed in learning or social interactions.[38,39]

- **Cognitive performance and mental development:** Infants with better sleep quality, including longer sleep duration and fewer nighttime awakenings, tend to perform better on cognitive tests, including the Bayley Scales of Infant Development, which assesses mental and motor skills.[40]

Because babies' brains develop when they're sleeping, facilitating good sleep allows them to make cognitive leaps and bounds. Of course, you want every advantage for your little one to be primed for success and thriving in this world. Helping them get great sleep can do just that.

Not only does sleep benefit their brain in so many positive ways, but parents also have more energy and motivation to avoid things like screen time, which we know is less than ideal for their developing brain. Of course, we're all going to turn on a show from time to time, but exhausted parents have a far higher likelihood of resorting to the mind-numbing TV as a "babysitter" when they're tired and ragged and just need a nap.

Learning to sleep well is a skill—a very important one. It simply isn't as inborn as other milestones our kids achieve effortlessly. We have to work at it. But it's a skill that will benefit your child for the rest of their life. Just like eating a variety of nutrient-rich foods, we have to give special focus to helping our kids develop a palette for vegetables more than we have to help them like cookies. But because it is important for their health and well-being, exerting that effort is well worth it. When you diligently assist your child to get quality sleep and facilitate their opportunity to learn independent sleep, you'll set them up on the path for success in a multitude of areas.

Chapter 5

Why Quality Sleep Matters for Parents

Sleep deprivation takes a huge mental and physical toll. In fact, it has been used as a form of torture for centuries. It's no secret that the adjustment to having a baby involves some sleep deprivation. But having a beautiful new baby in your home should not feel like torture.

Newborns don't come out with a developed circadian rhythm, and they usually need to eat every two to three hours around the clock. Depending on how long the feeding takes, it can mean you are losing several hours of sleep each night.

This adjustment period can be incredibly difficult for new parents. My aim is to keep this period as brief as possible. In the following chapters, I'll give you tools and resources to get great sleep as quickly and efficiently as possible.

Everything you hope for and dream of as a parent is more attainable when built on the foundation of good sleep. If you're the type of parent reading a book like this, I assume you have a vision for the kind of parent you'd like to be. What does that look like to you?

Your quality sleep is absolutely pivotal for your well-being *and* the well-being of your child.

Of course, your child's optimal well-being is your top priority. For example, you might fuel yourself on iced coffee and bagels, but you better believe that once Baby starts solids, you're going to make sure they have a great variety of fruits and vegetables. We want better for our kids than we sometimes do for ourselves.

However, quality sleep is critically important for you too. You might be tempted to make sacrifices for your kids and conclude that *your* quality of sleep doesn't matter as long as *they* are getting good sleep. But your quality of sleep directly impacts their well-being. It benefits every process in your body and brain, every aspect of your relationship with your partner and child, and every aspect of your well-being.[1] If you are thriving, it benefits your children.

Want to reduce your risk of cancer? Get better sleep.[2,3]

Want to reduce your risk of Alzheimer's,[4,5] diabetes,[6,7] and cardiovascular disease?[8] Get better sleep.

Want to reduce your risk of depression and anxiety?[9] Get better sleep.

Want to reduce your risk of divorce and improve your relationships with your children? Improve your sleep.[10,11]

As professor of neuroscience and psychology at UC Berkeley, Matthew Walker, PhD, put it, **"There does not seem to be one major organ within the body, or process within the brain, that isn't optimally enhanced by sleep (and detrimentally impaired when we don't get enough)."**[12]

Through literally thousands of research studies, the evidence is clear: **There is not one biological function that is not benefited by a good night's sleep.** "Sleep is the single most effective thing that we can do to reset our brain and body health each day."[13]

Somehow, when we have babies we seem to just accept poor sleep as the new way of life. Though, yes, your sleep quality will temporarily and inevitably reduce at first, it should be our number-one priority to get sleep back on track as quickly as possible, not only for your sake but for the sake of your children.

Worse yet, some advice givers in the anti-sleep training space make it seem like the *more* benevolent, loving thing is to just accept crappy sleep as a sacrifice you make for the sake of your children and that taking measures to improve *their* sleep so that *your* sleep can improve is inherently selfish. This line of thinking is not only wrong; it's harmful.

First, just because you're a parent now doesn't mean your needs don't matter anymore. Of course you will prioritize their needs over your own sometimes, but ideally you shouldn't have to choose their core needs versus yours very often. Second, your health and well-being directly impacts your baby.

Quality of Sleep Affects Your
Physical Health

The first, most obvious benefit of good sleep is your physical health. As we established in the previous chapter, you don't have to look far to find empirical data that supports a link between good sleep and any physical process. These same principles hold true for you too.

When you're not getting sufficient sleep, you're directly impacting your immune system functioning, even in the short term.[14,15] Insufficient sleep long term wreaks havoc on your health and longevity and is linked to cardiovascular disease, autoimmune diseases, cancer, and diabetes.[16,17]

During sleep your body is busy at work repairing tissues and inflammation, which assists in strength and recovery.[18,19] If you'd like to put this to the test, I challenge you to run a mile in the morning after a great night of sleep. Take note of how you feel. Then, run a mile after a poor night of sleep. Notice a difference? I assure you, you will. The same is true for weight lifting. Your body simply functions better with better sleep.

Big picture, you want to stay alive and healthy for your posterity for as long as possible. The cumulative effects of poor sleep over time are undeniable and are staggering. Even in the short term, if there was a way to reduce the length of colds and flus, or better yet skip some altogether, wouldn't you want that? Good news! These benefits can all be yours.

Quality sleep impacts your **hormone balance and weight control.**[20] Hunger and fullness cues, the kinds of food you crave, and how your body stores fat are impacted by sleep.

At a minimum it makes baby weight harder to shed. Not to mention the trickle-down effect of poor sleep reducing your energy and motivation to exercise, which is your next best bet to boost your health. The more regularly you exercise, the more energy you'll have. Your muscles and bones will be stronger, your heart will be healthier. You'll live longer and have an improved quality of life. You'll be the kind of parent who can get down on the floor to play with your kids or chase them on the soccer field.

Don't get me wrong; you're inevitably going to have moments of exhaustion from a long day of work where you give your kids a tablet and a drive-thru dinner and you park yourself on the couch and doomscroll. But sleeping well allows you to show up as the best version of yourself. The better you sleep, the healthier your lifestyle habits will be the majority of the time. The healthier you are, the healthier your children will be, because you are modeling to them their norm.

A University of Cambridge study[21] found that children who see their mothers exercise are far more likely to be active too. Your kids look to you as an example for everything. The more you prioritize sleep, healthy diet, exercise, and a healthy lifestyle, the more they will follow suit. All of these health benefits and outcomes are directly linked to and trickle down from quality of sleep.

The better you sleep, the healthier you'll be for your children, and the healthier they'll be in turn. Period.

Mental Health

If we take a quick ride back on the research train, there are a couple of things I'd like you to understand.

Sleep and mental health are *deeply* interconnected. During REM sleep, the brain is hard at work for your emotional well-being. Areas of the brain are active to process emotions and memories. Have you ever had a fight with a significant other, friend, or sibling only to wake up the next morning and feel less bothered by it? Thank you REM sleep and emotional processing!

Or maybe you realize that you got grumpy or offended *because* you were tired. That happens too. When we're sleep deprived, the amygdala (the emotional part of the brain) becomes overactive, and the prefrontal cortex (the logical part of the brain) starts to sputter and slow. The result? Irrational emotionality, misinterpretations, and impatience.

On this note, please disregard the old adage "Never go to bed angry." If you're emotionally dysregulated and it's late at night, just go to bed. Talk again in the morning when your brain chemistry is reset and it'll be far more productive.

During sleep our hormones balance and neurotransmitters replenish and repair.[22] Cortisol (stress hormone) is managed, and dopamine and serotonin (happy chemicals) restore and balance.

For all of my therapy clients, my initial prescription for boosting brain balance is:

1. Sleep
2. Fresh air and sunshine
3. Movement
4. Nutrient-rich foods
5. Water

Sleep is first, because everything else is easier to do when well-rested.

Again, in the upward cycle of positive outcomes: the better you sleep, the more energy and optimism you have, the better food choices you make, the more likely you are to exercise, the more likely you are to get outside in fresh air and sunshine and choose productive activities, the more dopamine and serotonin will be produced.

The bottom line is that sleep promotes happiness and emotional resilience.

Mother-Infant Bonding

The more Mom is thriving postpartum, the better off her baby will be. In fact, the bond between mother and baby is deeply impacted by Mom's mental health. And Mom's mental health is deeply impacted by her sleep.[23]

Depressed mothers often show subtle cues of their depression, by way of repressed expression of joy and warmth. They may exude sadness or overwhelm or be less affectionate.[24,25]

Think of the last time you saw your best friend and you knew something was wrong. How did you know? Most often, the answer is in the subtle cues. You just knew. The energy had shifted. They *seemed* sad or upset. Maybe their eyes looked different or their smile was muted.

Infants are masterful at noticing subtle cues, but they don't know how to make sense of them. Infants who have a mostly steady dose of "things are great, everyone's happy" have a more peaceful and calm demeanor than infants who perceive "something is wrong. Something isn't okay but I'm not sure what." Those infants are more on edge, anxious, and fussy. And the last thing a depressed or anxious parent needs is an extra fussy baby.[26]

Additionally, one component of mother-infant attachment consists of accurately interpreting and responding to baby's cues, both verbal and nonverbal, such as crying, smiling, reaching, and vocalizations.[27] Depressed (and exhausted) mothers are far more likely to miss those cues simply because they're zoned out and in their heads. Anxious and depressed mothers that feel disconnected from their babies feel *more* depressed as a result. They report feeling like they're failing and that there's something wrong with them, which perpetuates the vicious cycle.

Co-regulation refers to the act of your body and nervous system regulating your baby's. If your baby or child are stressed out, simply having you close can calm them. Your heart rate and breathing regulate and calm theirs. Their biology will match yours. Unfortunately, the same can happen in reverse. The more amped, agitated, and on edge we are, the more anxious our kids may be.[28]

Depressed and anxious mothers also are found to have reduced eye contact and social behaviors with their children.[29] Their lower energy can mean less engaged play, fewer stories read, fewer outings, and more screen time. Not only does this negatively impact Mom's brain chemistry, but it negatively impacts baby's brain chemistry.

Additionally, more engaged play, social smiles, shared activities, and eye contact boosts oxytocin for both parent and child, which is the chemical that makes us feel bonded, connected, and content.

In short, the better you're sleeping, the better off you'll be mentally. If you're thriving mentally, you'll have more energy and connection to give to your child, setting them up to thrive in a myriad of ways.

Parents' Relationship

Parents who are sleeping better have a better chance at relationship satisfaction.[30] Of course, having a healthy relationship relies on several factors and not only sleep in a vacuum, but as with everything else, sufficient sleep lays the foundation for success. Though not all parents are partnered and the dynamics may look different, the principle is the same: when you're rested, you're better able to handle the pressures of parenthood and nurture your relationships.

Typically after you have a baby, tensions are already high because both partners are sleep deprived and on edge. Plus, since you have a baby that needs a whole lot of love and attention, you have way less time for yourself, your chore list just quadrupled, and you're probably having way less sex. Add to that baseline hormone regulation being thrown off and stacking sleep deprivation, and you have the recipe for disconnection and bickering instead of the newborn bliss you were expecting.[31]

Remember how, when you're sleep deprived, the emotion parts of your brain heighten while your logic slows?[32] When you are tired, you are grumpier. Your subtle cues are shifted. You've moved into survival mode instead of cheerful thriving, and partners pick up on these nuances and often respond to them. If they are sleep deprived too, they're way more likely to personalize or take offense, and it may even take a bit to realize the cycle you just found yourselves in.[33]

If you've ever had a romantic partner, I assume you've determined the cause of more than one squabble in your relationship was sleep deprivation. I remember one instance in particular where I'd had a poor night of sleep with my baby. I was in survival mode dealing with a headache, and my husband came home and seemed snippy. After a series of short exchanges, I finally threw up my hands and said,

"Why are you so grumpy? Are you mad at me?"

Him "No, I'm bugged because *you're* grumpy!"

Me "No, I'm not! I wasn't even mad at *you* until you were mad at *me*."

Him "Wait, so you're not mad at me? You seemed so on edge when I got home."

Then we laughed at the series of misinterpretations and miscommunications we'd had simply because we were both tired.

Now add the stress of a baby into the mix. The pressure to be a "good enough" parent can make the stakes feel impossibly high. When you layer in sleep deprivation, it's easy to slip into survival mode instead of showing up as your best self.

If you have a baby that has a predictable schedule and can sleep in their own space, you can have freed up bandwidth to pour into yourself and your relationship. As a result, you will have more capacity to enjoy each other and the life you're building together.

Becoming parents together with your person is the fulfillment of a lifelong dream, and you deserve for it to be as magical and special as you've hoped it would be. Getting great sleep is the critical foundation for bringing this dream to life. More sleep = more love.

Job Performance and Cognitive Functioning

Remember how sleep deprivation most quickly impacts the prefrontal cortex? This is the place in the brain that is responsible for critical thinking, decision-making, and logical processes.[34]

The amount (and quality) of sleep that you get *is* going to affect your performance.[35] When you are sleep deprived, your cognitive abilities and even work performance deteriorate.[36] I remember a particularly humbling game of Yahtzee once in my postpartum fog. Despite feeling like I'm usually pretty smart, at the end of the game I stared at my score card and felt completely incapable of simple addition. When sleep deprived, you're significantly more likely to make cognitive errors, which can be physically or financially harmful to yourself or those you work with. In fact, an Illinois Department of Labor study found that 13% of workplace injuries are caused by fatigue.[37]

Other effects of fatigue include:

- Reduced alertness, attention, and vigilance
- Reduced ability to make decisions or process information
- Reduced ability to plan complexly
- Reduced communication skills
- Reduced productivity and performance
- Reduced ability to handle stress[38]

One mom I worked with was Katie, a C-suite executive at a prominent company. She told me:

"I couldn't believe how much of a zombie I was when I had my baby. I was responsible for managing a multimillion-dollar portfolio, and I'd get on work calls with the executive team barely able to form a coherent sentence. Things felt like they just went in one ear and out the other."

Her husband Brian said:

"Most of the time my wife handled the nighttime feedings but even so, I was exhausted and could barely function. Broken sleep took a toll even when I wasn't getting up. I found myself zoning out on my computer screen. Not to mention the guilt that consumed me—if I was this tired, she must be dying. I tried to take over as much as I could so she could get a break but we were both running on empty. My work definitely suffered those first few months!"

Even if you're not returning to work, the cognitive effects of sleep deprivation can negatively impact everyday activities like driving. A 2023 study compared the driving performance of mothers of infants with sleep issues, mothers of infants without sleep issues, and women without children. The results showed that sleep-deprived mothers drove significantly worse—they tended to drive at higher speeds, drifted out of their lanes more often, and were more likely to report being aware that their driving was impaired.[39]

Every aspect of your life as a parent can run more smoothly if you start from a foundation of good sleep. You owe it to yourselves to thrive, but you also owe it to your babies to give them the benefit of well-rested parents. Providing for optimal sleep is a gift to your baby, not something you're selfishly putting them through.

Chapter 6

Why Quality Baby Sleep Matters for the Rest of the Family

L ast but not least, let's briefly touch on why quality baby sleep matters for the rest of the family.

Put simply, the better Baby is sleeping, the better parents are sleeping, and the better you're showing up for your other kids. No one reaps the benefits of well-rested parents quite as much as your older kids.

When you have more than one child, there is no more "Sleep when the baby sleeps," so you have way less of an opportunity to catch up. Since most toddlers wake pretty early in the morning, there's no more sleeping in either. So this means all of the sleep deprivation that comes with a new baby gets compounded.

Your biggest parenting asset, especially with toddlers, is patience. Unfortunately, when you're exhausted, your patience is one of the first things to go.[1] Most parents already tend to feel an enormous amount of guilt when they have a second baby because of the time and energy they'll have to share now. (Don't worry, your capacity for love grows! Though you think you can't possibly love another child as much as your first, you'll find that you do and that a sibling is the most wonderful gift.)

Toddlers push boundaries, they don't always listen, they intentionally disobey sometimes, and they have big feelings. This is all very normal toddler behavior. The more sleep you have in your tank, the better equipped you are to handle all of this with patience and grace.

The attachment bond is still forming with toddlers, as is their personality and their sense of self. How you respond to your toddler and how they perceive you feel about them form the basis of their self-esteem and identity.[2]

Let's imagine two different scenarios:

A. A toddler wakes to find a well-rested mom, maybe already sipping coffee or just waking up herself. "Good morning!" she says with a big smile, eye contact, and a joyful hug. Their morning chatter is light and loving: "How did you sleep? Did you dream? I missed you! You look even more grown up today. I'm so lucky to be your mom." After breakfast and getting dressed, the day begins. Toddler moments still pop up, but Mom navigates them with patience and cheer instead of power struggles.

B. A toddler wakes to find an exhausted mom, still trying to squeeze in a few more minutes of sleep. The morning sounds more like: "Hi, sweetie . . . Mommy needs a little more rest. Want to watch a show? Just keep it quiet . . . turn it down . . . please stop kicking . . . okay, fine, I'm up." The rest of the morning is peppered with short, impatient exchanges. Small battles over the color of a breakfast bowl or putting shoes on quickly wear Mom down. From the outside, you might catch an eye roll or hear a heavy sigh as she struggles to respond to her toddler's endless requests.

How might scenario A versus B play out not just throughout the day but over the course of a few weeks or months? What subtle differences might these experiences create for the child? And how might that impact the parent's perception of parenthood or the child's view of themselves or their relationship?

I'll be honest, I've been both Mom A and Mom B. Thankfully, attachment is formed from thousands of interactions, so as long as you're A more often than B, it's all going to be fine. But I promise, the better you sleep, the easier it is to show up as the parent you hope to be.

The more rested you are, the more energy you'll have for engaged play. And no one needs engaged play more than a toddler. You'll have more energy to read, do puzzles, play tag, or take them to the park instead of parking them in front of the TV.

Not to mention, new babies sleep a ton, so if they nap predictably and independently, you'll still have plenty of one-on-one time with your little one.

When I had my fourth baby, I was already established on social media as @the.peaceful.sleeper. One evening for bedtime I propped up my phone to record a quick five-minute bedtime routine with a three-month old. What I captured instead were multiple interruptions from a too-loud two-year-old waking her sister every time she intruded. I whisper-yelled, "I'm getting your sister to sleep, go find Daddy!" She accidentally slammed the door every time, Baby started screaming, I had to yell to my husband for backup, and then it took 30 minutes to get an overstimulated newborn to sleep.

Unfortunately, some of that is inevitable in the newborn stage because they can't reliably put themselves to sleep yet. But boy did life feel 1,000 times easier after sleep training when I could just plop her in bed and return to the rest of my kids within minutes.

For the record, I still posted that video because it was all too real. Everyone needs to know that even the "experts" still have train-wreck moments!

Additionally, toddlers mimic all that you do, so your ability to model emotion regulation teaches them how to manage their emotions too.[3,4] Having emotionally regulated toddlers makes a world of difference. One of my proudest parenting wins would happen when

53

my toddlers would ask for a reset. They learned to recognize when they were overstimulated and needed a break. Instead of melting down, a "reset" meant they got their pacis and got to chill in the crib with soft music, stuffed animals, and books. I'd come back and get them when they were ready, whether that was 5 minutes or they were content for 40. To be clear, this was not a time-out or punishment; it was self-guided emotional awareness and coping.

And of course, even though toddler FOMO will sometimes make them think sleep is lame, the more you prioritize sleep as an important family value, the more they will see the value in it too, which sets them up for life. You can, in fact, have toddlers and young children who love sleep and ask for it. The benefits of sleep for our kids' intellectual, emotional, social, and physical development throughout their entire lives cannot be overstated. Well-rested families are happier families!

Quality sleep impacts everyone in the family system in a multitude of ways.[5] If you can get great sleep with your infant sooner rather than later, everyone in the family will immensely benefit. In the next section, we'll dive into a deeper understanding of core parenting principles at the heart of optimal child development. With that theoretical foundation, you'll then learn how to apply those principles to your sleep training journey. The result is a sleep training process that you can feel confident in.

Part III

Sleep Training in the Overall Parenting Picture

Chapter 7

Secure Attachment

I know that if you've picked up a book on sleep training, part of you just wants the instructions. "Tell me what to do so my baby will sleep!" I get it. You're exhausted, and quick solutions are appealing. But here's the thing: your baby isn't a robot, and one-size-fits-all methods don't always work. What I will give you is even better: the tools to think through these decisions the way I do. That way, instead of just following a formula, you'll know what to look for, how to make judgment calls, and how to adapt when your baby doesn't respond exactly as expected. That's what makes this book different.

So yes, we'll get to the nuts and bolts very soon. But first, we need to lay out a few more guiding principles. These aren't detours—they're the foundation that makes the steps actually work. Stick with me here. I promise, this part is worth it and it will all come together.

As mentioned in Chapter 1, sleep training the right way for your family is about so much more than just following a step-by-step formula. At its core, this approach provides a framework for authoritative parenting. When you understand these fundamental principles, you'll feel empowered to make the best choices for your family. The goal is to love and nurture your baby while also giving them the chance to grow into a resilient, confident, well-adjusted child.

There will be many junctures in your sleep training (and parenting) journey where more than one option could be right. In those times, you'll use this knowledge to discern what best fits your family. As you strengthen your connection with your baby and stay grounded in the broader framework, your instincts will sharpen. This is parenting with confidence.

Attachment

Attachment is the bond that an infant forms with their caregiver. It fosters a sense of security and emotional regulation and is formed through thousands of interactions. Through everyday behaviors like eye-contact, smiling, tone of voice, and responsiveness in meeting needs they learn that they are loved and taken care of.[1,2]

There's a lot of emphasis in the parenting space on building a secure attachment. And for good reason. There's a ton of research that connects a secure attachment with a host of positive outcomes. This includes things we want for our children like resilience, self-esteem, confidence, forming healthy relationships, and coping with disappointment. And it connects to lower rates of things we don't want for our children, like depression, anxiety, eating disorders, drug use, and more.[3,4,5]

But what exactly is a secure attachment, and how do we build it? Unfortunately, there's quite a bit of misinformation about attachment security that we need to wade through.

Let's start with how researchers define and assess secure attachment.

Attachment Theory

Dr. John Bowlby was a pioneer and thought leader in what we now call Attachment Theory. His work aimed to understand human relationships, specifically the relationships between children and caregivers and how that impacts long-term outcomes.[6]

One of the primary ways attachment security is studied is by an experiment called "The Strange Situation" developed by Mary Ainsworth in the 1970s.[7] It's been replicated thousands of times since then in attachment studies.

In this experiment, a mother and her infant go into a play space together, and the child begins to play with toys. A few minutes later, another care provider (a stranger) comes in, and the mother leaves. The infant's responses to their mother leaving and returning are then assessed. Of the infants studied, those determined to have a "secure attachment" were naturally upset when mom left but were later able to calm down without her there. When Mom returned, they were happy to see her. Children with an "anxious attachment" did not thrive while Mom was away. Instead, they stayed upset and agitated, unable to find calm within themselves or with a stranger even though they were safe. Sometimes those infants calmed down when their mother came back; some stayed agitated even after her return.

Parents today, for all the reasons we've discussed, put *way* too much pressure on themselves to be the "perfect" parent. Somehow this idea of perfection, presence, and making our kids feel loved and safe above all else has morphed into a phenomenon called *overparenting* or *snowplow parenting*, which, ironically, leads to more insecurity and anxiety in children. These parents intervene so much to take away struggle and avoid their children's experience of discomfort that they actually aren't able to develop the necessary grit and resilience for real-life struggles.[8,9]

Of course, you want to be there for your child and help them through life. But you also want them to feel confident, capable, and secure even when you're not physically present. Despite your best efforts, you are not going to be there to fight every hardship for them. So the kindest, most protective thing you can do is lovingly help them learn how to navigate difficulty and select struggles on their own.

There can and should be a balance where we can get the best of both worlds. This comes from building a secure attachment and becoming what they call in the research a *secure base*.[10]

Secure Base

A *secure base* means being a loving figure that children can explore from and return to.[11]

Children with a secure attachment are more confident to have distance from their parents. To illustrate, let's imagine you take a child to the park. You sit down on a park bench while they venture off to play. Every time they look to you, they see you sitting in the same spot watching them. With every passing minute, and with every subsequent trip to the park, they become more and more confident that you're right there. They'll still look to you to check in, and they'll circle back to tell you a story, but they are comfortable and confident playing on the equipment without you. As a result, they have confidence to try new things and have the security to know you'll embrace them with open arms if they need you.

Parents' responses to children lead to what we call an *internal working model*, or their own inner knowing and inner voice.[12] This later guides their feelings, thoughts, beliefs, and expectations as they grow. This is why secure attachment leads to all of the positive outcomes we hope for when trying to raise secure, confident, well-adjusted humans.[13] When your words and actions convey, "You've got this! I believe in you!" Our children's internal working model learns "I've got this. She believes in me." And then later, with more practice, "I believe in me, too." That, my friends, is mastery.

Thus, creating a secure attachment doesn't mean that we take away struggles and discomfort. It means that we lovingly equip them to face struggles and discomforts with confidence and support.[14,15] Some of this simply comes from practice.

We've all encountered protests while changing a diaper, giving a bath, taking away a choking hazard, or . . . the greatest injustice of all. . . . being buckled into a car seat. Do these things damage attachment? No, of course not! Clearly they're upset, but you are protecting them, nurturing them, and caring for them even if they don't like it or recognize it.

When they're a little older, they're going to wobble and fall while learning to walk or ride a bike. Of course, you will help them, but it delays their development if you don't give them an opportunity to try to work it out.

When Maddie was a baby, she was newly crawling, and I had this realization in my parenting journey. She was trying to get through a door that was only partly open. In her rush, she kept bumping it closed and growing more frustrated with each attempt. It would have been easy for me to step in, but instead I encouraged her: "You've got it! Try pulling it open wider." After a few more tries, she figured it out, and we both beamed with pride. That door was never a problem again.

As parents, it's tempting to jump in and fix things, but often the most helpful choice is to hold back. When we believe in our kids' abilities, they begin to believe in themselves.

A secure attachment is born from thousands of interactions wherein you are warm, loving, responsive, kind, and protective, and you meet their primary needs and many of their wants.

The attachment bond is formed through subtle and obvious ways all day long. It happens when you make eye contact, smile, pay attention to them, feed them when they're hungry, play with them, laugh with them, listen to their stories, or scoop them up in a snuggle when they get a bonk. It is also strengthened when you give them a carrot instead of a lollipop at dinner, stop them from running into the street, and prevent them from putting their fingers in sockets.

Building Resilience: Needs, Wants, and Protests

It's interesting to note that one of the primary indicators of a secure attachment in the "Strange Situation" study was the ability to bounce

Secure Attachment

back and be fine even when uncomfortable or without their parent.[16] But in modern parenting, there seems to be a strong, anxious drive to prevent our kids' discomfort at all costs in the name of "attachment" and "security."

Ironically, a common criticism from parents who oppose sleep training is the notion that "I want my child to know I'm always there for them" to promote a secure attachment, when in fact "secure attachment" is, in part, developed by resilience to insecure moments.

Just as an immune system strengthens as it's exposed to germs, attachment security strengthens when the bulk of interactions are warm, loving, and responsive, and a child is slowly tested. In fact, a recent study found that the most well-adjusted children were consistently disappointed by their parents in manageable ways, amid the backdrop of warmth, love, and responsiveness.[17] What a relief! We don't actually have to be perfect. In fact, it's better for them when we're not.

Sometimes they are tested when we can't meet their legitimate needs quickly enough. More than once, we've been out running errands, someone gets hungry or thirsty while I'm driving, and I realize I left my water bottle or extra snacks on the counter. It was a legitimate need, and I dropped the ball. If I usually provide food and drink, this one (or a few) times will not damage their trust in me. Will they learn to pack their own water or snacks because mom is forgetful? Probably. Will this make them feel abandoned, unloved, and uncared for? Gosh, I sure hope not.

Sometimes they are tested when meeting their *needs* clashes with what they *want*. Recently I took my family to the beach for spring break. Before we left the hotel room, I told them to line up so we could do sunscreen. Oh, how the protest chorus began. After a long winter, they've lost their tolerance for sunscreen. You would have thought I was rubbing them with torture lotion. Crying, spitting, and thrashing ensued but we got everyone greased up and ready to play.

Did this damage their attachment with me? No. I was calm, I was kind, I was gentle but firm. They were protected. And as soon as it was over, they were fine.

The following day, however, it was overcast, and I didn't think we'd be out long. When they protested about sunscreen, I backed down. They ended up sunburned, and I was filled with regret. I met their desire for comfort in the moment but unfortunately did not meet their needs. The result was *more* discomfort.

Sometimes, your actions will even accidentally but directly hurt your child. Even then, their attachment can be resilient and remain intact. Once with my sweet little London I was rushing too fast putting her pajamas on and I accidentally caught a tiny pinch of her skin as I was zipping them up. Another time, she toddled up next to me while I was looking for something in the refrigerator, but I didn't hear her. When I closed the fridge and turned, I knocked her over. Is her new narrative "Mommy pushes me"? No, of course not. Try as you might, you will have dozens of times where you'll step on their toes, play too rough, accidentally bonk heads, not hear them when they're calling for you, or miss the punchline of their joke because you're typing a work email. When the majority of your interactions are safe, loving, and responsive, attachment security is incredibly resilient.

Sometimes, meeting their needs pushes them outside of their comfort zone. But we do it anyway when it's important, especially in matters of safety and well-being. Let's take swimming lessons, for example. When I had my oldest, Maddie, we rarely went to the pool. We couldn't afford swimming lessons, and she had my undivided attention, so I had the ability to make up for her lack of skill and keep her safe. Though she got sporadic practice, she wasn't a safe swimmer until she was 7. By the time I had Nolan, my fourth, we practically lived at the pool in the summer, and I couldn't afford to *not* invest in swim lessons.

She needed some tools and skills of her own *in addition* to my conscientious efforts to keep her safe. Waiting to gradually teach Nolan to swim like I had with Maddie was simply not an option. Miss Sarah, her teacher, was patient and firm despite Nolan's protests. And boy, did she protest! She hollered and cried through her entire lesson sometimes. But her teacher was calm and unphased, gently guiding her through. Did it break my mama heart when she'd cling to me crying "I'm scared"? Absolutely it did! It was not comfortable for her or for me, but it was critically important for her well-being and I knew she was developmentally capable of learning. In just two weeks, with 10-minute lessons, she gained a skill to prevent drowning.

Did she give up on love and security because of this process? No, of course not. She learned she could do it. Despite her apprehension, she was safe and contained, and then she got confident and grew. What took Maddie until she was seven years old to master, Nolan had mastered by three years old.

Neither is inherently right or wrong. It was perfectly fine to take a gradual approach to learn to swim for Maddie when that felt right and to take an accelerated approach with Nolan. Despite her initial protest, fears, and apprehension, she beamed with confidence as she acquired her skills, and it opened up so much joy for her childhood. Swim lessons don't ruin attachment security, and neither does sleep training.

Attachment security flourishes when you tune into the needs of the child to provide warmth, support, and challenges to grow at a pace they can handle.[18] A dear friend of mine is a kindergarten teacher. She's described how this dynamic plays out during the first few weeks of school:

> *"During the first week of school there are kids who are dropped off unphased, kids who are upset but quickly recover, and a small number who cry for the first hour and*

then bounce back. Every so often there is a child who is beyond distraught. I've seen teachers pry the child from parents arms, and then sometimes they don't get over it. They have a horrendous day: sometimes unable to engage, even hitting teachers and screaming for their parents. Every child is different, and every child's readiness is different. Though there is value in pushing kids outside of their comfort zone, there is also a line where we don't want to push too hard, too fast."

Thus, it's a delicate dance that requires attunement. We push babies and kids slightly out of their comfort zone and then assess how it's going. Can they adjust and adapt eventually? If they genuinely can't, then we reevaluate our strategy. After a week of swim lessons, Nolan was demonstrating mastery, and her confidence increased. Sometimes things get worse before they get better, so we keep on keepin' on for a reasonable amount of time to hope the breakthroughs happen. If and when they don't, we reevaluate and pivot. This doesn't damage attachment either. Sometimes you don't know until you try, but if you're intentional, you're paying attention, you're trying your best, and you pivot when it's clear you need to pivot, everyone will be just fine.

Secure Attachment and Sleep Training

Now let's talk about attachment as it relates to sleep training. When babies vocally protest falling asleep independently, many parents get uncomfortable, just like I did with swim lessons. It's understandable—it's never enjoyable to hear our babies cry. We are biologically wired to feel stress when our kids are upset. It is an instinct to want to intervene. But that doesn't automatically mean intervening is what they need.

The great news is, sleep training actually has no bearing on their attachment security.[19,20,21,22,23] Yes, they may prefer your assistance to fall asleep or to fall back to sleep in the middle of the night during a sleep cycle transition, but sleep is one of our most important, and most beneficial, human needs. If they are developmentally ready to learn the skill of independent sleep initiation and maintenance, it is perfectly fine to give them space and time to figure it out. The benefit of consistently deep and restorative sleep massively outweighs any temporary frustration or discomfort in the learning process.

Unfortunately, sometimes in parenting circles the mere mention of words like *sleep training* or *cry it out* make people shut down. In the chapters to come, we will dive into the intricacies of this process, but I want to set your mind at ease. Whatever you have heard about sleep training or whatever your preconceived notions are, you don't have to do anything that you don't want to do. The objective is to guide our children to these skills and to good sleep patterns through whatever way **their learning** and **your teaching** is most effective.

Sleep training, as I approach it, is nuanced and attuned. Extreme "cry it out" methods got a bad rap because they ignored other cues about babies' needs and promoted a one-size-fits-all approach that didn't sit well with many loving parents. But that doesn't mean "crying it out" is inherently anti-attachment. Even through protest, your attachment can stay intact.

Many parents hesitate to sleep train because they're afraid it will damage their relationship with their baby. These fears are misguided. Attachment is a trusting relationship we work on all day (and all night) long. Sleep training no more harms infant emotional security than buckling them in a car seat or rubbing sunscreen on them. You don't have to choose an accelerated method, but don't avoid it because you're afraid it will damage them.

Attachment is all about being responsive to your baby's needs. That's how they learn that they are safe and protected in the world.

When it comes to sleep, we have to remember that a baby's *needs* and *wants* are different. They do actually *need* to sleep, they just don't really want to right now. Or they *want* you to help them to sleep but they are in fact capable of learning how to on their own. Supporting their sleep, despite protest, is an act of love because sleep matters so much.

Not only can attachment security thrive *despite* sleep training, it can actually strengthen *because* of it for all of the reasons we've discussed. Well-rested, sleep-trained babies tend to be easier and more predictable. When parents experience their babies as easy or difficult, their parenting styles shift accordingly, through toddlerhood and beyond.[24,25] Easier days and nights create space for joy in your relationship and allow you to show up and parent as the best version of yourself.

Chapter 8

The Gifts of Independence, Resilience, and Self-Soothing

The Gift of Independence

Fostering independence in our children is a gift for them and for us. When our children have some tools to help themselves, their needs are met faster, and we have freed up bandwidth to meet more of their wants. We get to be collaborative and supportive. The more independent they are, the lighter our burdens will eventually be.

Imagine two different babies in a car running errands around town: Sophia, six months old, loves her pacifier. Unfortunately, it falls out of her mouth while they are driving. She looks down, spots it next to her leg, grabs it, and pops it back into her mouth again. This might happen three more times during the drive, but each time it's a momentary setback that she easily navigates. Sophia and Mom or Dad arrive at the store, load up into the shopping cart and blow bubbles, giggle and play games as they complete their errand.

Arlo is six weeks old. He also loves his pacifier, but when it falls out during the drive, he cannot get it and starts to cry. His cries turn to screams while his mom or dad try to find any other way to console him while driving. He's not having it. Finally, exasperated, they pull over to put it back in. Five minutes later, it falls out again, and the charade continues. Once they get to the store, they're overstimulated and stressed before they even start shopping. Though subtle, there's likely a shift in how they interact through the store.

I imagine every new parent has experienced this chaos. What a relief it is when babies can get their own pacifiers. Everyone wins when they've achieved this independence milestone.

Similarly, potty-trained children don't have to sit in their own mess until Mom or Dad notice and clean them. Young children that can reach into the fridge to grab a cheese stick don't go hungry while they wait for a younger sibling to get settled before lunch. A young child that can read doesn't have to wait for parents to read them a story.

When kids are capable of meeting their own needs, those needs get met more efficiently. Of course, this doesn't mean we stop trying to help, but some things go much more smoothly when we can work together.

Big picture, small doses of independence like this lead to a construct we call *self-efficacy*. Self-efficacy is the belief in one's own ability to master and accomplish their goals.[1] It's the personal satisfaction and pride that can be seen on a toddler's beaming face when they exclaim "I did it!" This in turn leads to the development of optimism and self-esteem as well as reduced depression and anxiety.[2,3] When parents believe their children are powerful and capable, children will in turn believe this about themselves. Then, a great game of childhood and beyond becomes testing limits to increase ability and, in turn, self-efficacy and confidence.[4]

As parents, we must stand in a "Let's see what you're capable of" mindset instead of "I don't think you can" or "Mom or Dad will do it for you" mindset. Our kids are incredibly capable. Let's lovingly encourage them to see what they can do.

Early in my parenting journey, I remember one experience at the park. To be fully transparent, I tend to run on the anxious side, and it's a constant, conscientious effort to tame my own anxiety and not let *my fears* hold my kids back. As my almost two-year-old daughter climbed up the stairs to the big slide, I felt my own fear of heights kick it. *She's never done this before. Is this too high? Should I let her do it, or will she get hurt?*

As Paisley reached the top of the slide, I could see in her eyes that the height set in. She looked at the slide and down to me full of nerves. I swallowed my anxiety, determining that it was indeed safe, and smiled up at her. "It's high, huh? Do you think you can do it?" She looked back and forth as I stood up and walked closer to her. "I bet you can do it. You're so brave! Do you want me to wait at the bottom for you? You've got this!"

She sat at the top for an extra second and then pushed off. As she got to the bottom she was *beaming* with excitement and pride! I cheered; she smiled and then raced off to do it again. I returned to the park bench this time and gave her a big thumbs-up as she conquered the slide again and again.

A few minutes later, another mom sat on the park bench next to me. As her much older child approached the top of the big slide, she jumped up and frantically called, "No, no, no that's too high!" He immediately jumped back, startled and confused, and slowly backed away scared. At this point, Paisley was coming up the stairs to do the slide again. I watched as he scooted out of her way, bewildered and curious while he watched this little girl confidently do the big slide on repeat.

Look, I'm not here to judge another mom at the park. I'm sure that kid eventually learned to navigate a bigger slide, and he's going to grow up and turn out just fine. I'm also certain my anxiety has unknowingly crept up on me dozens of times and I've stopped my kids from doing something that would have been okay.

What was interesting to me about this moment was watching in real time as a child learned "You aren't capable of this" when in reality, he very likely was. In her attempts to prevent potential discomfort, his or her own, she delayed a growth opportunity and taught him to be scared when he might have otherwise learned to be brave.

71

The Gifts of Independence, Resilience, and Self-Soothing

Fortunately, learning like this happens over thousands and thousands of interactions. We're all going to miss opportunities sometimes; what matters most is that the overall trend in our parenting is that we're teaching "You are capable, you can figure this out, and I'm here for you if you need me. And sometimes if I think you can figure it out, I'm going to give you some space and time."

The Gift of Resilience

Sometimes there is struggle, trepidation, or discomfort when we stretch and grow. In fact, I would argue that there is always some struggle in growth and development. In his book *The Anxious Generation*, Jonathan Haidt mentions an experiment conducted in the early 1990s where researchers attempted to create a self-sustaining ecosystem in a bubble to see if we could eventually learn to support life on Mars.[5] It was complete with trees and plants as a source of oxygen. However, suddenly and inexplicably, the trees started to fall over and die. They just toppled over even though there was no disease or bug that killed them. What the researchers realized was that because there was no wind, the root systems were not given an opportunity to sufficiently strengthen enough to support their upward growth and weight. As trees encounter wind, there's *just enough* pressure to trigger roots to grow, develop, and widen in order to stabilize and withstand greater strain.

The trick is finding the right amount of struggle to optimize growth. To build on this metaphor, sometimes too much wind is damaging to trees. Some tree species, like palm trees, do fine with severe wind, while others may snap and die. Thus, we can't say there is one exact, perfect amount of wind for optimal thriving and growth. So much depends on individual factors.

The right amount of struggle is absolutely essential for growth, even if it's uncomfortable sometimes. Immune systems strengthen through sickness and exposure to germs; muscles get stronger when they strain. The key is to keep the struggle appropriate to what *your* child can handle. Because it's not possible to prevent all discomfort, it's much better to give our kids safe opportunities with "micro struggles" to learn how to navigate and build resilience and mastery. Of course, you'll offer support if they need it. This builds trust with you and confidence in themselves.

Gently nurturing independence to build self-esteem and self-efficacy is a parenting journey you'll navigate for life, but it starts in the groundwork you lay when they're small. You'll let them experience the annoyance of tummy time or strain to wiggle to a toy that's just out of reach to help them get stronger and more capable. Sleep training falls under this same umbrella. Though there may be some protest as they navigate this developmental task, when we allow space and time for our babies to figure it out, not only can they, but they're so much happier and sleep so much better.

One client, Gabrielle, enthusiastically reported, "I couldn't believe it! I was so nervous about the sleep training process. He cried through three timers the first night, but the second night he just played with his hands for five minutes, made some noises, and then rolled over and fell asleep. I thought it was going to be way worse." Blair's baby whined and babbled for seven minutes before falling asleep the first night. "I've just never even given him a chance," she realized.

As with all developmental growth areas, the short-term discomfort of sleep training is worth the long-term rewards of having a good sleeper. There is so much more peace of mind when you know your baby will sleep reasonably well regardless of the circumstances. Viewing them as independent and capable sets you on the path to gently nurture other aspects of self-reliance and independence, in turn building self-confidence and self-esteem.

73

The Gift of Self-Soothing

One of the main arguments we see against cry-it-out sleep training is the argument that the stress hormone cortisol spikes while babies are crying. And they worry that too much cortisol is not good for developing brains.

While there is indeed evidence that cortisol is raised during periods of CIO, studies indicate that these elevations are within a normal, healthy range. Additionally, in the follow-up study after CIO sleep training, there is no difference in cortisol levels between sleep-trained and non-sleep-trained babies; however, the sleep trained babies are sleeping better. They're getting more total sleep at night and waking up less often. Even if they do wake up, they put themselves back to sleep without waking their caregiver. Thus, there is a temporary increase in stress, but it is not long-lasting; it's within a normal, tolerable range; and it *is* productive.[6]

Cortisol is a stress hormone our babies and children are going to encounter their entire lives on a daily basis. Of course, we don't want too much stress on a constant basis, but stress to some degree is inevitable. It's much more beneficial to allow our children to experience small doses of stress and learn to calm themselves than to try to eliminate all stressors.

I'd much rather have a three-year-old that knows how to calm herself when she's angry she didn't get what she wanted than have a three-year-old who's always gotten what she wants and doesn't know how to share because she's rarely had to deal with that stressor.

As social psychologist Jonathan Haidt put it, "We must prepare our children for the road, not the road for the child."[7] Meaning, we cannot and should not eradicate every form of stress our kids might face. In fact, gently exposing them to stressors and then overcoming them helps their brains down-regulate cortisol, which is a gift for life. This resilience promotes optimism, confidence, and an internal locus of control. Momentary periods of fussing before falling asleep are a perfect opportunity to overcome a micro stressor and self-soothe.

The short-term, mild discomfort of facilitating independent sleep is well worth the inevitable discomforts of *not* teaching independent sleep skills.

Let me share two examples based on the thousands of families I have worked with:

- **Girl Interrupted:** Sarah has a seven-month-old baby who won't sleep with anyone else. Every nap requires her to nurse her baby to sleep and then hold him for 90 minutes. If she coughs, sneezes, or needs to go to the bathroom, her baby's sleep is interrupted. If a repair person comes to the door during naptime or she needs to sign for a package, it's game over. The rare times she's left her baby with someone else to care for, he's had short, fitful sleep and cries almost the whole time. While she's out, she's getting texts from her partner or babysitter asking for help and wondering when she'll be back. Even though it feels good to get away, it's so stressful it doesn't feel worth it. As a result, she does everything she can to not be gone too much. She skips lunches with girlfriends and doesn't do recharging activities like hair appointments, going to the gym, or going on dates with her partner. When she is inevitably gone sometimes, her baby has a much harder time. He doesn't thrive well without her.

  Even when she is home, Sarah is stretched thin and always feels chaotic and like she's running behind. The house feels messy, she's never sure when she's going to be able to shower, and at the end of the day she's tapped out and touched out.

- **Miss Independence:** Jane also has a seven-month-old baby, but her baby is sleep trained. Even though her baby is sad when she leaves sometimes, she quickly bounces back and is content with

The Gifts of Independence, Resilience, and Self-Soothing

a different care provider. Jane leaves her sitter instructions for naptime or bedtime that look something like this: "Nap at 1:30. Feed her, put on a sleep sack, turn on white noise machine, and close the curtains. Read two stories, and then put her in the crib. She should sleep until about 3. Help yourself to snacks in the pantry and feel free to watch TV." Jane feels completely at peace while she's out, and when she gets home, the babysitter reports that she's so easy and happy! Jane finds it way easier to make plans outside of the house and knows her baby can thrive in a variety of situations with a variety of trusted care providers.

Even when she's home, she can count on predictable breaks during the day while her baby is napping. This allows her to do things to still feel like herself. She can work out, get dressed and ready for the day, stay on top of chores and work, or just relax while her baby is napping. She invites girlfriends over for lunch while the baby naps so she can fill her tank and she loves being a mom.

Giving our children time and space to master new tasks, learn new skills, and encounter and overcome stress or other "negative" emotions within the context of a nurturing and supportive framework is not neglect; it's parenting. Our babies are going to feel temporarily stuck and bothered when learning to roll. They're going to fall a bunch when they first learn to walk. They might cry a bit when they're learning how to fall asleep independently. Frustration is part of growth.

It is okay for our kids to be mad or uncomfortable sometimes. In fact, it is a good thing. They can and will learn to tolerate those things and be unphased by them. Plus, usually the bulk of the sleep training process doesn't last longer than a week or two. It's a short-term intervention for a skillset that will benefit them for life.

Chapter 9

The Zone of Proximal Development

The *zone of proximal development* is an educational concept that describes how children learn new skills with the right kind of support. Developed by psychologist Lev Vygotsky in the early 1900s, it highlights the space between what a child can do independently and what they can achieve with support.[1]

Consider tasks and skills as falling into one of three categories:

1. Those we **can do independently**

2. Those we **cannot do even with assistance**

3. Those we **can do with some assistance**

This last category is what he calls our zone of proximal development, where optimal learning occurs. If we can already do the task independently, then learning is not happening. Similarly, if we are trying to learn something that is too difficult for our current ability, then learning will also not happen. Success in learning a new skill happens when we are being supported to learn something that is just slightly beyond what we can currently do.

For example, most two-year-olds can walk independently. Therefore, they are no longer *learning* to walk. It would be unnecessary in most instances to help them walk because they can do it on their own. However, a two-month-old doesn't even have the head and neck strength to support themselves or the coordination to purposefully put one foot in front of the other. Thus, it would be ludicrous to try to teach them to walk even with some assistance.

However, most 9- to 15-month-olds *are* in this zone of proximal development for learning to walk. First they master rolling, then sitting, then crawling, and then pulling up to a stand. Once the groundwork has been laid by mastering these prior skills, they are ready to take steps with support, usually walking while holding on to furniture, a caregiver's hands, or a walker toy. As they build strength, we can gradually release that support, and they can learn to do this task independently.

It is the same with teaching our kids how to read or swim. With reading, first we start with identifying letters and sounds; then blending sounds and sight words; and then stacking on new tasks as they're ready. With swimming, we teach them to get comfortable in the water, splash, learn to hold their breath, blow bubbles, and kick. We support them while we teach the structure and then gradually release that support so they can learn to do it on their own.

So it is with sleep training. As I will detail in the following chapters, in the first four months of life we are laying the groundwork for optimal sleep by doing things like helping them orient day and night, watching awake windows to prevent overtiredness, rocking to sleep, helping naps lengthen, treating sources of discomfort, helping them back to sleep in the middle of the night, and more. Around four months of age, a baby's sleep architecture is more developed, and they are now more equipped to learn the skill of independent sleep initiation and lengthening. This does not mean that every baby right at four months is ready to sleep through the night, just like every 11-month-old is not automatically ready to walk. But the vast majority are ready to learn more sleep skills, so we test them gently to see what they can do. First we set the stage for sleep learning, and then we gradually release support to see what they're capable of, jumping in to offer support and assistance as needed.

Overparenting

In a recent study published out of Yale University researchers looked at the dynamic that they call *overparenting*.[2] That is, stepping in to offer assistance when a child could try to complete the task themselves. I get it, it can feel really hard and frustrating to stand by and watch a child struggle to complete a task you know you could do quickly. This study found a few relevant takeaways:

- **Growth stagnation:** Previous research has linked overparenting behavior to decreased mental health, self-regulation, and motivation in children.[3,4] This makes sense—when we jump in to rescue our kids, we inadvertently teach them that they cannot do something on their own. When they believe themselves to be incapable, they feel more anxious and less confident. In turn, growth stagnates and physical and emotional dependence remain high.

- **Learning opportunity:** Overparenting behaviors were drastically reduced when the parents viewed the task and the resulting struggle as a learning opportunity.

- **Buy-in:** The importance of parent's "buy-in" about what was to be learned directly correlated to the child achieving independence sooner.

In the experiment, children were given the complex multistep task of putting on hockey gear and then playing a game. In one group, the parents were told that their kids putting on this hockey gear would help them "gain a deeper interaction with the sports museum," an outcome they likely don't care too deeply about. In the second group, the parents were told that putting on the hockey gear would help them "gain important skills like problem solving and confidence." They found that while parents still stepped in at some

79

points, the parents in the second group stepped in far less, suggesting that parent's mindset about learning opportunities significantly reduced overparenting behaviors.

This is why it's been so important up until this point to establish not only that quality sleep is vitally important for your child and family system's well-being but that the learning process also helps them, and you, achieve outcomes you want like confidence and resilience.

When you believe your child is capable of doing hard things, they will believe it of themselves,. This is a belief that sets them up for life. The more anxious parents are, the more anxious their kids will be, unless you conscientiously work to override your anxiety. I know, I know. I say this as an anxious mother myself, and I remind myself daily that my kids are capable and resilient. This is one of the biggest shifts we've seen in parenting in the last 30 years: parents today take on ownership for every one of our children's outcomes, and yet the result is that our children seem to be struggling more than ever.[5]

This parenting paradigm can start young. Look for opportunities where you can stand back, encourage, and let them figure things out instead of jumping in to rescue. It can be tricky to stand down while you let a baby or young toddler try to open a door, dress themselves, strap on their own shoes, or pour milk into their cereal, especially if you're running late and especially if *they* are struggling and want assistance. But even so, sometimes we should step aside and let them figure it out.

Even as I'm writing this book, I still catch myself in the struggle to not jump in and over-assist my four children. This will be a parenting dynamic for life, I promise.

Recently my 12-year-old got contact lenses for the first time. What feels effortless and automatic to me after decades of practice was frustrating and slow for her at first. Though it was painful to not be able to jump in and help, I knew she needed space to figure it out. So I stayed on the sidelines, offering encouragement and a few tips while she worked through it. The very next day, she proudly reported how much faster she'd gotten them in. Moments like this remind us that kids often need our support more than our interference. The chance to struggle a little is what leads to real mastery.

Of course, with our young babies, it's way harder to remember the importance of holding ourselves back sometimes and harder to recognize how capable they actually are since they seem so little. Maybe you've always rocked your baby to sleep, and you know if you stepped in, you could rock them to sleep in minutes. They might be protesting or annoyed, and they probably want you to help them too. But they *can* figure out how to fall asleep on their own, and it's remarkable how quickly most babies progress. Once they get the skills to fall asleep independently, they'll be able to work toward sleeping all night long without support too. Most babies I work with fall asleep in less than 30 minutes on night one.

Less than an hour of struggle on the first night, followed by less and less struggle in the coming days, to learn a skill that will drastically shift everyone's sleep quality almost immediately and set them up for success? Yes, please. When everyone is getting deep, restorative sleep, everyone wins! They can do it, and the benefits for the entire family are profound.

Part IV

Establishing a Strong Sleep Foundation (0–4 Months)

Chapter 10

Understanding Newborn Sleep

In the prior sections we've covered why good sleep is important and how providing a good sleep foundation for your children sets them up for lifelong well-being. Now let's dive into actionable tips to make great sleep a reality for your family. Though, yes, the rumors are true and you will experience some sleepless nights when you have a newborn, my aim is to help you navigate this phase with confidence to get through the hard parts as quickly as possible.

The reality is that your newborn is neurologically immature. You can implement every strategy perfectly, but you're still at the mercy of their developing biology to some degree. They develop at incredible rates, but everything they do is brand new, and sometimes it's clunky. There are lots of things you can try, and I'll teach you everything we know, but sometimes it just takes time for the kinks to get worked out. Overall, have patience. Don't assume that if your baby is fussy that must mean you're doing something wrong or that you have a hard baby.

The truth is that some babies are just easier than others. Some babies come out of the womb with what researchers call an *easy temperament*. They're just relatively chill and content. About 40% of babies fall into this category.[1] You still need to focus on optimal newborn care but with these babies, it often feels like everything you do just works. Things fall into place, and stretches of sleep at night lengthen naturally. Another 25% of babies fall into "difficult/spirited" and "slow to warm up" categories.[2] These babies are more easily agitated, are harder to keep content, and keep you on your toes wondering what it is they need to be happy.

There's also a tricky overlap that we'll dive into in the sections to come. Approximately 35% of babies have a "mixed" presentation.[3] Think of it like a Venn diagram with a wide space in the middle. These babies *are* very chill, sweet, and "easy," but at times they're not. They seem to have something bothering them that gets in the way of being content. We'll always play detective with our children to figure out what they need and how to best respond—but especially in the first year there may be a lot of guess work and trial and error as you get to know your baby.

Rest assured, if you're doing your best, you are good enough. The newborn stage can feel overwhelming, and it may not always feel like things are clicking. In the pages ahead, you'll learn the four key pillars of newborn sleep, the framework that will guide you through these early months and set the foundation for long-term success. Don't get discouraged by comparisons; every baby is different, and if you lean on these pillars, you'll be giving your little one exactly what they need.

First, let's understand what's happening for our newborns and what reasonable expectations can be.

Sleep Needs

Brand-new newborns need about 18 hours of sleep in a 24-hour period.[4] Their time in the womb was almost exclusively spent sleeping, so don't be dismayed if it seems like that's all they do. In the first few weeks their only "awake time" might still seem incredibly drowsy. Similarly, as long as it's not affecting night sleep, don't worry about a newborn sleeping too much. We call the first three months of life their "fourth trimester" because they're still rapidly changing and developing, but now it's happening in the outside world instead of in the womb.[5] The more you can mimic that womb-like environment, the happier they'll be.

Around four to six weeks of age they'll start to become more alert and engaged. Their eyes can focus, they'll stay open longer, and their awake time just feels more *awake*. By three months they'll have more predictable cycles. Though you may not have a concrete schedule yet, you can start to see some sleep and awake patterns taking shape. At this age Baby is still typically needing approximately 16 hours of sleep per day.[6]

Orienting Day and Night

Because newborns don't yet have a developed circadian rhythm,[7] you may need to help them orient day and night. Though there's no such thing as "too much sleep," the last thing we want is a newborn who sleeps deeply all day long and then naps at night. During day sleep, awake time follows a nap and feeding. In the middle of the night, we want them to go right back to sleep after feeding.

Day/night confusion is typically a short-term hurdle and can be resolved in the first few weeks of life. There are a few simple yet important strategies you can implement to easily get them adjusted.

Daytime:

- Keep day sleep light, bright, and noisy. The vast majority of newborns do not yet need a dark, quiet sleep space. They have enough sleep pressure to sleep in the living room or the grocery store and be undisturbed by regular life noises. Leave the blackout curtains and sound machine for now. Once they're more alert and engaged around 8–12 weeks, those tools will come in handy for naptime.

- Get outside during the day. When natural sunlight hits our eyeballs, it signals to the brain that it's daytime. This helps reinforce their day/night orientation.[8]

- Don't let Baby nap for longer than two to three hours at a time during the day. I hate to wake a sleeping baby, so if you want to let a nap go longer than two hours every once in a while, that's fine. But once you push 3+ hours, you run the risk of an awake stretch in the middle of the night. After a long nap, try to get active awake-time. Overnight, at first you may still need to wake your baby every three to four hours to feed, but put them right back to bed.

Nighttime:

- Overnight, keep the environment dark and quiet. This will signal to them that day and night feel completely different. Use a night light to see instead of turning on lamps and overhead lights. Similarly, refrain from turning on the TV, as the bright flashing lights can be stimulating. If you want to watch a show during a middle of the night feeding, do so on your phone with headphones so your baby doesn't think it's party time.

- Use a sound machine overnight. I know I said you don't need it for naps until later, but sound machines come in handy overnight. Since you'll likely have Baby sharing a room with you for the first few months, a sound machine can be helpful to neutralize the environment. If Baby is in a lighter sleep phase, the last thing you want is the sound of you rolling over to wake them up. It also can help signal a difference between night and day sleep.

Self-Soothing

Newborns are not yet capable of self-soothing.[9] Their brains and nervous system are still immature, so they need help calming down when they are upset. The good news: they aren't capable of getting "bad habits" either, so you cannot spoil them. In fact, when you help soothe them, it teaches their brain the pathways to calming down. Through thousands of instances of your assistance to get calm, you are teaching them the neural framework to later do it themselves, like water carving a path through rocks.

They will need support to establish a good sleep structure. Think back to what we learned about the zone of proximal development: when we are building a skill, first we help our children accomplish that task *with support*. Then later, we gradually release support so they can do it independently. The first four months of your baby's life, you are fully supporting their good sleep foundation.

That means you are likely rocking them to sleep for every nap and even holding them for some naps. You can, of course, practice laying Baby down drowsy but awake and see if they can practice falling asleep with minimal intervention, but this is just practice and often works better for babies with an easy temperament. Practice is always helpful, but don't bog yourself down with unrealistic expectations. Independent sleep is not the goal yet. A quality sleep foundation with support as needed is what we're aiming for.

Your job right now is to get to know them. Learn all of their little nuances and cues. Meet their needs as efficiently as possible, and help them comfortably adjust to this new big world outside of the womb.

For optimal newborn sleep we need to build on four main pillars:

1. **Feeding:** This means offering as much breastmilk or formula as they can comfortably take at each meal. Early on, you'll work to prevent dozing so they don't fall asleep before they're full and getting a good latch so that eating happens efficiently and painlessly. When they are able to get full feedings at each meal, they'll maximize their caloric intake during the day, leading to less frequent night awakening.[10]

Understanding Newborn Sleep

2. **Timing:** If you can master your baby's optimal timing, their sleep unfolds effortlessly. You'll primarily do this by identifying their ideal awake windows, recognizing their sleepy cues and most importantly, and preventing overtiredness. When you nail the timing, babies can be rocked to sleep in seconds or minutes.[11]

3. **Calming:** When you tune into your baby, you learn their needs on a deep level and can respond to them quickly and efficiently. When you can effortlessly keep your baby calm, the cascade of positivity is kicked off. Better sleep and more newborn bliss.

4. **Treating discomfort:** Since your baby is brand new, with immature biology and an immature nervous system, there is some detective work involved in figuring out if Baby is discontent just because they're having a fussy moment or if they are signaling that something is amiss. You can learn to collaborate with your care team to support Baby the best way possible to be comfortable and content.

4 PILLARS OF A GREAT SLEEP FOUNDATION

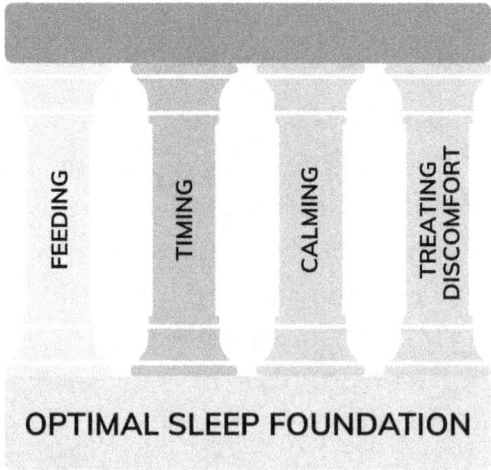

FEEDING TIMING CALMING TREATING DISCOMFORT

OPTIMAL SLEEP FOUNDATION

Think of the four pillars of newborn sleep as the support beams of a sturdy structure. With them in place, you're laying a strong foundation for quality, independent sleep to follow. In the early months, your baby relies fully on your support, like training wheels on a bike, but each well-supported moment is strengthening the pattern of great sleep. When you consistently strengthen these four pillars, not only will your baby sleep better sooner, but the eventual transition to independent sleep will feel seamless.

Chapter 11

Feeding and Timing

In this chapter, we'll tackle the first two pillars of a great sleep foundation for your newborn: the power of optimizing feedings at each meal and preventing overtiredness.

Pillar #1: Feeding

Our first pillar to ensure an optimal newborn sleep foundation is giving a full feeding every time. We want to ensure that Baby takes in as much as they comfortably can at each meal. Why? In short, because the better they eat during the day, the less they'll need to eat at night.[1,2]

If they fill up at each meal, they'll get more calories and fat, which will last them longer. You'll also get more structure in your day, with predictable feeds every three hours. You'll wonder less about their other sources of frustration between meals, and because you'll know if they're hungry or not, you can tune into other patterns and discern other needs more efficiently. Hunger isn't the only discomfort newborns deal with. Sometimes when parents resort to feeding at every squawk, we miss other important cues and start a snacking habit.

Please keep in mind that although feeding every three hours is a helpful guideline, there is no need to be rigid about it. Feed your baby when they're hungry. Anywhere from every two to four hours between feeds during the day is fine. If it seems like your newborn is hungry more often than every two hours, you might need to try to stretch them to get fuller meals each sitting and play detective to see if their agitation is about something other than hunger.

According to the American Association of Pediatrics (AAP), a newborn will typically eat 2–3 ounces per feeding by two weeks of age, and up to 3–4 ounces per feeding by one month.[3]

**BABY FEEDING CHART
FOR NEWBORN TO 12 MONTHS**

AGE OF BABY	AVERAGE AMOUNT OF BREAST MILK OR FORMULA PER FEEDING	EXPECTED NUMBER OF FEEDINGS PER DAY
Newborn	1 to 2 ounces	8 to 12 feedings
2 weeks	2 to 3 ounces	8 to 12 feedings
1 month	3 to 4 ounces	8 to 10 feedings
2 months	4 to 5 ounces	6 to 8 feedings
4 months	4 to 6 ounces	6 to 8 feedings
6–12 months	7 to 8 ounces	4 to 6 feedings

How Often and How Much Should Your Baby Eat? *American Academy of Pediatrics.* 2024.

Prevent Dozy Feeds

In the first few weeks, newborns are typically *very* sleepy. This is because their brains still have an enormous amount of development to do, and brains develop most during sleep. Many animals come out of the womb ready to take their first steps. Alas, humans aren't one of them. Human infants are developed enough to survive outside of the womb but are far from fully developed. Thus, the first three months of an infant's life are often referred to as the *fourth trimester.*[4]

This intense sleep pressure means your biggest hurdle in getting a full feeding is that as soon as milk starts flowing, they'll likely start to relax and doze. Though we aren't letting newborns "cry it out" at this stage, it's perfectly fine to let them fuss for two to three minutes before a feeding, especially in the middle of the night, to ensure they're really awake and ready to eat a full meal.

As soon as you get your baby latched on the breast or bottle, start gently engaging with them. Talk to them, make eye contact, and wiggle their arms and legs. It's a whole lot easier to keep a newborn awake from the beginning of a feeding than it is to try to wake them up once they start heavily dozing. It's like trying to stop a runaway train. You can even gently tickle their ears, tap their face, or undress an arm or two to keep them from getting too sleepy. If they're eating from a bottle, you can wiggle it gently to encourage them to keep sucking.

Try to refrain from having your newborn swaddled during a feeding in the first month or two. This isn't *that* important, so don't overly stress, but it can be a helpful little tidbit so Baby doesn't get too snug and sleepy before they're finished eating. If you are feeding Baby in the middle of the night, I suggest unwrapping the swaddle, feeding fully on one side or 75% of the bottle, and then changing their diaper, reswaddling, and offering the other breast or the last 25% of the bottle.

Feeding length varies from nursing mother to nursing mother and from baby to baby. Typically in the first month, a feeding session lasts about 30–45 minutes. As they get older, they will become more efficient and more alert during feedings.

Recognize the Signs

I sat down with Kary Rappaport from Solid Starts to understand more about infant feeding issues. She's a pediatric occupational therapist, an international board–certified lactation consultant, a feeding and swallowing specialist, and she has helped thousands of babies and their parents. The goal with newborns, she says, is to help Baby "take the maximum amount they comfortably can during each meal." But because newborns are neurologically immature, their cues can be unreliable at first. "It will take some experimentation to strike the balance," Kary explains.

Like everything, that learning process begins with tuning into and discerning Baby's signals. Hunger cues often start subtly and become more obvious if missed. **Early signs** that Baby is ready to eat include:

- Rooting (turning the head side to side, opening the mouth, or sticking out the tongue)
- Stretching or increased movement upon waking
- Bringing hands to the mouth or sucking on fingers or lips
- Soft fussing, babbling sounds or smacking lips

If these cues are missed, some babies, especially more sensitive ones, may escalate quickly to full-on crying. However, keep in mind that newborns are neurologically immature and are drawn to sucking for soothing as well as for eating. If it's been less than two hours since they last ate, you may offer a pacifier to soothe their need for sucking if they aren't ready for a meal yet.

Fullness cues can also be nuanced. Kary notes that babies may:

- Slow their sucking or take longer pauses
- Shift to quick, shallow, non-nutritive sucking
- Fall asleep during the feed
- Let go of the breast or bottle
- Turn, push away, or simply appear disinterested

Of course, these cues don't always mean the same thing. Falling asleep, for example, might signal fullness—or just fatigue. Try again after a small break to see if they might take in more before concluding they're full. "It's definitely a bit of a puzzle early on, trying to figure out how to keep Baby maximally engaged and awake," Kary says. "Skin-to-skin care may help babies stay neurologically more organized and calm prior to the feeding so that they're awake, alert, and ready to engage in eating."

Ensure a Good Latch

There are several reasons why getting a good latch is super important. The first, most obvious one, is a nursing mother's pain when breast-feeding. Breastfeeding isn't supposed to hurt.

Now let me pause and tell you that even when I had a good latch (or what I thought was a good latch), nursing was still excruciatingly painful for the first two weeks. I stressed that my pain was a sign that I was doing something wrong, but actually my body was just getting used to a cute little leech with powerful suction on a sensitive body part. It was just an adjustment.

Work with a lactation consultant to make sure you're on the right track. This is a new thing you've never done before—you're not supposed to be good at it. Even if you've had babies before, it's a new nursing relationship with *this* baby. Getting additional support when you need it is a sign of strength, not weakness. There's no need to struggle alone.

A poor latch can also lead to the breast not being fully, evenly emptied, which can lead to issues like plugged ducts and mastitis. One sign to look for is the shape of the nipple after feeding. It should look more like chapstick than lipstick, symmetrical instead of flattened on one side. If it's lipstick shaped, that can be an indication of oral ties that you might want to get assessed. It means that the tongue is not fully drawing the nipple into the mouth to extract milk optimally. Not only will a poor latch cause you pain, but it may also prevent your little one from eating efficiently.[5]

If the latch isn't great , there are a couple of things that can happen that may impact a full feeding:

1. Baby wears out once they're not hungry anymore, but before they're completely full.

2. They get more foremilk and less hindmilk.

3. They swallow so much air that they start to become uncomfortable while eating.

Not to mention, if the breast isn't fully emptied, then mother's milk supply may be negatively impacted. Keeping Mom's breastmilk supply up and Baby eating well are the two top priorities of an early nursing relationship.

Feeding Fatigue

If your baby has an improper latch, it takes a great deal more effort to extract milk from the breast or bottle. The more effort it takes, the quicker they wear out. The last thing we want is a baby who could eat more but stops just because they've gotten tired of eating. Additionally, some babies "chomp" at the breast instead of taking full draws, so they're working hard but not necessarily taking in a whole lot of milk with their efforts.

Not to put myself on blast, but it's kind of like me at the gym: if the trainer calls for 20 push-ups, I'll probably call it good at 12, take long breaks, or do half-reps. If he doesn't notice, I get away with less, but I also lose out on the full benefit. It's a strategy that works great for me when I'm phoning in a workout but not a pattern we want to let our tiny, hungry babies fall into.

Foremilk Versus Hindmilk

The first milk expressed from the breast is called *foremilk*. This is a much more watery version of breastmilk, more like skim milk. It doesn't have as much fat content or as many calories. As the feeding continues, babies get to the hind milk. Hind milk is more like cream. It has a higher fat content, more calories, and keeps babies fuller longer. If you've ever seen expressed breastmilk, you can typically see the difference.

Solid Starts feeding experts like Kary recommend feeding fully from one side at each meal to get both foremilk and hindmilk and then offer the second breast if they're still hungry so that we can maximize their ability to eat what they need from each meal.

Green stools, gassiness and fussiness, shorter sleep stretches, and frequent, short feedings may all be indicators that Baby is getting more foremilk than the balance with hindmilk we're hoping for. Additionally, the higher fat content milk is more calorie rich and keeps babies fuller longer, allowing for longer night stretches.

Swallowing Air

Have you ever swallowed too much air while you've been eating or drinking? It's the worst. Just last week I was starving after a long day of work and scarfed down a brisket-loaded, twice-baked potato. Delicious. But all that starch and air left me with painful hiccups and a giant stomach bubble. For about 12 seconds, I thought I might die. Dramatic, but true. So imagine what this would be like for a newborn brand new to digestion and air bubbles.

Babies with an improper latch swallow extra air with each gulp. Sometimes they're proficient at moving air through, but often they need to take breaks and be burped while feeding. If we don't catch those air bubbles, they squirm and cry in pain, or refrain from eating more because it's starting to feel uncomfortable.

Even bottle and formula fed babies can struggle with latch, wear out too quickly and swallow too much air while eating. Often these babies are still gaining weight just fine, so there may not be a direct concern from your pediatrician. Please remember that your pediatrician is a physician, primarily focused on tracking your infant's growth and development and being the first-line professional to identify and treat a health *problem*. If your newborn is gaining weight well but snacking, waking frequently at night, or squirmy and fussy, this isn't technically a health problem, but it doesn't mean it's not worth addressing.

Talk to your doctor or a lactation consultant if you have concerns about your infant's feeding and expand your pool of resources more if needed. You can and should create a village of support if you are struggling with a discontent baby. Though they will likely eat more fully and efficiently as they grow, there are resources to help you in the meantime.

Pillar #2: Timing

I once had the privilege of being interviewed on *Good Morning America* to share baby sleep tips. In perhaps the proudest moment of my professional career, I shared some soothing tips and then rocked that baby to sleep on camera in 34 seconds.

I'll share the soothing tricks with you in the next section, but the most important part of that equation was actually the timing. When you time it right, soothing your newborn to sleep is significantly easier.

We nail infant timing by focusing on three areas:

- Preventing overtiredness and overstimulation
- Scheduling
- Recognizing sleepy cues

Preventing Overtiredness

Preventing overtiredness is the cornerstone of happy, blissful sleep. The trick is actually to help Baby to sleep as soon as they're sleepy but before they've gotten overtired.

The biggest mistake parents make when it comes to sleep for their baby is underestimating how much they actually need and when they need it. Or thinking that if we keep them awake for longer, they'll sleep better. This may be true for toddlers and adults, but it is the opposite for young babies, especially newborns.[6] Keep in mind the phrase "Sleep begets sleep," introduced by the legend Dr. Marc Weissbluth.[7] Meaning, the more babies sleep, the better they'll usually sleep.

The human brain produces neurochemicals and hormones to regulate sleep. Some signal to the brain that you're tired and ready to sleep, and some tell the brain to power through and override sleepiness if need be. Melatonin and cortisol are two of these chemicals, and their processes are complex, so for the sake of ease, I'll call these processes "sleepy chemicals" and "awake chemicals."

The adult brain can typically regulate these processes with ease. We can stay out late for a concert or snap awake at 3 a.m. if a child needs you and then fall asleep with relative ease. Our sleep systems can power up and down as needed, for the most part. A newborn's neurology just isn't that coordinated yet.

Our little, tiny baby brains are wired to have some of these processes, but they're clunky. Just like their little arms flail and whack themselves in the face, their brain chemicals can fire willy-nilly if they get too activated.

We can help newborns by syncing sleep times with when their brains start producing those sleepy chemicals. If we miss that window, awake chemicals can take over, and they struggle to find the "off switch," leading to an overtired, overstimulated state I call "wired and tired." Overstimulation is a newborn's Achilles' heel: their immature brains can't process too much input, so instead of shutting down to sleep, they ramp up and melt down.

I'm sure at some point you'll encounter this: a big, exciting day where your happy little babe will stay awake for hours and then completely melt down later. That's overstimulation. Don't worry, it happens to all of us.

I learned the hard way when I confidently took my two-month-old to a Rangers game, assuming she'd sleep in the baby wrap. Instead, she was entranced by the noise and lights, stayed wide awake, and then lost her mind. She screamed while I paced the stadium, we finally left, and then we both cried the whole way home. Never again. Overstimulation can sneak up anywhere: at the store, on a walk, or even around siblings. When a baby's brain chooses excitement over sleep, the crash always follows.

There's a lot of nuance here that relies on individual personality factors and family dynamics. I'm incredibly extroverted, so I'm always looking for an excuse to get out of the house. Some of my babies acquired this FOMO energy and would do anything to stay awake and experience it all. Some didn't care and would easily sleep on the go when they got tired. With my FOMO babies, I had to watch very closely so I could help them power down when it was time.

I hear lots of parents say they don't want to be *those* kinds of parents that revolve their whole life around their baby's sleep. I hate to break it to you, but this might not be up to you. Some babies drift off easily even if you're still out and about or you've missed their signals. Some will make you pay dearly if you throw them off track. To preserve your sanity and everyone's well-being, you might become *those* people. Don't worry, add it to the growing list of things you said you'd never do until you got there. It's about to get long.

In the first six weeks, newborns typically have a strong sleep drive that overpowers the urge to experience the excitement. Once they start to be more alert around six to eight weeks, it's important to be mindful of sleep times and patterns. If your baby isn't falling asleep amidst the excitement when they usually would, you know to intervene and get them somewhere dark and quiet.

If you can time it right and help soothe them to sleep when their brain is signaling that it wants sleep, this process is significantly easier. If we miss their cues, we have an uphill battle to get them to sleep.

Keep in mind that babies move from sleepy to tired to overtired and eventually to exhausted. Sometimes exhaustion tricks us: your baby may crash hard and take a decent nap, making it seem like everything is fine. But if evenings are chaotic from 6 to 8 p.m. or nights fall apart around 3 to 5 a.m., daytime overtiredness is often the culprit. Even babies who look flexible in the moment can have their overtiredness catch up with them later. The good news? Once you learn to spot the signs and protect their sleep, you'll start to see calmer days and more sleep at night.

Scheduling

One powerful tool to assist you in this process of preventing overtiredness is tracking awake windows. That is, the amount of time your baby is awake in between naps. In the first 6–12 weeks, you likely won't have a predictable schedule yet. This is okay. Newborns don't have an established circadian rhythm yet, so it's totally fine if every day looks slightly different than the day before. You can, however, start to establish more predictable *cycles*.

Some parents do much better with predictability and would like to be on a schedule sooner rather than later. If you are this parent, great. Start with a consistent wake-up time, and the rest of the day will flow from there. Keep Baby in bed until, say, 7 a.m. Some mornings you might wake them up, and some mornings you might bring them into bed with you for a few minutes to stretch the time. Other parents get overwhelmed by rigid schedules and would prefer to go with the flow and let the day unfold as it does. The great news is, either option is fine. Do what works best for you.

The only thing that matters is tracking their awake windows and trying to help naps be long enough. Generally, in the first six weeks newborns will stay awake for 45–90 minutes at a time and nap for 1–2 hours. Loosely aim for 60 minutes of awake time and experiment from there. Try not to let naps be shorter than one hour or longer than three hours.

If you want a quick rule of thumb, plan on **one hour awake** and then **at least one hour asleep.** Rinse and repeat all day long. They might have up to two hours of awake time before they go to sleep for the night. Newborn bedtime should align with yours. They'll get the longest stretch of sleep first at night, so plan to go to bed as soon as they do so you can capitalize on those Zs. Usually it's sometime between 9 and 11 p.m.

If you're the schedule kind of parent, here you go. Follow these as a loose template:

6 WEEK OLD
SAMPLE SCHEDULE

Wake up and feed	7:00 a.m.
Nap 1	8:00–9:30
Nap 2	10:30–12:00
Nap 3	1:00–2:30
Nap 4	3:30–5:00
Nap 5	6:30–8:00
Bedtime	9:30–10:00 p.m.

The Peaceful Sleeper

6 WEEK OLD
SAMPLE SCHEDULE
OPTION 2

Wake up and feed	7:00 a.m.
Nap 1	8:00–9:00
Nap 2	10:00–11:00
Nap 3	12:00–1:00
Nap 4	2:00–3:00
Nap 5	4:00–5:00
Nap 6	6:00–7:00
Nap 7	8:00–9:00
Bedtime	10:30–11:00 p.m.

If rigid schedules stress you out and make you feel like you're failing because your baby doesn't align perfectly with what's expected, pretend that chart doesn't exist. Remember, one hour awake, at least one hour asleep. Rinse and repeat. Easy peasy.

Sometimes newborns need help to lengthen their naps. This is perfectly fine. Remember, you cannot spoil a newborn. If you find joy in holding your newborn for their naps, fantastic. Enjoy those contact naps. If having a baby sleeping on you all the time makes you feel "nap trapped," that's allowed too. Many loving parents feel overwhelmed by contact naps, and it *is* possible to get your baby napping well in their own space. There's no shame either way.

I personally was a blend of both. Sometimes I loved nothing more than snuggling up with my squishy baby and laying around reminding myself that everything else can wait because my most important job is right here, and these moments go by so fast.

Feeding and Timing

Of course, I wanted to cherish every minute. But also . . . of course I wanted to take a shower, put on clothes, do a chore, or do something for myself. You can "cherish every moment" better when you haven't lost yourself along the way in motherhood. It's perfectly fine to not want to contact nap for every sleep.

Remember that we're not expecting babies to be able to fall asleep on their own yet. If they can, fantastic. But sometimes there's more luck than skill involved here. If you'd like to try, get your baby calm and drowsy, and then try to lay them down *drowsy but awake*. This means they're about 70–90% of the way to sleep. Keep them close to your body for as long as possible while you lay them down so they don't feel like they're falling and then gently lay your hand on their chest and rock them if needed to help them fall asleep the rest of the way. Keep practicing this and see if you can get away with less and less intervention over time.

If you can't get them to fall asleep this way, just pick back up, rock to sleep and hold them for the first 5–10 minutes. If you hold them for longer than 10 minutes they might be in a more shallow phase of their sleep cycle and may wake easier in the transition to the bassinet. If you hold them for less than five minutes, they might not be deep enough into sleep to navigate the transfer. Just keep practicing. One day soon, they can learn to fall asleep independently.

Many newborns can do their first nap cycle in their own space but need to be held or rocked back to sleep to lengthen the nap past 45 minutes. This is also normal. You have a few options:

- Keep trying. Plan on the first part of the nap, or nap cycle, in the bassinet. When they wake, spend 10–15 minutes trying to rock them back to sleep and lay them down again.

- Plan on the first part of the nap in the bassinet and the second half of the nap in your arms.

- Plan on finishing the nap in a safe sleep aid, like a moving bassinet or in a wrap so you can be hands free.

Even if it requires support to get the nap to be longer than 60 minutes, the investment will pay off in dividends when it's time to sleep train at four months because Baby will already have the pattern of longer naps established.

Sleepy Cues

Catching sleepy cues is a second tool used closely in conjunction with tracking awake windows. They're Batman and Robin. Sometimes we watch the clock; sometimes we watch the signals Baby is giving to know how to time it right.

The trick is to catch the sleepy cues *before* they become tired cues. That's right: there's a difference. Sleepy cues are the first signs that your baby is ready for sleep. These signs include:

- Eyes are staring off into the distance
- A calm, peaceful demeanor
- A subtle yawn
- Reddish hue on their eyebrows and eyelids

Tired cues, on the other hand, indicate that you're getting close to missing the optimal "sleepy" window and your baby is at risk of becoming overtired. Tired cues are usually:

- Fussing
- Rubbing their eyes
- Tugging on their ears

- Avoiding eye contact
- Arching their back
- Getting rigid
- Jerky flailing limbs

SLEEPY CUES	TIRED CUES
Eyes staring off into the distance	Fussing
A calm, peaceful demeanor	Rubbing their eyes
A subtle yawn	Tugging on their ears
Reddish hue on their eyebrows and eyelids	Avoiding eye contact
	Arching their back
	Getting rigid
	Jerky flailing limbs

If you can catch the timing right, assisting your baby to sleep can be quick and easy. Think of sleepy cues like the first alarm bell. First just notice and cross-check that awareness with the clock. Does this timing make sense for a nap? If so, start to move toward naptime. Depending on the temperament of your baby, you might have 2 minutes or 20 minutes before you need to put them down. Once they start lightly fussing, ideally just before, it's time to deploy your soothing strategies and help them to sleep.

Chapter 12

Calming Strategies and Treating Discomfort

Before I had kids of my own, I remember hanging out with friends who already had babies. When their little one started to fuss, they'd confidently, almost casually, identify the source and spring into action. What sounded like any other squawk to me led my friend to turn to her partner and say, "He's hungry, can you make him a bottle?" If I got a chance to hold the baby, she'd gently coach me about his preferences along with other helpful tips. I was amazed—how did they just *know* these things?

The truth is, when you know what to look for, reading your baby's cues becomes a roadmap to their comfort and happiness. As you learn to efficiently meet their needs, you're not only soothing them in the moment, you're also building the deep sense of attunement that becomes parental intuition.

Pillar #3: Calming Strategies

Ready to learn these magical calming tricks? Of course you are! These soothing strategies are helpful to get your baby to sleep but are also great to help them stay calm and content throughout the day.

Remember how we call the first three months of Baby's life the "fourth trimester"? Through these strategies we're mimicking the sensations they had while they were still in the womb and capitalizing on some of their infant reflexes.

Dr. Harvey Karp popularized the idea of the five Ss in his book *The Happiest Baby on the Block*.[1] These are infant strategies parents have been using for centuries. I'll expound on them and add my own, sixth S for infant soothing.

1. **Sucking:** Babies love to suck—it's one of the quickest ways for them to calm down. Even non-nutritive sucking, like on a pacifier or their own fingers, helps activate the parasympathetic nervous system, the body's *rest and digest* mode. This activation steadies the heart rate, supports relaxation, and brings a soothing sense of calm.[2,3] Some babies naturally figure this out, pressing their tongue against the roof of their mouth and pursing their lips into the sweetest little duck face while their cheeks and chin bob. Others find comfort in sucking on a fist, thumb, fingers, a pacifier, or the breast to get that same calming effect.

   I recommend introducing a pacifier within the first two weeks. Though some parents worry about "nipple confusion," offering a pacifier ultimately gives Baby extra practice to master a sucking rhythm, leading to more efficient feedings sooner.[4] Though there's no *problem* with comfort nursing, I prefer to reserve the breast for full feedings or for situations that require above and beyond soothing. Offer a pacifier liberally so Baby can get the nervous system benefits of sucking and the breast doesn't become the only option to calm. After all, sometimes the breast just isn't available, like if you're driving, or Mom is away.

   Babies are incredibly uncoordinated, so introducing the pacifier might take practice and patience at first. The tongue does a wave-like, figure-8 motion while sucking: going down and out and then scoops up and in. To frustrated parents it can look like they are trying to spit the pacifier out, when in reality, they're trying to scoop it in. To help solve this, hold it gently in place and let their tongue clumsily roll around it until they figure it out.

2. **Swaddling:** Babies love to be snug! In the womb, they were snuggled close to you, with their flailing arms and legs tucked tightly to their bodies. Newborns have tons of involuntary jerking movements that can be incredibly disruptive to their sleep. Imagine you're drifting off into a peaceful sleep and your partner comes over and shoves you. You'd be deeply offended, right? Newborn's bodies are constantly firing off randomly, and if they're not swaddled, they run the risk of waking themselves up and being grumpy about it.

   Additionally, that snug feeling reminds them of the comfort of the womb. Everything was warm and easy then, with nothing to do except sleep and grow.

   Some parents think their babies don't like to be swaddled because they squirm and fuss more after they're swaddled. In the thousands of babies I've worked with in my career, I have yet to meet a newborn baby who genuinely does not do better swaddled. They may resist it at first, but keep implementing the rest of your soothing strategies. If you've gotten the timing right and eradicated other discomforts, they should be asleep within 15 minutes.

   Oftentimes, the issue is that the swaddle isn't quite snug enough. You want to be able to easily put your hand between your baby's chest and the swaddle blanket, and make sure it's loose around their hips, but otherwise it should firmly keep their arms tucked closely to their bodies.

   I vividly remember the nurse in the hospital seemingly flopping my precious newborn around swaddling her up. *She's not a burrito!* I thought. But actually, she was thrilled to be a burrito. The most precious baby burrito I'd ever seen.

Fortunately for you, mastering the perfect swaddle is easy now with dozens of tutorials online. Spoiler alert, the first tuck is the most important. Don't just lay the blanket across their chest, tuck it back behind them. Feel free to sing "the first tuck is the deepest" to the tune of Cat Steven's "the first cut is the deepest" to remind you. If that still overwhelms you, find one of many swaddle alternatives like a Velcro sleep sack.

3. **Shushing:** In the womb, your baby had so much constant noise and motion, the sound of your heart beating and blood flow was constantly whooshing through. They could hear that sound over everything else echoing through from the outside. As a result, when they're agitated or ready to sleep, a whooshing, *shhhhhhh* sound drowns out other noises that might disturb them. I usually find myself sssh-ing to the beat of my rocking motions.

4. **Side positioning:** When you're rocking your baby to sleep or to calm them down when they're agitated, make sure they're on their side pressing into your body, not on their backs resting on your arms. If they're not on their side, it kicks off their moro reflex and makes them feel like they're falling, which is anything but calming. It startles them into agitation instead of lulling them to sleep like you're hoping.

Some babies do better facing away from you so they can see the outside environment, but I find that 95% of the time they do best when facing into your body with nothing to see but your shirt, your face, or a ceiling fan. This also helps keep a pacifier locked into place against your chest.

5. **Swinging:** Remember how your baby was in almost constant motion in your womb? They swayed along with every step you took. And not surprisingly, they still love to move. When sleepy, their focus will latch onto one particular thing and while you sway you'll see their eyes dart back and forth,

mimicking REM sleep and further encouraging them into a sleep cycle.

Swing side to side, bounce up and down or do a little combo dance move of both. You'll find your rhythm. Sometimes it's a more overt side to side motion, sometimes it can just be a little jostle, almost as if you were sitting on top of a dryer.

6. **Stroking:** This one is my signature move. Maybe you've figured it out on your own, but our eyes instinctively shut when something gets close to them. Once you've done your other five Ss, gently trace your fingers across your baby's eyebrows, from the top of their forehead to the tip of their nose. You'll see them melt into it and close their eyes underneath your touch. Once they have their eyes closed, it's like you just reminded them how sleepy they are and how good it feels to keep their eyes closed and drift off.

Last but not least, B for Bonus: the **Booty pat.** In the womb, your heart beat gently thudded against your baby's bum. They were most likely positioned head down, booty up so they constantly got a gentle pat, pat, pat with every beat of your heart. While you're swinging and shushing your baby, mimic that feeling.

The more agitated your baby is, the bigger and louder your movements can be. Shush louder and take a wider swinging stance or bounce with more oomph. Meet them where they're at and slowly bring them down. As they calm down, you do too, until your shush is a whisper and your swing is a gentle rock in a rocking chair.

If you've gotten the timing right, these calming strategies will be the ace up your sleeve. If you're sure Baby is full, you're guided by awake windows and tuned into sleepy cues, and these calming strategies *don't* reliably work to keep your baby happy and content, it's time to assess other sources of discomfort.

Calming Strategies and Treating Discomfort

Pillar #4: Treating Discomfort

Newborns can sometimes be little balls of mystery! Unfortunately, their primary mode of communication is crying, and sometimes we struggle to discern if the cry means they're tired, hungry, need to be changed, cold, in pain, or just being a baby that cries.

The better you are sleeping and the more support you have, the more bandwidth you'll have to play detective out of curiosity and not from a place of exasperation and overwhelm. Enlist support during these newborn days. You've heard that "It takes a village," but sometimes you'll feel defeated and want to cry "Where are they?" You might have to find, create, and utilize your village. They may not come running. I hope they do, but they might not. Track them down.

Coming from a busy mom of four kids with multiple businesses, if a friend of mine asked me to come snuggle her newborn so she could take a nap, I would absolutely jump at the chance. When you don't have little babies anymore, there is nothing in the world more precious than having a little bug curl up in your arms. When you're the mom with the tiny baby, you think it's an imposition to ask for a different set of arms to hold them while they sleep. I promise you, it's a gift.

A few weeks after I had my second baby, my best friend Sydney asked how she could help. I told her to just stop by. When Paisley started fussing, as she often did, Sydney offered to jump in and help out. After a few minutes she looked at me and said, "I think she's got reflux. Blythe was exactly this way. You should talk to Dr. Mitchell about it—do you want me to call him for you?" Right in front of me on speaker phone, she got an appointment scheduled. I never would have known the signs so quickly myself, but she had been through it with her first and had paved the path for me. Instead of waiting for weeks with a discontented baby, my village came with insight, tools and support exactly where I didn't know I needed them. Find that friend, and be that friend.

About 30% of babies are just trickier. Some have a naturally "spirited" or "difficult" temperament,[5] but I believe many of these babies just have something bugging them that we haven't figured out yet. "Colic" has been kind of a catchall term describing babies who cry all the time but will eventually grow out of it.

Colic isn't entirely understood. It's often defined by the "rule of threes": crying more than three hours a day, three days a week, for three weeks or more in an otherwise healthy baby.[6] We know newborns are neurologically and digestively immature, so theories about colic include digestive discomfort, immature nervous system regulation, or heightened sensitivity to stimulation.[7] The good news is, they will outgrow it. But can we keep looking to find treatments and resources until that happens? Yes.

Before we dive in and explore sources of newborn discomfort, please remember that one of the most important resources you have in your parenting journey is a skilled and collaborative healthcare provider. While I will aim to pass along what I've learned from experts in their fields, I am not a doctor and this is in no way an exhaustive list designed to diagnose or suggest medical treatments.

I'll also give you the reminder that every Psych 101 professor gives their classes: don't diagnose yourself with everything you're about to learn about. Often sleep regressions and overstimulation can present with many of these same symptoms. If you think your baby may be struggling with some of these challenges, let's get you empowered to find the right resources for them instead of just waiting it out.

There are a handful of common sources of discomfort you may encounter with your newborn:

- Gas
- Reflux

Calming Strategies and Treating Discomfort

- Food intolerances
- Oral ties
- Other sensory needs

Gas

Your newborn's digestive system is brand new! Sometimes they have a food intolerance or oral tie contributing to increased gas; sometimes it's caused by a forceful let down, latch, or feeding problem; and sometimes they are gassy just because they are. If gas is a consistent problem, it may be worth diving deeper to find underlying causes of their upset.

How Do You Know If It's Gas?

Gassy cries often look and sound different. You might have a baby that's sleeping peacefully and then they utter a loud sharp cry while they squirm and grimace. Babies often scrunch their legs up to their bellies. You may even hear a loud, sharp cry followed by a toot.

When newborns have a particularly grunty-squirmy stint from 3 to 5 a.m., I suspect gas first. This is because they've been lying relatively still all night and haven't had great opportunities for air bubbles to move through. Additionally, tired parents don't always get the best burps out when we're trying to get back to bed quickly.

Gassy bellies feel more firm and bloated instead of soft and squishy.

What Can You Do About It?

First, work to improve latch. When their latch is poor, they swallow more air, which will contribute to more gas.

Second, try to get a good burp during every feeding. You might even find it helpful to burp your baby halfway through a bottle or when you switch sides while breastfeeding. When burping your baby, there are two tried and true strategies:

1. Scrunch their knees up to their chest, placing light pressure on the bottom of their belly, and then bring them up to your shoulder. Give a hearty pat, starting from the bottom of their back and working your way up. Many parents do a gentle, sweet, pat pat pat, but if you've got a stubborn burper, they might need a little more oomph.

2. The "magic burp." The idea here is that if babies are straightened out, gas can flow through more easily. Placing them in a sitting position on your lap, cup your hand gently below their jawbone and press your hand on their back, gently straightening their spine instead of being scrunched. Hold in this straightened position for 10–60 seconds. A huge burp can effortlessly arise. It truly is magical.

Thirdly, tummy time is incredibly helpful to work gas out of both ends. It provides a little bit of gentle pressure on their bellies while

Calming Strategies and Treating Discomfort

also giving them an opportunity to move and squirm, which gets things moving through. Wait about 20–30 minutes after eating before doing tummy time to avoid large amounts of spit-up.

Fourth, massages. Before sleep times, especially in the evening before bedtime, do some deliberate belly massage activities. The "I love you" massage is my very favorite. Bicycle kicks and windshield wipers can be incredibly effective as well.

In the "I love you" massage, you are going to follow the path of their intestines to help bubbles move through. Starting with *their* left side, drag your thumb in a straight line down the side of their stomach from just below their ribcage to just above their hip bone. This is the "I." An upside down "L" is next. Drag your thumb from right to left across the top of their stomach, and then down following the same path you did your previous "I." Next, an upside "U" or a rainbow shape from their right side hip bone, up to their ribcage, arching back down to their left hip bone. "I-Love-You" you can repeat with each movement, repeating three to five times and followed by full-hand clockwise massage movements. Bonus, this works like a charm for adults too if you ever have stuck, painful gas. It's wild, because sometimes you can feel the air bubbles crackling under the pressure of your fingers. You're welcome.

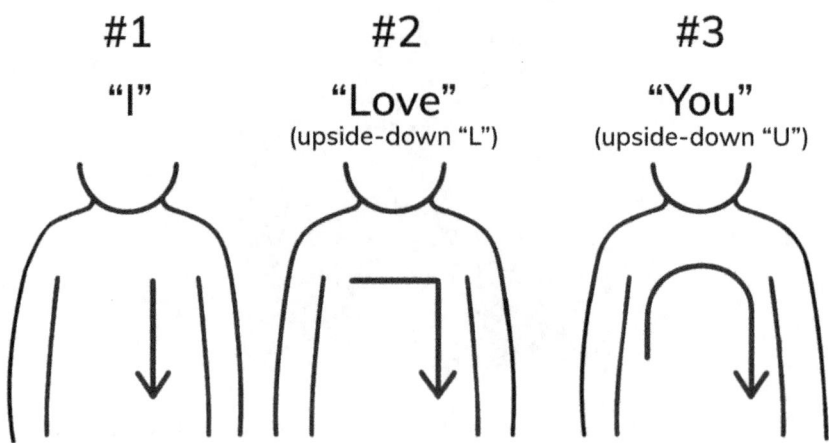

#1	#2	#3
"I"	"Love" (upside-down "L")	"You" (upside-down "U")

Any activities where knees are bent up to the chest can be good for gas to escape. In bicycle kicks, you'll alternate bringing one knee to the chest at a time. For windshield wipers, bring both knees up at the same time and slowly wiggle them back and forth. Other times that you're sitting with them or holding them, look for opportunities for a knees to chest position.

Last but not least, if approved by your pediatrician, you could try gas drops, infant probiotics, or other over-the-counter supplements designed to alleviate gas.

Acid Reflux

Keep in mind that spitting up is totally normal and, in and of itself, is nothing to be concerned about. There's a small muscle between the stomach and esophagus called the *esophageal sphincter* that, like everything else in a newborn's body, is fairly weak and underdeveloped at first. Babies will inevitably swallow some air while eating, and it's common for some milk to come back up with the air bubble when they burp.

This spit-up shouldn't be painful though. Babies who spit up a lot can be called "happy spitters." It might seem like a lot sometimes, but as long as they're growing well, it usually isn't anything to be concerned about.

Acid reflux, though, is caused by an overproduction of stomach acid along with that weak esophageal sphincter and is another common culprit that throws parents through a loop because Baby seems utterly inconsolable.[8] A complaint I hear from parents is that "My baby just won't sleep unless he's held." The first thing that I wonder is if reflux is at play.

More specifically, if your baby won't sleep or be calm unless they're held in *just* the right upright position, it could be a sign of reflux. If they won't calm cradled in your arms but they will when you hold them upright, cheek to cheek, that could be a signal. Reflux babies might sleep terribly in a crib or bassinet but will sleep like a dream in the car seat.

Calming Strategies and Treating Discomfort

Some other signs to look for:

- **Stinky breath and sour spit up:** You should be oddly intoxicated by the smell of your newborn. Their spit up smell should be fairly neutral, even sweet. If you smell your baby and they smell gross like sour milk, it might be reflux.

- **Cottage cheese consistency:** For the most part, spit up should look more like milk than cottage cheese. Some chunks are normal because there is acid in the stomach, but if it has a very chunky consistency, that may be an indicator of excessive acid.

- **Discomfort while feeding:** During and immediately after a feeding, your baby should be the happiest and most content. If your baby pulls off your breast or the bottle to cry and squirm, it's likely reflux or gas.

- **Arching back, head and neck:** If your baby is arching their head back when they cry, they might be trying to stretch and elongate that space. I remember doing this exact movement when I was pregnant and had heartburn. It was almost like I was trying to stretch away from the acid creeping back up.

- **Burps followed by crying:** A burp in and of itself shouldn't be uncomfortable. Usually, if anything you'll get a cry *before* the burp because the gas bubble caused a little pain before it came up. If the cry was *after* the burp, that tells me it might have had a little bit of burning spit-up accompanying it, even if it didn't come out. This is called *silent reflux*.

If you suspect that reflux is a problem, talk to your doctor about it. They'll probably first recommend eliminating some things from your diet or changing their formula. If that doesn't help, you can try some over the counter remedies or even ask for a temporary prescription for reflux medications while you wait for them to grow out of it.

Babies will typically outgrow acid reflux by age four to six months when the esophageal sphincter has gotten stronger and more effective at keeping stomach contents in the stomach. Tummy time can help a lot here to strengthen head and back muscles, which then also strengthens the core.

I'll admit, I do tend to have a bias toward trying medication so we can get Baby out of pain as quickly as possible while we try other solutions to treat the source of the problem. But I'm not a doctor, and I'm definitely not *your baby's* doctor, so I highly recommend you consult with them.

Infant chiropractic care, craniosacral therapy, and releasing oral ties can be other helpful bodywork practices if you've got a chronically upset baby that seems to be in pain.

Oral Ties

I didn't even know that oral ties were a thing until my fourth baby, Nolan, came along. She became increasingly fussy, often throwing her head back and crying, sometimes to the point of being inconsolable. To me, it looked like the telltale signs of reflux. Looking back, I now know there are subtle signs that can point to oral restrictions: things like the mouth hanging open during sleep, noisy or nasal-sounding breathing, blisters on the lips, or feedings that tire a baby out after just a few minutes. At the time, I had no idea those were red flags.

I posted a picture and video on social media, as well as my suspicions that she might have reflux, in hopes that it might be helpful for others dealing with the same thing. What I did not expect was the response from hundreds of moms encouraging me to explore oral ties. What I learned is that, for some babies, the tissue that connects to the bottom of the tongue or the top lip can be too tight, leading to restricted mobility and functioning.[9] Oral restrictions can be the cause of pain issues like gas and reflux, and if we treat the problem at the root cause, Nolan might feel better. Bonus: the plugged ducts and mastitis I was experiencing might get better too.

As Dr. Radhika Kapoor, a pediatric dentist, explained to me, it's not just about spotting a visible "string" under the tongue. It's about evaluating how the tongue actually *functions* during feeding, breathing, and rest. That's why she encourages families to work with a team, often a lactation consultant, a bodywork provider, a feeding therapist, and a pediatric dentist, to get a complete picture before deciding on treatment.

We got Nolan's ties released, did some other body work like chiropractic care and craniosacral therapy, combined with a low dose of reflux medication, and suddenly I had a happy and content baby on my hands again.

Tongue position matters beyond gas and feeding fatigue, says Dr. Kapoor. "Where a baby's tongue rests actually communicates with the *vagus nerve*, a major nerve that helps regulate the parasympathetic and sympathetic nervous system to keep us calm, rest, and digest. When the tongue rests fully against the roof of the mouth, it stimulates this nerve and supports a calm, regulated state. If the tongue can't reach or maintain that position because of a tie, weakness, or poor mobility, babies may have more trouble settling, even after a full feeding."

Oral Function Insights: Key Takeaways from Dr. Kapoor, Pediatric Dentist and Infant Oral Function Specialist

1. Resting Tongue Position Matters

When the tongue rests on the roof of the mouth, it stimulates the parasympathetic nervous system, which helps babies feel calm and settled.

2. **Look for Functional Clues, Not Just a "String"**

It's not just about seeing a tie; it's about whether the tongue can move the way it needs to for feeding, breathing, and rest.

3. **Notice Patterns Over Time**

Signs like the mouth hanging open during sleep, noisy breathing, lip blisters, short or tiring feeds, or frequent gassiness can point to oral restrictions, especially if they happen consistently.

4. **Build Your "Village"**

Work with a team: a lactation consultant, a bodywork provider, a feeding therapist, and a pediatric dentist who collaborate with your pediatrician to find the root cause of discomfort and give you options and resources.

Food Intolerances and Other Sensory Needs

Gas, reflux, and skin issues like eczema *can* be associated with food sensitivities, but they aren't definitive on their own. According to Solid Starts expert Kary Rappaport, the clearest and most reliable sign of a true food intolerance, such as a cow's milk protein intolerance, is blood in the stool.

Kary also offered a gentle reminder to parents: in our well-meaning quest to do everything right, it's easy to assume something must be wrong if Baby is fussy and seems discontent. We jump from one theory to the next, cutting foods, treating reflux, and questioning milk supply, when sometimes the real answer is simply time. "Babies are neurologically immature," she emphasized, and much of the early fussiness or feeding difficulty resolves as their systems catch up. These signs are important to watch, but we also need to temper vigilance with patience. Not every bump is a crisis, and not every challenge needs a fix. Sometimes, babies are just hard for a little while, and it won't last forever. If you have a particularly fussy baby, don't lose hope. You will get through this period, and it won't always be this hard. Please don't let the suggestions and insights in this chapter overwhelm you. Sidestep the narrative that there is something "wrong" with your baby or with your approach, and instead explore from a confident place what your baby might be trying to tell you. Get curious about the why and reach out for help; there is a plethora of resources out there to support you. If you can't figure it out quickly, that's okay! You're in this together, and you'll figure it out one day at a time.

Summary

The newborn stage sometimes requires an "all hands on deck" approach. They don't have the ability to do much at all on their own, so you are supporting them in establishing a solid sleep foundation and slowly seeing what they're capable of. Each time you help them settle and sleep well, their brain is learning and reinforcing the pathways toward a calm, peaceful demeanor and restful sleep.

By focusing on the four pillars of newborn sleep, you can ensure a solid launching point to then scale back on your level of intervention and begin to teach independent sleep skills.

When you get full feedings, optimize their schedule, learn how to soothe efficiently, and treat sources of discomfort, you can experience the "newborn bliss" you've always dreamed of. By six to eight weeks following this method, many newborns can be sleeping six to eight hours stretches or more in the middle of the night.

Part V

Sleep Training

Chapter 13

The Importance of Four Months and Teaching Independent Sleep

Woot-woot, you made it! We're finally at the four-month mark when sleep training (read: teaching your baby independent sleep skills) becomes an option. Life is about to get so much more streamlined when you can simply lay Baby down in their crib with confidence, knowing they'll get the restorative sleep they need.

Before we dive in, let's address the question: what's so noteworthy about the four-month mark?

We often hear about the dreaded "four-month sleep regression," so I sat down with Dr. Sujay Kansagra, MD, director of the Child Neurology Sleep Medicine program at Duke University, to get more clarity on baby sleep structures and what is happening in their brains.

It's not that at this defined point in time baby sleep patterns shift, he explained.

> *"Between six weeks and four months, the brain's sleep architecture continues to evolve. Melatonin production and more robust circadian patterns form around six weeks of age, and the majority of sleep shifts to night sleep. By six months of age, these sleep patterns have matured enough to be observed and labeled easily in a sleep study as different stages."*[1]

There's not one marked shift from one day to the next; their sleep is continuously developing over time.[2]

What we do know is that in the newborn stage, sleep cycles aren't very predictable or structured. It's relatively easy for them to fall asleep, but it may not be that deep or restorative. That's one reason they needed so much of it. Around four months, they've developed into more mature sleep patterns. They can start to take longer naps and sleep longer stretches at night, but they might not know *how* to yet.

I often hear from parents that their baby used to be sleeping way better, and now it's seemingly falling apart. "My baby was such a great sleeper until the four-month regression, and now they're up every three hours at night and their naps are 40 minutes." This exasperated conundrum fills my inbox daily in the hundreds of messages we receive. Why is this?

Over time, their deep, restorative sleep is harder to get into, and sleep cycle transitions can feel like a whole new beast.

"What's different is that babies begin cycling through light and deep sleep in more structured waves. These sleep cycle transitions can lead to awakenings—especially if they haven't yet learned the skills to settle back to sleep on their own," says Dr. Kansagra.

After four months, babies need a new level of skill to stay asleep through sleep cycle transitions. If your baby relies on your help to go from fully awake to fully asleep, they'll also need your help each time they stir between cycles. But if they've learned to fall asleep independently, they can also link these cycles on their own. This means longer naps and fewer nighttime awakenings.

BABY SLEEP CYCLES

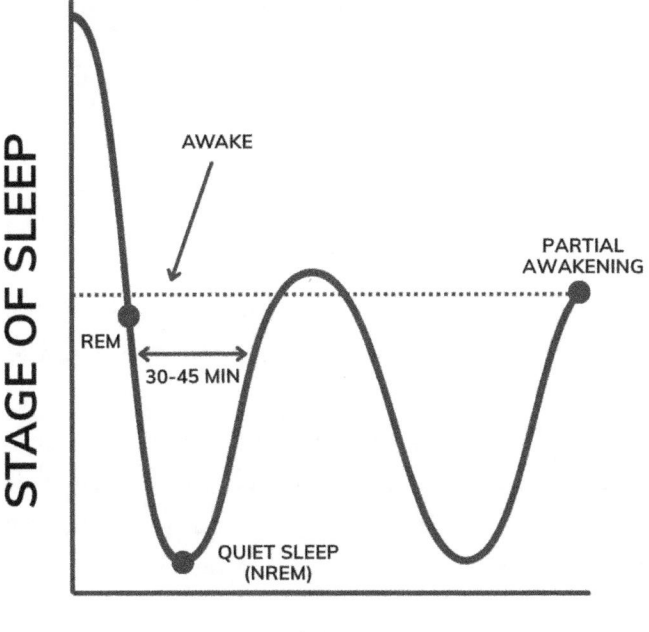

Why Is Independent Sleep So Great?

Independent sleep is better sleep.[3] If they can fall asleep and stay asleep independently, they'll get better overall sleep and so will you. There are so many benefits to this!

For one, it'll free up your evenings to hang out with your partner after bedtime or do some self-care instead of spending hours trying to get your little one to sleep. Though beautiful, the transition to being a

129

The Importance of Four Months

parent of a newborn has likely meant that you've spent all day and night caring for someone else. It feels really nice to be "off the clock" for a few hours to recharge your batteries, knowing that their needs are still perfectly cared for.

I love the pictures I get from clients after sleep training featuring a smiling couple on the couch with takeout, a glass of wine, and a movie, with the baby monitor in the background. A perfect date night in.

It also actually helps your baby fall asleep more quickly long term. As they get older, they are more likely to get stimulated by you as you're trying to help them wind down. Think of how much later you stay up when you're at a sleepover or on a girls trip. You're tired, but you're also excited to hang out.

What starts off like really sweet quality time and bonding starts to become more terse as they get older and you get less patient. You might have this ideal in your mind of gentle quiet bedtimes while your baby or toddler angelically drifts off to sleep whispering "I love yous." And that *does* happen. But what also happens is stern commands to "Stop moving! No more talking! Lay down! GO TO SLEEP!" These extended bedtime routines leave parents exhausted and empty.

Or maybe you gladly give every last ounce of yourself to your little one and you're brimming with patience for them, but because you're running on empty, you have nothing left to give your partner when they brush up on your leg in just that way that signals they want to connect.

I once heard a speaker share how, after a profound loss, she began every morning by saying, "Today is going to be a great day." It struck me because, despite being grateful for my beautiful life, the first word out of my mouth most mornings was. . ."f****." I'd drag myself out of bed exhausted, bracing for another long cycle of wake-ups and nap battles. I still smiled when I greeted my daughter, but inside I was running on empty. Once she started sleeping through the night, though, everything changed. I woke up with joy, genuinely excited to see her, like I was greeting my best friend after time apart.

Everybody in the family system wins when you can have a beautiful, connected, joyous, and loving 10-minute bedtime routine, and then you can have your evening while your baby falls asleep independently.

"But I love the snuggles!" I often hear. Yes, of course you do. I do too, actually. I'm an incredibly snuggly mom, and there is a ton of time during the day to snuggle. You can have the best of both worlds.

You don't sacrifice quality time and affection when you teach your children to fall asleep independently. In fact, you get a way better version of it because your cup is full. Instead of feeling "I love you so much, but I'm utterly exhausted by this," you just get "Holy cow, I love you so much, and I am so lucky you're mine."

This is why it's important to teach the skill of independent sleep initiation. Sure, it makes your life easier too when they can fall asleep and fall back to sleep with less support, but the one who benefits the most is your baby. This is something you're doing *for* them, not something you're doing *to* them.

When they have the ability to fall asleep independently and stay asleep all night long, they are the biggest winners. After the first few months of life, babies don't *need* to eat all night long. They can redistribute their calories to get what they need during the day so they're actually just as disturbed by the middle of the night awakenings as you are. Remember when you were pregnant and had to wake up multiple times in the middle of the night to pee? Ideally you could go right back to sleep, but it was annoying, right? Sleeping through the night without disruption, or with only one feeding, is preferable for them too.

Your baby would rather be sleeping through the night! Yes, if they wake up from true hunger, we'll feed them. But often they're actually just waking up because they're in a sleep cycle transition and need help getting back into the next sleep cycle.

Sleep training is a gift. There might be some clunkiness when it's brand new, but that is the same with every developmental milestone. Your child will protest and get frustrated when they're learning to walk, read, swim, and sleep independently. But all of these independent milestones are massively beneficial to their lives, so the temporary frustration is worth it. And when you do it right, it can be fairly smooth and easy.

So how do we teach a baby to fall asleep independently when they're used to being rocked to sleep? By building on the foundation you've already set and giving them the space to practice doing it themselves.

Imagine building a block tower: the stronger the base, the sturdier the whole structure can be. So it is with sleep training. The foundation you've built through the newborn stage is critical and remains crucial through the process.

That foundation comes from four pillars you've already learned:

- Full feedings to maximize daily intake
- Mastering timing: preventing overtiredness, awake windows, sleepy cues
- Calming strategies: discerning and meeting needs efficiently all day long
- Identifying and treating sources of discomfort

And now, in this next phase, we focus on three pillars of "sleep training."

- Falling asleep unassisted
- Lengthening naps
- Sleeping through the night

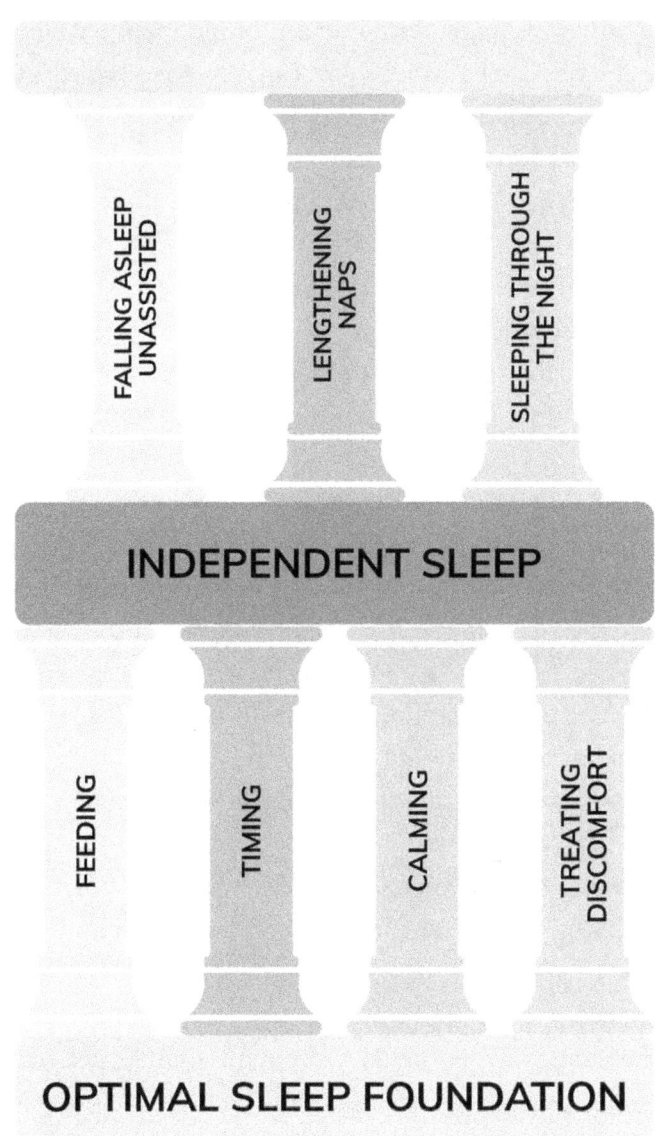

FALLING ASLEEP UNASSISTED

LENGTHENING NAPS

SLEEPING THROUGH THE NIGHT

INDEPENDENT SLEEP

FEEDING

TIMING

CALMING

TREATING DISCOMFORT

OPTIMAL SLEEP FOUNDATION

The newborn sleep foundation pillars remain essential during sleep training and beyond. When sleep training "doesn't work," it's often because something in the foundation still needs shoring up.

The Importance of Four Months

Now that we are ready for the phase of independent sleep, mentally carve out one to two weeks you can devote to the process. This should be a time without major travel and without too many commitments that will disrupt naps or bedtime.

In as little as three days, we can see massive progress! For about 90% of the thousands of babies we've worked with directly, we see up to 75% improvement in sleep in just three days. That means falling asleep unassisted, taking naps longer than one hour, and eradicating middle-of-the-night awakenings that aren't due to hunger. It usually takes another week or two of consistency to iron out the rest of the kinks.

Even an A+ sleeper is going to have rough naps from time to time, struggle to fall asleep at night, or wake up randomly in the middle of the night for a few days. Keep providing consistency in the process, and they'll bounce back. Remember, even professional baseball players don't bat 100%. Pro basketball players miss free throws all the time. The key is that they bounce back, they keep trying, and they don't catastrophize the misses.

So, how do we arrive at this glorious new milestone of having a sleep-trained baby? One that you can gently plop in the crib, smile and say goodnight, and you're confident you won't hear from them for 12 hours? The baby you can lay down for a nap and you know it'll be about 90 minutes?

The simple answer is: 10-minute timers. After optimizing your sleep foundation, you'll do a regular bedtime routine and set them in their crib awake. Through a series of 10-minute timers you'll give them space and time to work on falling asleep independently with soothing intervals between.

Again, babies aren't robots. There's quite a bit more nuance I will teach you about, and as every baby is different, you can choose if one of my other methods is a better fit. The bottom line is, I will teach you what you need to know so you can sleep train with confidence.

Chapter 14

The 10-Minute Method

Falling asleep unassisted is the first pillar of sleep training. As we've discussed, if they have the skill to go from completely awake to completely asleep independently, they will also be able to sleep cycle transition on their own.

BABY SLEEP CYCLES

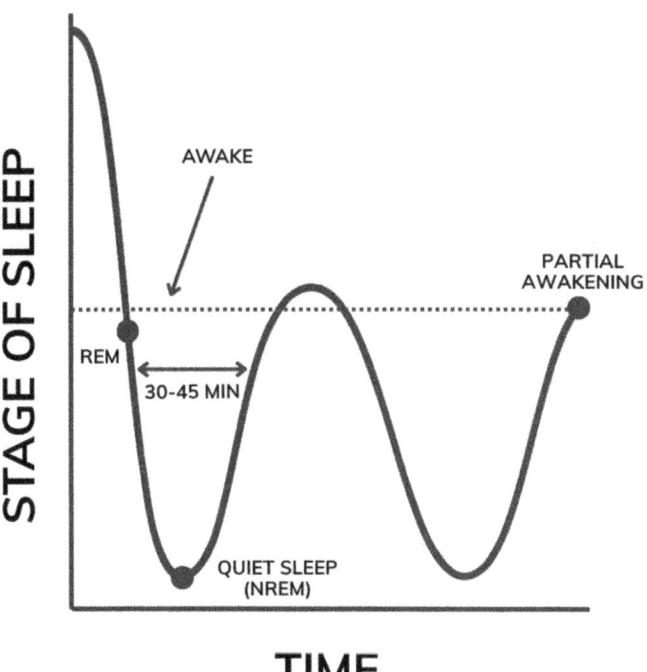

TIME

I often hear parents who love to rock or feed their baby to sleep; they just wish they would sleep through the night or take better naps. But, unfortunately, it doesn't work like that most of the time. We have to progress in order. If they can fall asleep on their own for the beginning of their sleep, they'll be able to do the rest too.

Thus, independent sleep initiation, or falling asleep unassisted, must come first.

So how do you do it? Grab a highlighter, bookmark this chapter, and read on!

On the day that you start, and the one to two days prior, do whatever you need to do to get good naps during the day. We want to start off with a nice, full sleep tank. Well-rested babies do much better than chronically overtired babies.

The Snapshot for Bedtime

- After your bedtime routine and last feeding, place your baby in the crib awake and leave the room.
- Once they start fussing, set a 10-minute timer and watch the monitor closely to assess soothing behaviors.
- When the 10-minute timer is complete, go in and soothe until calm.
- Place Baby back in the crib, and set another 10-minute timer.
- Repeat this pattern for up to five timers.
- If Baby is not asleep by the end of the fifth timer, rock to sleep. That's enough practice for tonight.

The Full Picture for Bedtime
Bedtime Routine

At this point, bedtime should have naturally started to move closer to 7 p.m. If not, we can adjust their schedule as part of this process. For night 1, just do bedtime whatever time you have been up until this point.

A bedtime routine is helpful to signal to your baby that sleep is coming soon, but it can be as involved or as minimal as you have bandwidth for. In fact, your play in the evening before bed is arguably more important to set you up for success than the bedtime routine itself. Evening playtime should be active. With our younger babies, you may still have to watch for overstimulation, but that will disappear as they get older. Activities like tummy time, bicycle kicks, and windshield wipers can move gas through. Rough and tumble play, deep squeezes, bear hugs, and standing or jumping with support can provide valuable sensory input to activate the parasympathetic nervous system. This lowers cortisol, regulates heart rate, and instills a feeling of peace, calm, and security in the body and brain.[1]

Baths can be a nice part of the bedtime routine because the warm water furthers a calming feeling, and it's a great way to get last wiggles, eye contact, and laughter. A quick massage with lotion further provides sensory input to infuse their body with calm, and a book is a great way to unwind, snuggle, and support language development.

If your baby typically falls asleep during that last feeding, we want to prevent this. You have a few options:

- Move your process up 15 minutes earlier.
- Feed in the living room where there's more activity.
- Feed in the nursery with the lights still on.
- Feed before the bath or pajamas.

You'll have one last bedtime snuggle and then gently put them in their crib and walk away. If you have a baby that takes a pacifier, feel free to give it to them when you put them down. It may fall out, and that's okay.

The First 10-Minute Timer

This is where all babies are different and we're learning about *your* baby.

Some babies will play with their hands, coo, practice rolling, and just hang out for a few minutes. Some babies will cry as soon as you leave the room, offended that you missed the last step and didn't rock them to sleep. Like "excuse me, hello—get back here!"

Once Baby starts fussing, set a 10-minute timer.

Through a series of 10-minute timers, we are giving Baby space and time to figure out how to self-soothe and fall asleep. We learn a great deal from these intervals, and so do they.

More important than the amount of time you set on the timers is what you see unfolding during the process. We're not just allowing crying for the sake of crying, this is an active part of learning for you as well as your baby. There are three main factors to assess:

- Variability in crying

- Self-soothing behaviors

- Ease of soothing with caregiver support

Variability

It's most helpful to think of your baby's noises and cries on a scale of 0–10. Zero is no crying at all. They're just cooing, playing with their hands, or staring off silently. Level 2 might be making noise, but you're not sure if they're cooing or fussing. Level 9–10 is the siren alarm kind of crying. They're screaming, and they're *upset*.

Typically, babies will vacillate through a whole range during this 10-minute timer, mostly staying between levels 4–7. Sometimes they'll pop up to a 9 or 10 for a minute, but they should come back down at different points.

Every time they bring themselves down a level, even if only for a few seconds or minutes, they're putting a piece of the self-soothing puzzle into place. Think of the sleep training process like building a 500-piece puzzle of the Grand Canyon. Some pieces fall into place easily, sometimes it seems like no progress is being made, and sometimes things come together and consolidate in huge sections. It's just a process that unfolds one small piece at a time, but the big picture comes together.

The main sign of progress we're hoping for is **variability.** This variability is baby vacillating from a level 7 to a 4, up to an 8, down to a 6 and so on.

If you're seeing great variability, long moments of calm, or a strong downward trajectory in their level of escalation, you may consider extending your timer. After all, we don't want to interrupt their progress. If Baby is quiet and settling, more time may ultimately be more helpful than you stepping in. For example, if Baby was at a 0–3 for five minutes or they were initially at a 7 or 8 but now they're much more calm, I'll add five more minutes to the timer to see how it unfolds.

On the contrary, if Baby is getting madder and madder, there's little to no variability, and increasing escalation, I might cut the timer off at seven or eight minutes and go in to soothe. It doesn't seem like more time to work it out is going to be helpful. **The objective is to tune in and help when they need it, while giving an opportunity for growth when they can handle it.**

On the first night, you're not likely to see a whole lot of variability in your first two timers. They're mostly just blowing off steam. Around the third or fourth timer, you should start to see some good signs of winding down.

If you have a baby that quickly gets up to a level 9 or 10 and stays there, take note. We may still complete the 10-minute timers to see if anything changes and develops during the first night, but a baby with high escalation and no variability might ultimately need a different strategy. We'll discuss modified options in Chapter 17.

Self-Soothing Behaviors

The next thing you're observing during a timer is their self-soothing behavior. Once they move through their initial upset, you'll start to see some self-soothing behaviors popping through. They may display these while they're highly escalated, but you'll see more of them when they start to calm. Common self-soothing behaviors might be:

- Rolling their head from side to side. Think of a dog walking in circles on a pillow before plopping down, or maybe your own behaviors when you get into bed, adjust your pillows, blanket, and get comfortable. They're settling into their bodies and their space.

- Rocking their head from side to side. This may be a more vigorous side-to-side motion that can seem disconcerting but is totally normal and good. They are activating their own vestibular sensation and rocking themselves to sleep.

- Chewing on their hands, sucking on their thumb or fingers, or sucking on a pacifier. Babies have a strong oral soothing response.

- Playing with their sleep sack, touching the sheets or playing with their ears.

- Trying to roll.

- Dozing eyes.

- "The position." Having watched thousands of babies learn to fall asleep independently, I've noticed a trend that I can't explain but makes me chuckle. If they can't roll onto their bellies yet (a position most babies will choose once they can roll), they *often* fall asleep with their head to the left and their right arm out at a 90-degree angle. Sometimes babies will still be crying when the timer is up and I'll say "wait—they're in position. Let's give them two more minutes" and, sure enough, they fall asleep.

Some escalated babies will clench their fists, hold their bodies rigid, and scream. Though this might be typical of babies in the first or second timer or our babies with a feisty, fiery personality, if they're not moving through that upset and displaying any soothing behaviors as the timers go on, this may be an indicator that we need to shorten timers or there's something else going on. More on that later.

Soothing Your Baby Between Timers

After the 10-minute timer is complete, go back in and soothe your baby in whatever way they need to calm down, aside from feeding. They just got a full meal before bedtime, so they shouldn't have legitimate hunger. Feel free to pick them up if they need it and offer a pacifier if they want one.

The next behavior to watch for and learn from is how they soothe when you're in there helping them. How they calm down between timers with your assistance can teach you a lot.

Soothing with Caregiver Support

I've worked with thousands of babies at this point, and they're truly all different.

Some babies will stop crying and start smiling as soon as they hear the door open. You can simply pat their belly, say hello, whisper some encouragement, and step back out again. This tells me that they probably have an easier temperament and will probably learn this process relatively quickly. Maybe the check-in was helpful, or

141

maybe they could have gone longer before checking in because they didn't really seem to need anything.

Some babies will holler and scream during the timer but will calm immediately when they're picked up. There are no tears, no snot, no heavy breathing. They were just yelling, not even distressed. This tells me that they were more pissed and annoyed than truly upset. They're protesting, but they're okay. This gives me confidence to move forward with timers, or even lengthen timers. I'm okay with babies being a little bit uncomfortable or even mad and frustrated. We don't want them to be overly distressed.

Some babies will take a full five minutes to calm down. They may have gotten very upset. They are breathing heavily, they have tears and snot, and even when you're soothing them, they struggle to get regulated. We take special note here. The goal is to let them protest and work it out as long as it's productive. We don't want to push them too hard too fast. We're not going to give up yet, but we are going to be mindful to not push them past their window of tolerance. If they get so upset they can't resettle and stop scream-crying within five minutes with your support, they may have gotten too upset.

Most babies will fall somewhere in the middle. They'll probably be crying and will need to be picked up, rocked, and bounced to get calm again. Hold them close, offer a pacifier, give kisses on their cheek, and whisper encouragement and reassurances. Ideally, keep these check-ins less than two to three minutes if you can. The goal is to support them as much as they *need* in order to feel calm, without doing more than necessary. If all they need to calm is a hand on the chest, great. Some methods say to never pick them up or only soothe verbally without touching, but those rules are arbitrary. What matters is helping them calm with the amount of support they actually need.

Once they're calm and their breathing is regulated, place them back in the crib and set your next 10-minute timer.

You'll follow this pattern for five cycles and will keep watching for variability, self-soothing behavior, and how they soothe with caregiver support.

Helping Baby Over the Finish Line

About 90% of babies who aren't chronically overtired or have underlying issues like gas or reflux will fall asleep in the third or fourth timer on the first night. If, for some reason, they do *not* fall asleep by the end of the fifth timer, just rock them to sleep. If this happens, don't get discouraged.

I like to think about basketball here. If you went to the driveway and shot 100 free throws but didn't make a single one, you still laid some groundwork to get better at basketball. Instead of staying outside in the cold and dark trying repeatedly, you can decide that's enough practice for one night and get back out there tomorrow.

We want to give babies an opportunity to practice and struggle to obtain a new skill, but we don't need to push them too hard, too fast. Whereas pure extinction methods suggest that you're "caving" or slowing down the process by intervening, we actually know that optimal learning occurs when we strike the right balance of struggle and support.

You've spent the last four months supporting their sleep. This helped strengthen really important neural connections in the brain and carved the path for good sleep. Now you're giving them bursts of opportunity to explore independence, but you'll help them over the finish line after sufficient practice if they haven't gotten there on their own.

The Jerk

Just when your baby is finally calming and drifting toward sleep, you may see it—a full body involuntary twitch that startles them awake. I call it the jerk.

Annoying as it is, it's totally normal, and they can learn to sleep through it. You and I usually do it too. As the brain is relaxing and *falling* asleep, there's often a misfire where the brain isn't sure if it's falling asleep or actually falling. It won't be a problem forever, but the first night or two it will get in the way.

When this happens, give them a few minutes to try to resettle. If you have a baby that's woken themselves up repeatedly just as they're falling asleep, they may get increasingly agitated. If you have one of those babies that's gotten close but ultimately woken themselves up a dozen times, just go in and help them over the hump. Usually these babies can be soothed to sleep in the crib. Place both hands on their chest as they finish falling asleep.

The best way to prevent this is to do lots of body work in the afternoon and evening before bed. Do massages, deep squeezes, tummy time, and hold their hands to let them balance on their legs in your lap. Anything that gets pushing and pulling movements will help their body settle.

I find that the most active parents have the most jerky babies. It makes sense—these are people with a high need for movement for the body to feel calm and regulated. As kids get older, they are better able to meet their own need for movement and bodily sensory input. These are the kids who don't walk; they run or skip from place to place. They twirl, jump on couches, hang upside down, wrestle with siblings or friends, and want to be involved in every sport. Until then, they need your help getting the input they need to relax.

Rolling is the good news here. Once babies can roll onto their tummies to fall asleep, this jerking reflex will be way less disruptive. Of course, always remember that *back is best*. Place your baby in the crib on their back, but if they roll on their own, they are strong enough to be safe sleeping that way. Practicing tummy time is the fastest way to expedite that process.

A Framework for Learning

Recently, we took a family trip to a water park. My four-year-old, Nolan, had passed the 25-meter swim test, but this was a new environment with lots of excitement. When she slipped off a log obstacle, I saw her start to panic. I crouched down close, locked eyes, and calmly said, "You've got this! Find your float." She tried, but when it was clear she needed help, I nodded to my husband, who scooped her up before it got too scary.

There are a couple of things to note from this example:

1. **Allow for struggle:** Big picture, she was significantly better off because we allowed her to struggle an appropriate amount. If I'd have jumped in the second she panicked, she wouldn't have faced an important learning moment. As the swim season kicked off, she needed reminders about her skills and the importance of implementing them. Struggle, within safe limits, is what builds confidence and skill.

2. **Ensure safety and calm:** It was important that I did *not* panic even though she was. I knew the situation was 100% under control. In children's moments of overwhelm and fear, they learn confidence and security when you are cool, calm, and collected. If I'd been panicking with her, she would have gotten more scared.

3. **Intervene mindfully:** Intervene at the right time in the right way. I intervened when the struggle was no longer productive. When it turned from "I wonder if she can do it" to "Nope, she definitely can't," it was time to step in. She needed me to get her out of the pool—but she didn't need me to leave the water park or postpone swimming to next year.

4. Try again: The hard moment and support intervention is just a stepping stone. It's important to try again. She cried, we snuggled, she took some deep breaths, and then she ran off to try it again. This time, when she fell off, she effortlessly found her float and kicked to the side. We celebrated her win, and then she did the log obstacle course 100 more times.

We follow this same framework when setting timers during sleep training.

1. Allow for struggle.

First, you have to get grounded in your decision to sleep train, or you'll fold when it gets hard. It's never easy to let your child struggle, but it's manageable when you trust the value in it. Good sleep matters. Babies that have the skill of independent sleep initiation and maintenance get better sleep than babies who need support to fall asleep and stay asleep.[2] Parents with sleep-trained babies get significantly better sleep. *And good sleep is* **directly linked** *to better physical and mental health outcomes for the entire family system.*

2. Ensure calm and safety.

Yes, it is uncomfortable when your baby is crying. Remember, your baby will feed off of your energy. If you are confident in them, they will become confident in themselves. Throughout their entire lives, starting even now, your children will look to you to learn about their capabilities. "If Mom and Dad believe I can do this, then I bet I can. If they don't think I can, then I probably can't."

If you are grounded in theory and keep a watchful eye through the process, you can stay calm and confident in their abilities to master this new skill. You are a good, loving parent trying to provide the best possible outcomes for them. You've demonstrated your love and responsiveness through thousands of interactions thus far in their little life and millions more to come.

3. **Intervene mindfully.**

This is perhaps the most critical and nuanced step in the process. The timers themselves provide a framework for the intervention, but there is no exact *magic* in 10-minute timers. What they accomplish is giving parents a reasonable amount of time to let your baby protest and giving Baby enough space and time to work on things. You can deviate outside of this 10-minute framework as needed to better tune into the needs of your baby. Anywhere from 7 minutes to 20 minutes is fine.

There's usually little value in consistently setting timers for less than five minutes. Some parents prefer to start the sleep training process with two to three minutes at a time, but often we see that interrupts more than supports them. Imagine if you laid down at night and someone came in every three minutes to see if you were falling asleep okay. It would probably be incredibly frustrating. If checks are too frequent without enough time to make progress, your baby may be more agitated and have a harder time learning.

4. **Try again.**

Once you've gotten Baby calm, give them an opportunity to try again. What may seem like a failure might actually be an important stepping stone toward success. These moments of protest and subsequent calming are crucial elements in their learning process. It is just like tipping over while learning to sit or stand strengthens the muscles needed for balance. Growth isn't linear. It doesn't always unfold seamlessly the first time. If you end up needing to rock your baby to sleep after the fifth timer on night 1, try again tomorrow.

If you haven't seen *any* measurable successes self-soothing or falling asleep independently after three days of practice at bedtime and naptime, you may want to consider a different approach. I'll detail other options in Chapter 17. But give it some time and some repeated practice before concluding it's not the right fit.

As all babies are different, there will be some individualized refinement, but ultimately, giving them space and time to figure it out *is* how they figure it out. As I say in therapy, "Sometimes the only way through is through." **Either we give space for babies to learn on their own or they will keep needing us.** When we find their zone of proximal development, growth happens, and attachment security blossoms.

When we over-support, we risk unintentionally holding our kids back. I recently worked with a family with an eight-month-old. As bedtime approached, he'd fidget, jerk, arch his head back, squirm, and cry. Rocking him to sleep could take up to an hour and felt like a wrestling match. When I was there and this started to happen during the bedtime routine, I said "Alright, let's just plop him in the crib and see what he does." To their shock, he rolled around cooing for four minutes and then fell asleep. Their support was well-intentioned, but it turned out he just wanted to be put down.

All babies are going to present slightly differently in this process, so it's hard to tell you exactly how night 1 for *your baby* is going to go. What I do know is that for about 90% of the babies we work with who have a strong sleep foundation, we see pretty good variability on night 1. They'll be upset when you go in to soothe them, but they *can* be soothed. As the timers go on, they get closer and closer, demonstrating lots of different self-soothing behaviors until they eventually fall asleep. Even if they startle and flinch as they enter the active sleep phase, they can overcome those hurdles. Even if they ultimately need support, they power through that phase better and better over the course of the next few days as they learn to initiate sleep independently.

Overnight

In the first few days, our primary objective is to help them learn to fall asleep independently. Once they can do that, they will learn to sleep-cycle transition independently too. Independent sleep *initiation* comes before independent sleep *maintenance.*

So, for the first few nights we're not doing a whole lot of intervention in the middle of the night. I know sleeping through the night is probably your biggest goal, and we'll get there. But if you take the steps in the right order, you'll get there faster with way less drama.

Once your baby has fallen asleep for the night, the only thing you're going to do for the rest of the night is a single 10-minute timer each time they wake. Set **one 10-minute timer and then intervene as needed to get them back to sleep.** That's all we're doing in the middle of the night for the first few days. We'll do a deep dive on sleeping through the night in Chapter 16.

If it's been less than three hours since their last feeding, rock or soothe them back to sleep without feeding. If it's been more than three hours since their last feeding, go ahead and feed them.

One of the reasons sleep training has gotten a bad rap over the years is that a lot of methods went out of order and were more intense than they needed to be. There was no emphasis on building a sleep foundation or looking at individual factors like temperament or eradicating issues of discomfort. The objective wasn't to scaffold skills to achieve the milestone of sleeping through the night; the goal was just to stop feeding overnight. So as soon as you were ready to start, you were instructed to just skip all overnight feedings and let Baby cry themselves back to sleep, even if it took hours.

That is the biggest difference with my approach. First we build a solid sleep foundation. Then we scaffold skills. One builds on top of the next until we reach that final milestone we're after: sleeping through the night. Baby learns to fall asleep on their own; then they learn how to lengthen naps on their own, which teaches them to sleep cycle transition independently. Once they have some skills for initiating and maintaining sleep, the overnight awakenings that aren't due to legitimate hunger will drop off.

Many parents are okay with one overnight feeding remaining if their baby needs it. The most exhausting issue is when bedtime takes hours, when naps are hit and miss, and when they're woken up multiple times at night. One quick feeding isn't *that* disruptive.

I recently met with Nicole, mom of two boys. She summed it up perfectly:

> *Overnight wouldn't be so exhausting if I wasn't running myself ragged all day long. I see other moms that seem to be thriving and I am not. I don't even know who I am anymore. I don't have time to shower, much less exercise, arrange a playdate, or meet friends for lunch. I have no idea when naps are going to be. But if he doesn't sleep well, everything is worse. He's grumpy, fussy, and I feel like I'm failing. Every day it's a whole song and dance, and I also have a toddler running around. I feel terrible brushing him off or turning on a show. So I'm constantly trading off—his well-being versus his brother's well-being. I'm okay going last, but I'm not even on the map right now. I'm running on empty. It's stressful all day long, and then he's up multiple times at night. If he still needs one feeding but everything else gets better, that's more than doable.*

When you have a baby that can reliably fall asleep on their own, it opens up a whole new world of freedom and ease. You're still meeting all of their needs; it's just become significantly easier to do so. In the following chapters, we'll dive into the other two pillars of independent sleep: improving naps and sleeping through the night. We'll also discuss alternative approaches including "no cry" if this 10-minute method isn't the right fit for your family.

Chapter 15

Naps

The eventual goal for naps is that we can lay Baby down awake, and they can fall asleep on their own and nap for at least an hour.

On day 2, you're going to start working on initiating independent sleep for naptime as well. Last night for bedtime you allowed for up to five timers to help Baby learn to fall asleep on their own. When they woke in the middle of the night, you just did one 10-minute timer and then rocked or fed back to sleep.

Today and beyond for all naps, you'll allow up to *three* timers for Baby to fall asleep and/or sleep cycle transition on their own.

You'll follow the same bedtime format for naptime initiation.

The Snapshot for Naptime

- After your nap routine, place your baby in the crib awake and leave the room.
- Once they start fussing, set a 10-minute timer and watch the monitor closely to assess soothing behaviors.
- When the 10-minute timer is complete, go in and soothe until calm.
- Place Baby back in the crib, and set another 10-minute timer.
- Repeat this pattern for up to three timers.

- If Baby is not asleep by the end of the third timer, rock to sleep. That's enough practice for this nap.
- If Baby falls asleep independently but wakes before the nap has lasted an hour, you can use your remaining timers or assist them back to sleep so the nap is restorative.

The Full Picture for Naptime

Naptime Routine

After an appropriate awake window, you're going to do an intentional but brief naptime routine. This may include one last feeding, but it's important that Baby does *not* fall asleep during this feeding. Feed them out in the living room or in the nursery with all of the lights on, and engage with Baby during this time. Talk to them, wiggle their arms, stroke their cheek, and don't rock too much while you're feeding.

Change their diaper, put on a sleep sack, sing a song or read a story if you want, and prepare their room for sleep. After four months of age, blackout curtains and white noise machines become especially helpful tools to neutralize the sleep environment, signal that it's sleep time, and support longer naps by eliminating disruptions. Close the curtains, turn on the sound machine, give a last snuggle, and then gently place them in the crib and leave the room.

Timers and Soothing

Just as with bedtime, you're going to allow time and space for Baby to settle and fall asleep on their own, soothing between as needed. You'll follow nearly the exact process you did last night. Again, the three main factors to assess during this process are:

- Variability in crying
- Self-soothing behaviors
- Ease of soothing with caregiver support

Helping Baby Over the Finish Line

Because we don't want to risk pushing your baby over the line of overtiredness, we're just going to do three timers for naps instead of the five timers we do at bedtime. If Baby has not fallen asleep on their own after the third timer, go in and help them fall asleep.

Again, we're looking to support them to sleep with as little intervention as possible. If they got really close to falling asleep, you may be able to rock them gently in the crib instead of picking them up to rock to sleep.

However, if Baby got very worked up, they might need to be taken out of the crib and fully rocked to sleep. Once asleep, within 10–15 minutes, attempt to transfer them back to the crib. They will likely stir in the transfer and may need some more support in the crib, like resting your hands on their chest, to help them stay asleep.

Sometimes your baby will wake up immediately when you set them back in the crib. Use your best judgment to decide if you should give one more 10-minute timer, rock to sleep and try to transfer one more time, or just finish this nap as a contact nap. Though having them sleep in the crib is ideal, either option is perfectly fine.

Nap Lengthening

What if they wake up after 30 minutes?

If your baby usually wakes after just one sleep cycle, this will very likely happen. What you do next depends on how hard it was to get them to sleep for the nap initially.

We don't want to push babies too hard, too fast. The last thing we want is to feel like we're letting them fuss all day long. For this reason, we're allocating three timers *total* for each nap.

If it took your baby three timers to finally fall asleep or if after the third timer you had to help them get to sleep, you'll probably need to support the rest of the nap. You may still want to wait a few minutes to assess the likelihood that they can fall back to sleep independently. Give them the chance if it seems promising; otherwise, just go in and rock back to sleep. Once asleep, within 10–15 minutes attempt to put them back down in the crib. If they wake during this transition and you can't support them to sleep in the crib, just finish the nap as a contact nap. The goal is for each nap to be at least one hour.

If you go in to rock them back to sleep and they simply won't do it, attempt for 15–20 minutes and then move on with your day. We'll try again at the next nap.

If your baby fell asleep in fewer than three timers to *start* the nap, use your remaining timers to *lengthen* the nap.

Let's say, hypothetically, that Baby fussed for 10 minutes, then you went in to soothe, and they were able to fall asleep on their own during the second timer. You technically have two timers left to utilize.

When they wake up after less than an hour, set a 10-minute timer once they start fussing. Again, you're watching for variability and self-soothing signals, and then go in to soothe after the timer is up. Set Baby back in the crib once calm and do one more 10-minute timer. If they haven't fallen back to sleep at that point, go in and support to sleep.

Again, you may try to set them back in the crib after 10–15 minutes of sleeping in your arms, or you may finish this nap as a contact nap.

- The goal is for each nap to be at least one hour. Again, if you go in to rock to sleep and they simply won't do it, attempt for 15–20 minutes and then move on with your day. We'll try again at the next nap.

If I've helped Baby to sleep, how do I transfer them?

If you have helped Baby fall asleep or fall *back* to sleep, it's important to try to set them down within 10–15 minutes if you're going to attempt to transfer them to the crib. This is because a typical nap cycle lasts 30–45 minutes. We want to transfer them while they're still early on in the trajectory of heading toward deep sleep. If you hold them for too long, you risk waking them up right when they're in the deep sleep stage or on the tail end of the deep sleep stage. When this happens, it's harder to get them back to sleep. They may startle or feel *rested enough* so they'll wake up completely feeling like they got a power nap.

Baby Nap Cycle

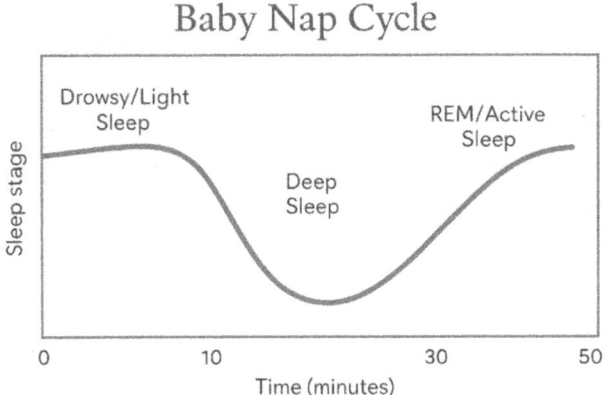

There is a finesse to transferring a sleeping baby without waking them. You might feel absolutely ridiculous, but this works, so it's worth it.

The key is preventing their startle reflex from activating. If Baby gets the sensation that they're falling while they're being lowered into the crib, they will startle and wake up. To prevent this, hold Baby snug against your body. Squeeze them a little tighter while you're moving than you just were. This reminds the brain that they are secure and supported even though they are being lowered.

Take this process *slowly!* Keep your baby pressed against your body as you lower them. Get your hips right up against the crib or bassinet and lean into the crib with them as far as you can go. Short mamas like

157

Naps

me can even use a step stool next to the crib. Instead of them feeling like they're free-falling 24 inches or more as you're lowering them, you're going with them most of the way so you only have 6–8 inches left where they're away from your body as they're being lowered.

Gently move your hands out from under them, starting with the hand that's under their head. Gently lower their head onto the mattress and then move your other hand that was supporting their lower body. If they start to stir, immediately put both hands onto their belly and hold still with medium pressure or rock gently. Place the paci back in their mouth if they take it, make a shushing sound, and use one hand to gently stroke their eyebrows. Once they fall back to sleep, gently decrease pressure and walk away slowly.

The eventual goal, of course, is that they'll have the skills to initiate sleep on their own, so you'll rarely be rocking them to sleep and worrying about transferring them. This is just a tool to bridge the gap.

Naps unfold for babies on a wide spectrum. Some babies quickly consolidate naps within a few days; some babies take two to four weeks to consolidate their naps. You should ideally master naptime sleep *initiation* within a few days, but independent nap lengthening may take a few weeks. If you're on the longer end of this range, don't be dismayed.

Once Baby wakes up from their nap, do your next awake window. Getting outside during this process is incredibly beneficial for them. Go on walks or take toys outside and play on a picnic blanket. When it's time for the next nap after an appropriate awake window, you'll follow the same steps as earlier.

You'll give Baby up to three timers total to work on independent sleep initiation and nap lengthening.

Depending on the age of your baby when you start, you might have 1–4 naps per day, with awake windows ranging from 75 minutes to 5 hours. Of course, all babies are different, and some have higher sleep needs and lower sleep needs. This chart of averages is meant to be a general reference. We'll talk more about scheduling in Chapter 18.

AGE	NUMBER OF NAPS PER DAY	IDEAL LENGTH OF NAPS	AWAKE TIME BETWEEN NAPS	AWAKE TIME BEFORE BED	AVERAGE AMOUNT OF DAYTIME SLEEP	AVERAGE AMOUNT OF NIGHTTIME SLEEP	AVERAGE AMOUNT OF TOTAL SLEEP
0–3 months	4–7	1–3 hours	60–90 min	1–2 hours	5–6 hours	9–10 hours*	16–18 hours
4 months	4	60+ min	90 min	2 hours	3.5–5 hours	10–11 hours*	15–16 hours
5 months	3	60+ min	2 hours	2.5 hours	3.5–4.5 hours	11–12 hours*	14–16 hours
7 months	2	1–2 hours	2–3 hours	4 hours	3–4 hours	11–12 hours	14–15 hours
14 months	1	2 hours	5 hours	5 hours	2–3 hours	11–12 hours	13–14 hours

*broken for feedings

Naps

If your baby is younger than six months and has had a difficult time through the first few naps of the day, you may want to consider fully supporting them for the last nap before bedtime. You can rock to sleep and transfer to the crib or just do the whole nap as a contact nap if you'd like.

The first day of nap training is the most trying. During the first naps of the day they've gotten sufficient practice, and it's most beneficial to give them the snuggles and reset they need so they'll be ready to try again at bedtime. They're better off when they're well-rested and have a nice, full sleep tank before bed.

If your baby has done fine throughout the day, they might not need additional support, and the last nap of the day can be exactly like the others.

As the days go on, you should expect to see improvement in falling asleep for the nap within one to two timers. Some babies will always fuss for a few minutes before naps. These are usually our more alert, FOMO babies who just want to experience everything. Some babies always have some extra steam to burn off, so they'll cry for a few minutes as part of their process. Some babies will babble, coo, and play with their hands until they fall asleep. If your baby consistently cries every time you put them down for sleep but it lasts fewer than 10–15 minutes, you notice good variability and self-soothing behaviors, and they do fall asleep unassisted, it's probably just a personality thing, and you don't need to change anything.

Within one to two weeks, most families see 75–90% improvement in lap lengthening. The goal is for all naps (except nap 3 or 4) to be at least an hour. If you are not seeing improvement in nap lengthening after two to four weeks, you might consider adjusting the schedule.

The Crib as a Developmental Playground

Some parents feel bad letting their baby stay in the crib if they're awake, even if they're not crying. Within reason, keep in mind that the crib is a developmental playground. If they are content, it's perfectly fine to let them hang out in the crib for 10–20 minutes. In the crib they practice skills like talking, rolling, sitting, pulling to a stand, and more. They also get to wind down or wake up slowly. I imagine sometimes it takes a few minutes for you to fall asleep or wake up slowly, and you're not distressed about the quiet relaxation. Some parents will say, "I feel bad just letting him sit in there. Is he lonely?" If he's acting fine, then he is fine. Of course, don't leave your baby in the crib for hours on end if they're not sleeping, but there's no need to feel guilty letting them get a few minutes of quiet time either.

Now that you know everything you need to know about independent naps, it's time for the final (and most beloved by parents!) pillar of independent sleep: sleeping through the night.

Chapter 16

Sleeping Through the Night

Remember that although sleeping through the night is often the biggest goal of sleep training, it's the final piece of the puzzle. We are scaffolding skills, and we only reliably get to this milestone when the rest of the foundation is secure. Once we have discomfort treated, a good schedule in place, and babies have the skills to initiate sleep independently and they're taking good naps, sleeping through the night can fall into place.

For the first few days, the primary objective was giving Baby an opportunity to learn how to fall asleep on their own.

Typically, the unnecessary night awakenings will drop off on their own through this process. When Baby previously woke simply because they were sleep cycle transitioning, they now have skills to get into the next sleep cycle so they won't need your assistance.

Once Baby is falling asleep independently for bedtime and naptime with relative ease, we can focus more heavily on dropping night awakenings. This might happen after two days or after a few weeks. You get to decide how important it is to you that Baby sleeps completely through the night.

You'll want your pediatrician to weigh in here. Up until this point in the sleep training process, babies of any weight and size can do this process because we're not changing much about eating habits. Sleep training for these first two phases has been only about learning to fall asleep independently for naptime and bedtime and taking good, long naps.

Yes, we allowed them to fuss for 10 minutes in the middle of the night before feeding them, but if that's all it took to drop a wake-up, we can rest assured they didn't need to eat.

If your baby has low weight or difficulty meeting their caloric goals throughout the day, they may advise that you keep one feeding overnight. You may choose to keep one feeding in the middle of the night even if they are on a good growth trajectory simply because it doesn't feel worth it to drop it yet. You may wait until it drops on its own as they grow or make a bigger push when they're older.

Every Family Is Different

For my own babies, I made the initial push for sleep training at four or five months. I had so much more bandwidth and energy from the other wins that I was fine keeping one night feeding for a while.

All four of my babies had a slightly different process. These differences were a combination of their personality differences and my life factors. My oldest held on to a 5 a.m. feeding until 10 months. At that point I was positive she was big enough, she was meeting her caloric needs throughout the day, and it was simply a habit that wasn't working for us anymore. She didn't *need* it, and the negative impact wasn't worth it.

My second followed a similar pattern. London, my third, dropped the night feeding on her own at seven months. There was no intervention or cry-it-out process; she just stopped waking up for it. Bless her, my forever angel child. Everything with her thus far is just easy.

By the time I had Nolan, I obviously had three other kids. My disrupted sleep was a bigger issue for me and for my other children. My kids got a better version of me if I slept through the night. At six months I knew she could drop the feeding, so we did a more intentional push. Within four days she was sleeping through the night.

All parents have different preferences here, and I don't have an agenda. If you'd like to keep a middle-of-the-night feeding until they're older, great. If you'd like to do the big push now and drop the middle-of-the-night feedings, that's fine too.

Most parents I work with are somewhere in the middle. I often hear, "I don't *mind* one middle-of-the-night feeding if they need it. But I'd also be thrilled to sleep through the night if we can." With these parents, we opt for a medium push to see if we can drop it without too much stress.

For Amanda, sleeping through the night was the goal sooner rather than later. She told me:

> *"He's ready. He's 19 pounds, eats great all day, and is 4 months old. A middle-of-the-night waking just isn't sustainable. I have trouble falling back asleep, so if he wakes at 3 a.m., I'm up for the day and dragging. My husband travels for work, so it's usually just me, and when I'm that tired, I hate how I'm showing up for my toddler. I don't have the energy to play like I used to. And with work starting again in two weeks, there's no way I can do my job on five hours of sleep."*

She was right; he was ready. Within two days her baby was sleeping through the night. She said she felt like an entirely different person. She began waking up happy and felt genuinely excited to hang out with her boys all day long. They just both needed some support to make the push.

Keep in mind, we're not actually "dropping" a feeding; we're just redistributing calories. Babies will take a bigger feeding in the morning and eat a little more at each interval throughout the day so they still can get the caloric intake they need.

On the other hand, Allison, mother of two, cherished that quiet time in the middle of the night. She told me:

"Honestly, that time is so special to me. The whole rest of the day I have another kid running around demanding my attention. I'm always scattered and distracted. During that feeding at 4 a.m. it's just me and my baby. The whole house is quiet, and it feels like sacred time."

She opted not to drop the feeding until 18 months, when she realized neither of them was benefitting from it anymore. This approach was fine too.

Keep in mind that older babies tend to protest harder when things change. You'll have more peace of mind and assurance knowing that their needs are met and the protest is just protest, but they are bigger, louder, and more willful.

McKenna, like most parents I work with, was on the fence. Her baby was waking every 90 minutes, and she was exhausted, but she wanted to do what was truly best for him:

"I know it can get better than this. I can't keep doing wake-ups every 90 minutes. But if he needs to eat once or twice—or even three times—I can handle it. I'll do whatever he actually needs."

Since she'd already been hesitant about allowing for protest, we opted for a light to medium push in the middle of the night. He was sleeping through the night four days later!

If you don't have a clear agenda:

- Take it one day at a time.
- Learn from them about what they need and what they can do.
- Try to decrease intervention and see if you can get away with it.

Every Baby Is Different

When the rest of the foundation is in place, **there are three main strategies for cutting out night awakenings:**

1. **Adjust timers:** Give longer timers or more timers before feeding. You can allow Baby to protest and try to work it out for up to 60 minutes before feeding in the middle of the night. This might be three 20-minute timers, two 30-minute timers, or one 60-minute timer.

2. **Decrease feeds:** Feed less during middle of the night feeds (i.e., offer 2 ounces instead of 5).

3. **Simplify support:** Support getting back to sleep without feeding (i.e., offer a pacifier, pat in crib, rock back to sleep, etc.).

Start with a 10-minute timer in the middle of the night when Baby wakes up; then intervene with as little support as you can get away with. For example if you can offer a pacifier without picking them up, or if they're content with 1–2 ounces, try that. Gently push them a little bit more each night, even adding more time before you go in, and see how it goes.

This will unfold slightly differently for each baby. To illustrate this, I'll share some stories of different babies I've worked with and how they arrived at sleeping through the night. Remember, we learn through trial and error. When we try new strategies, we'll get either *progress* or *information*. The objective is to keep learning about *your* baby to know the next right steps.

McKenna

As I shared earlier, with McKenna's baby we opted for a light to medium push. Since he had great variability when he woke, we let him fuss for 15 minutes before intervening. Instead of feeding right away, she offered his pacifier and a quick pat, and he immediately resettled. This repeated several times that night until she finally nursed at 4 a.m.

The following night, she placed several pacifiers in the crib. Sometimes he found one on his own; other times she stepped in after 20 minutes to help him resettle. By the third night, most wakeups required little or no assistance, and by the fourth night he slept straight through.

Jenna and Michelle

Sometimes I work with small groups of parents to sleep train their babies together. Jenna and Michelle both had 4.5-month-old babies and started with a simple plan: one 10-minute timer followed by a feed. Both babies woke at 10 and 4 but went back to sleep easily after feeding. Because the other pillars of sleep training were solidifying seamlessly, we decided to focus more on dropping night awakenings.

At the 10 p.m. wake, Michelle offered a reduced feed. Her baby resettled quickly and slept until 4 a.m., where she offered a full feeding. Over the next few nights, she cut back gradually and found the sweet spot: no feed at 10 p.m. and a small feed at 4 a.m.

Jenna's baby responded differently. When she reduced the 10 p.m. feed, he woke more frequently. The breakthrough came when she tried a full bottle at 10 p.m. After that, he slept until 7 a.m. Over time, she cut the 10 p.m. feeding back and eventually dropped it entirely with some timers.

Two babies, two families, two slightly different paths, but both reached the same goal of sleeping through the night.

Tiffany

Tiffany came to me exhausted by her five-month-old's frequent night wakings. The night before we started, he'd woken up 12 times and needed to be fed back to sleep each time. Daytime wasn't the issue: he was easy to nurse to sleep for naps and bedtime. She was fine doing contact naps all day because she had only one baby and didn't mind the snuggles. But at night, she worried he was eating too much and throwing off his daytime appetite.

She had tried a "gentle" no-cry approach, but it wasn't working. "He's not happy either. I can see how tired he is," she told me. So we decided to use the standard 10-minute method, taking it one night at a time.

The first night was rough. After a 10-minute timer, he would fall asleep in her arms but wake when set down, leading to repeated attempts to rock, soothe, and sometimes feed. She was exhausted but trusted the process. The next night, she let the timers go a few minutes longer, and to her surprise he fell asleep on his own after 12 minutes. This happened a few more times, but he was falling back to sleep on his own. At 5 a.m. when he cried, she planned to feed him but tested soothing first. He settled without feeding and woke up happy at 7 a.m.

From there, progress snowballed. He had a few nights of small wake-ups lasting less than five minutes, and within days, he was sleeping through the night. Tiffany was stunned at the transformation. "It's like a whole new level of happiness unlocked for him too," she said.

Often in this process, it might feel like it's not working in the moment, but the payoff comes later. Tiffany's brutal night of multiple wake-ups still facilitated the progress she got the next night.

Tricky Babies

Cora's baby was colicky as a newborn, and we tried everything under the sun: infant chiropractor, probiotics, lactation consulting, switching formulas, reflux medication, meeting frequently with her pediatrician, and more. To get to sleep, she needed to be bounced on a yoga ball for 40 minutes and, even then, would usually wake up after 27 minutes. To add a layer of complexity, her dad has horrible sleep issues. Without sleep medication, he could stay up for days and then crash.

As we dove in, I was curious if there might be a genetic, biological, or neurological factor at play. Because sleep is critical for her development, we needed to find the most effective path forward even if that looked different from the "average" baby's experience.

The only way to learn is to dive in and try some things. With the first timer the first night she was highly upset when we put her down but soothed quickly and started cooing and playing with her hands. She didn't fuss again for five minutes and had great variability. But after the first soothing interval, she unraveled.

She immediately jumped to a level 10 scream. We intervened earlier than usual, not wanting her to stay escalated for long. After several rounds of soothing and shorter timers, she finally fell asleep and then surprised us by sleeping through the entire night.

Over the next couple of days, we discovered she did best with longer timers and minimal check-ins. With this approach, she quickly learned to fall asleep in 15 minutes or less and was consistently sleeping through the night. The baby who once woke eight times a night was suddenly sleeping soundly. It felt like a miracle.

Naps, however, remained a challenge. She could fall asleep independently but struggled to connect sleep cycles, rarely napping longer than 37 minutes. For three weeks, we kept the plan consistent: one or two mid-nap timers followed by a contact nap. Eventually, it clicked. Sophia started lengthening her naps on her own, and the whole family finally found their rhythm.

These stories show that while the details vary, the principles remain the same. Their processes all unfolded slightly differently, and yours will too, but when you tune in, allow some space, and then support as needed, your baby can learn to be a fantastic sleeper.

The Final Push: Dropping the Last Feeding

While I hope your process can be one of the seamless ones to achieve sleeping all the way through the night, sometimes dropping the last feeding needs to be more intentional. If you want to make a bigger push to drop the last feeding, prepare yourself for one hour of protest every night for a week. Of course, make sure you've eradicated pain and discomfort, your schedule is good, and they're initiating sleep independently and taking good long naps. If you need to do a bigger push, usually longer timers are going to work better. Do three 20-minute timers, two 30-minute timers, or one 60-minute timer.

Middle-of-the-night timers often feel harder than daytime ones for a few reasons. Babies usually show less variability at night, especially older babies who may seem straight-up pissed—they're tired, disoriented, and just want to go back to sleep. On your end, being jolted awake comes with a rush of adrenaline, and because your logical, problem-solving brain is still half asleep, you're operating mostly from the emotional "survival brain," which makes everything feel more urgent. Unlike daytime when you can distract yourself with dishes, laundry, or a show while the timer runs, at night you're left in silence listening to your baby cry, which naturally feels more uncomfortable.

If you're going to go for the last push, I recommend getting headphones and an audiobook or podcast. You've already mentally decided to give your baby 20–60 minutes to try to fall back to sleep on their own, and you'll feed them after an hour if they haven't. What is in the middle is just the messy middle.

When Baby wakes up, set your timer for 20, 30, or 60 minutes. Choose whatever feels right for you and your baby based on what you've seen from them so far. Do you both do better with check-ins, or might the check-ins be more interruptive to their process? Set your timer, mute the monitor, and turn on something else to listen to.

When your timer goes off, go in and soothe. If they need to be picked up, keep them upright and snuggle cheek to cheek. Whisper reassurances and love and then place them back in the crib once calm or asleep and set your next timer if needed.

After 60 minutes, feed and put back down if they haven't fallen back to sleep yet. Following this pattern nightly for one week will almost always eliminate that awakening. Older babies or extra spirited babies may take more work. If, for some reason, the night awakening has not dropped yet after one week, you may consider adding a week if you feel you're making progress. If after two weeks the feeding still has not dropped, let's pause and try again next month.

Addressing Criticism of "Cry It Out"

One criticism of sleep training is that babies still awaken in the middle of the night; they just don't call out for their caregiver. This part is true—if you have a monitor that records your baby all night long, you will see periods of time that their eyes open and they seem to be awake but they don't cry and then fall back to sleep. However, the narrative that sleep-trained babies don't cry when they wake up because of learned helplessness is false. Please remember it is normal for babies to awaken during a sleep cycle transition. If they can fall back to sleep unassisted because they don't need anything, that's the beauty of sleep training!

Rest assured, if you have a baby that signals their needs and wants all day long, they have not given up hope on your love and responsiveness. If you smile when you lock eyes, giggle together, feed them when they're hungry, change them when they're dirty, and are otherwise responsive and engaged, their attachment security flourishes. Nothing in the sleep training process changes that. Remember, how much protest you allow is optional. Please be empowered to make the choices that are best for your family and give others the grace to do the same.

Of course, it is uncomfortable to allow your baby to protest. But this is a very short-term discomfort that allows for massive long-term benefit. Quality sleep affects *every* measure of physical and emotional well-being for *every* member of your family. Your baby deserves the positive benefit that comes from quality sleep, and they deserve parents and caregivers that are well-rested.

The thing I love about this framework is that it works! When it's the right fit, it works quickly and efficiently. We've worked with thousands of families with this method, and about 90% who try it see progress within the first 24 hours. In as little as three days, they see 50–70% improvement in independent sleep initiation and maintenance.

Chapter 17

The Other Three Methods and Special Considerations

O f course, not every baby is easy. Some babies, despite all of your best efforts, couldn't get a strong sleep foundation even with support. If you have a tricky baby, sleep is *really* difficult, or your baby requires an exhausting amount of support, don't lose hope. You may not be sure if there's an underlying issue, and you may be wondering if you can still move forward with trying to sleep train.

You've likely already talked to your pediatrician several times about your concerns. Get their input, and if they say yes, I recommend you give it a shot. Sometimes the biggest issue babies experience is that they're chronically overtired, so once they've got some sleep skills, other fussiness subsides. Thus, sometimes sleep training *is* the solution.

Sometimes it's not. But it's often worth trying. If you're on the fence, try it for three days. If you see zero progress in that time, it still gives you *a ton* of valuable information. It's time to pivot or modify your sleep strategy and widen your resource network to figure out how to best support your baby.

The process outlined thus far is what fits best and works most efficiently for the vast majority of babies. For about 85% of babies and families, this framework of 10-minute timers is the right cadence because it includes enough nuance and flexibility to support the most common challenges.

However, just because this standard approach works best for *most* babies does not mean it's the right approach for *your* baby.

When it comes to facilitating independent sleep initiation, there are four variations you can choose from:

- Accelerated (CIO)
- Modified-accelerated (modified CIO) aka the "10-minute method"
- Modified-modified
- Gradual

So, why would you consider a method other than the 10-minute method?

First, let's take a quick statistics refresher. A bell curve is a representation of how most things in life are distributed. The middle is where most people land. It's the average, the "typical," the most common experience.

As you move away from the middle, out to the sides, you find fewer and fewer people.

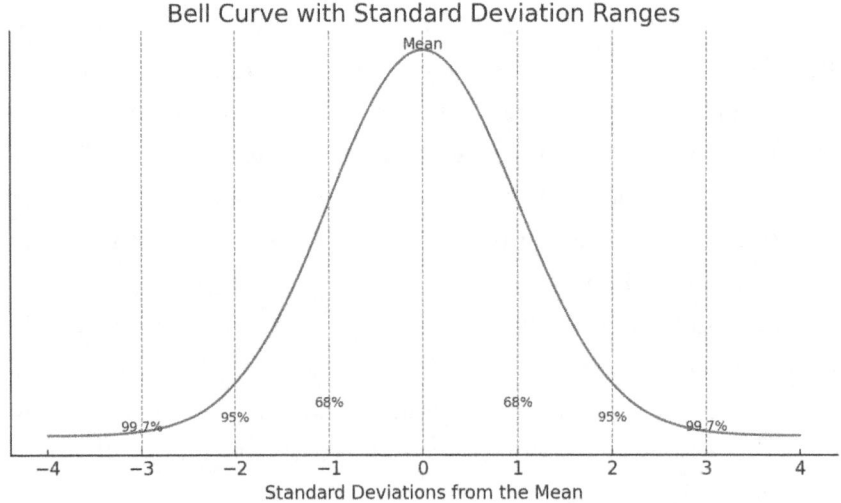

The Peaceful Sleeper

On one side, you might have babies who are extra sensitive and need a gentler, slower approach. On the other side, you might have babies who adapt quickly or do better with a more accelerated approach. Both ends are completely normal; they're just less common.

The 10-minute method tends to work for most families: those who fall in that big middle part of the curve. And if that's you, great. You'll likely see solid results pretty quickly. But if you're more on one of the edges, it doesn't mean anything is wrong; it just means your baby is a little more unique, and we may need to adjust the approach. That's not a failure. It's just part of working with real, individual human beings.

When choosing the "right" method, **the goal is to line up your best style of teaching with their best style of learning. You must be tuned into your baby and tuned into yourself to assess what's working, assess what isn't, and pivot when needed.**

This is what responsive parenting is all about. We tune into our children to discern what is going on and what is needed. Then we tune into ourselves to see what resources we have and how we can best help them navigate whatever challenge they're facing. Next, we assess how it's going and make changes when needed. This is how you'll help them in every aspect of their development from now until they leave for college and beyond—whether it's learning to clean up after themselves, share, play sports, excel academically, and more.

My team and I have worked with thousands of families over the past seven years. This graph represents the approximate breakdown of which method has worked best for them.

The Other Three Methods and Special Considerations

HOW BABIES RESPOND TO SLEEP TRAINING

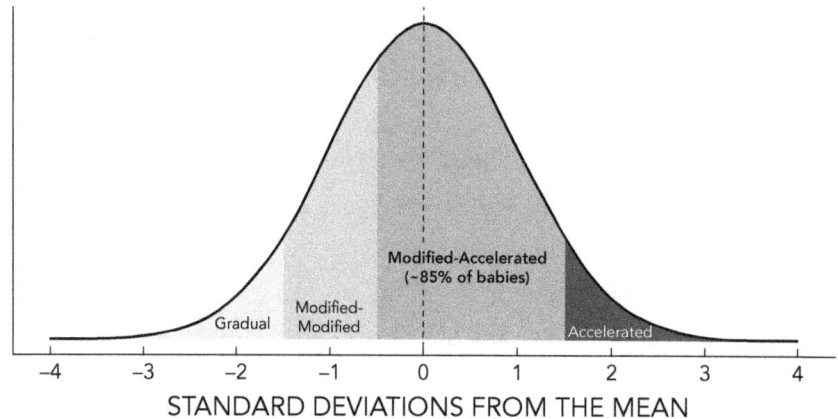

STANDARD DEVIATIONS FROM THE MEAN

If you are interested in learning how to implement the other three methods, the rest of this chapter is for you. In the Appendix 1 at the end of this book, you'll find a quiz to help you pick your approach.

Accelerated

As with all sleep training approaches, we must start with a good sleep foundation. An accelerated approach works well only when we are confident these four areas are buttoned up.

- Full feedings to maximize daily intake
- Mastering timing: preventing overtiredness, awake windows, sleepy cues
- Calming strategies: discerning and meeting needs efficiently all day long
- Identifying and treating sources of discomfort

The accelerated approach follows the same structure as modified accelerated, but we're doing fewer check-ins. We'll still cap our timers at 1 hour for bedtime and 40 minutes before naps, but instead of going in every 10 minutes to check on Baby and calm them down, you're setting timers for 20–60 minutes.

When I was first learning about sleep training, the advice was to let them cry until they fell asleep. In a popular sleep training book, it was advised to let them cry without checks, even if it took up to four hours. Though I'm sure that worked, after working with thousands of babies, I can confidently say that it just doesn't need to be that intense. One hour of allowing for protest is plenty to give them sufficient space and time to learn the skills. Then go help them to sleep. Even if they don't fall asleep without support the first few nights, they're still getting valuable practice.

Again, the most important markers we're looking for are:

- Variability in crying
- Demonstrating self-soothing behaviors
- Ease of calming with caregiver support

Although the accelerated approach is the least chosen option among the families that we work with, it nevertheless might be good place to start if:

- You need bigger, quicker progress ASAP. Maybe your family system isn't thriving and there's little bandwidth to have a plan drawn out over weeks. You need to see progress within days.

- You feel completely comfortable with allowing your baby 60 minutes to work on sleep initiation as long as they are in their zone of proximal development (there is very good variability, they are showing signs of self-soothing, and they're maintaining a regulated state).

179

- You have an older baby. Babies older than 10–12 months typically protest more and might benefit from timers longer than 10 minutes.

If you started with the 10-minute method described earlier, you may consider pivoting *to* this approach if:

- Your baby was showing great variability and it feels like they'd benefit from longer timers.
- Going in to soothe seems to interrupt their process and make it worse. They were close to falling asleep and seemed to be more awake or madder after a check-in.
- You have a baby that does fall asleep but keeps jerking themselves awake.
- You have a baby that's relatively calm and there's very little escalated fussing; they just seem to take a while to wind down.

You may consider pivoting *away* from this approach if:

- Your baby is not showing great variability; they are not self-soothing and/or become very dysregulated.
- Your baby was very upset for a long time and now is incredibly difficult to soothe; they may have gone past their window of tolerance and would benefit from check-ins sooner.

Modified-Accelerated (The 10-Minute Method)

Modified-Accelerated is the approach we've already discussed in detail. Though most babies thrive with this path, some babies either don't do well with check-ins or simply are not yet able to learn to self-soothe.

If you're unsure of the right path for your little one, I recommend you start here and pivot after a few days if you're seeing no signs of progress.

It might be a good place to start if:

- You've worked to establish a strong sleep foundation.
- Your baby has a good temperament during the day.
- You are looking for quick progress.
- You know protest serves a purpose and feel your baby will benefit from having room to work things out on their own.

If your baby is demonstrating variability in timers and signs of self-soothing, your checks appear to be helpful, sleep is improving, and you feel responsive and connected, you're probably on the right path.

If you started with another method, you may consider pivoting *to* this approach if:

- You started with a gradual approach, but now progress is stalled, and you think Baby might benefit from more space and time to work things out. Sometimes our good intentions to help actually slow them down.
- You started with a more accelerated approach and your baby became too escalated during the long timer and was very hard to soothe after.
- Your baby soothed well with a check-in after a long timer, and you think you could get the same results quicker with a 10-minute timer instead of a longer one.

The Other Three Methods and Special Considerations

You may consider pivoting _away_ from this approach if:

- It feels like your baby gets disrupted with check-ins. (They may benefit from longer timers).

- If your baby shows high escalation, little variability, very few self-soothing behaviors, and has difficulty soothing even with caregiver support. (They may benefit from shorter timers.)

- If your baby gets so worked up that they vomit or hold their breath. (They may benefit from shorter timers or no timers.)

- If you're concerned that they have an unresolved pain issue or neurodivergence preventing them from learning to self-soothe, a more gradual approach might be a better fit.

Modified-Modified

The modified-modified approach is a middle ground between the 10-minute method and a gentle/"no-cry" option. It might be a better option for parents or babies with high anxiety or sensitivity. Instead of five 10-minute timers before bedtime and three 10-minute timers before naps, you're going to do 45 minutes of timers before bed, and 30 minutes of timers before naps. These timers will be 5–10 minutes, depending on your comfort level and Baby's progress. Rock to sleep or soothe to sleep in the crib after that if Baby still needs support.

Give yourself grace and permission to modify and adapt this as needed for your baby. I find that timers shorter than five minutes are rarely productive, but with this approach you're focusing slightly less on the timer and more on the levels of variability. You're giving Baby more space and time when they're more calm and going in sooner if they get too escalated. You might still give them a minute to see if they'll calm down on their own, but you're going in to soothe when you feel like they're getting outside of their window of tolerance.

You may also stay with your baby for longer during those soothing intervals. Still avoid feeding to calm if you can, but you may take a few minutes to snuggle before you place Baby back in the crib. You may also soothe in the crib for a few minutes before leaving again to start the next timer.

The modified-modified approach is a good place to start if:

- 10-minute timers feel too long.

- You are open to some protest to let your baby work things out on their own, but the crying makes you uncomfortable, anxious, or feel guilty.

- Your baby had past (but now resolved) health issues, you have a high sensitivity baby, or they tend to get escalated and not calm easily.

- Your baby experienced trauma.

- Your baby was exposed to drugs or alcohol in utero.

- You are okay with this process taking a little longer.

You may consider pivoting *to* this approach if:

- You started with a more accelerated approach, but you find that the more escalated your baby gets, the less productive it becomes.

- If you started with a "no-cry" approach, but you're not making progress.

The Other Three Methods and Special Considerations

You may consider pivoting *away* from this approach if:

- They become more escalated after a check-in, or if progress has stalled. (They may benefit from longer timers.)

- They show high escalation, little variability, very few self-soothing behaviors, and have difficulty soothing even with caregiver support. (They may benefit from a gradual approach.)

- If your baby gets so worked up that they vomit or hold their breath. (They may benefit from a gradual approach.)

- If you're concerned that they have an unresolved pain issue or neurodivergence preventing them from learning to self-soothe, a more gradual approach might be a better fit.

Gradual/"No-Cry"

I would like to make it very clear that you do not *have* to utilize timers, allow room for protest, or cry it out. There's way too much judgment and criticism in the parenting space, and as much as some parents feel deeply shamed for sleep training, other parents feel deeply shamed for not wanting to sleep train. You still deserve great sleep, and you can get there over time with a more gradual approach.

Allowing for protest doesn't fit for some parents, and it doesn't fit for some babies. In theory, a gradual, no-cry approach sounds like the option everyone would want; listening to your baby cry sucks, and it's stressful. With this in mind, please be advised of two things:

1. **There is more work:** Gradual, no-cry options require much more work and diligence on your part, but for many parents it's totally worth it.

2. **There is still crying:** "No cry" does not mean your baby will not cry. All babies cry for a myriad of reasons, and it's just part

of being a baby. It is basically their only form of communication and doesn't necessarily signal an unmet need. What "no cry" actually means is that you are either mitigating the tears or staying physically with them if they cry before falling asleep.

The gradual/"no cry" approach is a good place to start if:

- Your baby has or had significant medical issues. It may not be advised to allow room for independent protest. Always talk to your doctor before starting sleep training.

- CIO doesn't align with the way you want to parent your child. Follow your instinct, and do what you feel is best for your family.

- You have a baby with a traumatic history or a foster baby/ adopted baby with an unknown history. It may not be advised to allow room for independent protest. They may not be able to downregulate their stress and learn to self-soothe yet.

- You have trauma. I once worked with a mother who grew up in a violent home. Allowing her baby to cry before falling asleep gave her flashbacks to a time when, as a young child, she heard her baby brother being abused in the next room and was unable to help him. Listening to her baby cry, even though she knew he was fine, pushed her outside *her* window of tolerance and was therefore not the right option.

- Your baby was exposed to drugs or alcohol in utero.

- You enjoy co-sleeping and plan to share a family bed. You don't have a timeline for success, so you're fine with their sleep unfolding at a gradual pace.

- There are some indicators of neurodivergence. Some babies simply are not capable of self-soothing and will need your help to fall asleep and stay asleep until they're older.

The Other Three Methods and Special Considerations

The important things to remember are to prevent overtiredness and maintain realistic expectations regarding time. There isn't a no-cry approach that works in three days. The timeframe really depends on your baby and how quickly you step down the levels of intervention, but plan on anywhere from six weeks to six months.

There are two different approaches as to what "no-cry" means:

1. Have as few tears around sleep times as possible. Establish habits, scheduling, and foundation, but independent sleep initiation isn't a priority. They'll learn it on their own eventually.

2. Slowly teach independent sleep initiation in more gradual steps, but you're *with* Baby when they're protesting.

Basically, "no cry" means you soothe your baby as much as they want/need until they fall asleep. Once you have a good foundation of long naps and easy sleep initiation, you can scale back the level of intervention required to get Baby to sleep so they're doing the sleep initiation more independently over time.

The "sleep training" part of it focuses on scheduling, establishing a good sleep environment, and getting into good sleep patterns. Mom or Dad's involvement in helping Baby to get sleep is very high and stays that way longer-term. It's a lot of work, but many parents don't mind that. This is a popular option for first-time parents who don't have other kids or demands on their time and can afford to spend that extra time with their baby.

Sometimes moving to a clock-based schedule sooner rather than later can help this solidify more easily.

Age	Wake Up	1st Nap	2nd Nap	3rd Nap	Bedtime
0–3 Months	6–8 a.m.	Nap lengths vary from 1 to 3 hours. Rely more on awake windows than a clock-based schedule.			10–11 p.m.
4–9 Months	7 a.m.	9 a.m.	12:30 p.m.	3:30 p.m.	7 p.m.
9–16 Months	7 a.m.	9 a.m.	2 p.m.	–	7 p.m.
16–24 Months	7 a.m.	12:30 p.m.	–	–	7 p.m.
2–3 Years	7 a.m.	12:30 p.m. (But may start to drop naps)	–	–	8 p.m.
3 Years +	7 a.m.	–	–	–	8:30 p.m.

The Other Three Methods and Special Considerations

Then we use a gradual step-down approach. Skip any steps you'd like or add any extras in. This part doesn't have to be an exact formula, so just tune into your baby and get creative.

Phase 1: Get on a more predictable schedule. Rock to sleep instead of nursing to sleep and hold for naps.

Phase 2: Rock to sleep, put down, and jostle back to sleep if they wake in the transition.

Phase 3: Rock to mostly drowsy, put down, and jostle to sleep in the crib. I like to think about percentages here. In phases 1 and 2, you were soothing 100% to sleep. Now you're soothing to 70–80% sleepy in your arms and getting them 100% asleep in the crib.

Phase 4: Rock until 40–50% drowsy, put down, and hold your hand on their chest until they're completely asleep.

Phase 5: Rock to 30–50% drowsy and put down. Slowly scale back the level of intervention over time and let Baby fall asleep in the crib independently.

Once you're in this phase, here are some ideas of interventions to try. Get creative!

- Cheek stroke eyebrow/face stroke.
- Palm on cheek.
- Lean over crib singing songs or shushing, but not touching baby.
- Sit next to the crib.
- Sit in a chair in the corner.
- Hold paci in place.

- Hold finger.
- If you're co-sleeping, you can go cheek to cheek.
- Lay on the floor and hold hands through the crib bars.
- Lay on the floor quietly or singing songs without touching.
- Move chair closer to the door, then move chair outside open door, and then sit outside closed door (singing or something so they know you're still there).
- Allow little bits of fussing.

For night wakings, feed or rock back to sleep as needed, gently trying to stretch the intervals between feeds. Remember that all babies cry. It's part of how they communicate. With this approach, the goal isn't zero fussing but to *be there* as your baby learns and works things out. Many parents find moments where their baby is protesting but clearly fine, and their presence isn't adding value. In those cases, stepping away for short increments is okay. You're not being "inconsistent"; you're adapting.

You may consider pivoting *to* this approach if:

- Your baby doesn't show signs that timers are helpful or productive.

You may consider pivoting *away* from this approach if:

- Your baby shows signs of being capable of self-soothing and wanting/needing some time and space to work through learning this skill on their own.
- If your progress has stalled or you and your baby are no longer thriving with your current sleep situation.

The Other Three Methods and Special Considerations

The heart of the Peaceful Sleeper method is collaboration with your baby. It's not about rigidly sticking to one approach but about observing, tweaking, and responding in ways that fit both you and your child. Sometimes being present is soothing; other times, space actually helps. That's why there are four approaches, *not because one is "best" but because every baby and parent is different.* When you understand the principles and trust yourself to adapt, you'll find the path that works. Every baby can get better sleep—it's simply a matter of choosing the method that aligns best for you and your little one.

Part VI

Life After Sleep Training

Chapter 18

Scheduling

After two weeks of sleep training and keeping a sleep log, usually you'll start to see some patterns develop. At this point, it is helpful to transition to a clock-based schedule. In Appendix 2, you'll find detailed instructions about how to create your own sleep log, a blank template for your use, and my own personal sleep logs when sleep training two of my kids so you can see it in action.

Some families prefer flexibility and to keep orienting sleep times around wake windows, so if that's you, that's fine. As long as your baby is getting the sleep they need and you are thriving, that's all that matters.

For those parents and babies who thrive with some predictability, let's talk about scheduling. Remember that everything you're about to read is based on averages. Some babies have higher sleep needs, and others have lower sleep needs. What matters is figuring out *your* baby and providing the right space and time for them to get the sleep they need.

Sample Schedules

Remember, at around four months we're probably still on four naps a day. At around five months (or while sleep training), we'll move to three naps a day. Then at around seven to nine months, we drop to two naps a day, and then at 12–16 months is when we drop to a single nap. More on nap dropping later. I'll give you some sample schedules so you can get a rough idea of what to aim for and how the day might look:

4 NAP SCHEDULE
(4 MONTHS OLD)

Wake up	7:00 a.m.
Nap 1	8:30–9:30
Nap 2	11:00–12:00
Nap 3	1:30–2:30
Nap 4	4:00–5:00 p.m.
Bedtime	7:00 p.m.

3 NAP SCHEDULE
(5 MONTHS OLD)

Wake up	7:00 a.m.
Nap 1	9:00 a.m.
Nap 2	12:30 p.m.
Nap 3	3:30 p.m.
Bedtime	7:00 p.m.

2 NAP SCHEDULE
(7 MONTHS OLD)

Wake up	7:00 a.m.
Nap 1	9:00 a.m.
Nap 2	2:00 p.m.
Bedtime	7:00 p.m.

The Peaceful Sleeper

1 NAP SCHEDULE
(14 MONTHS OLD)

Wake up	7:00 a.m.
Nap 1	12:30 p.m.
Bedtime	7:00 p.m.

Consistent Yet Flexible

Every day may look a little different. After all, your own sleep needs fluctuate too. Even if you have a consistent routine, you probably don't go to bed at exactly 9 p.m. every night. Therefore, even a "consistent" schedule can have 15–30 minutes of wiggle room. One goal of this whole approach is to increase your feeling of ease when it comes to sleep. If the first nap is usually at 9 but Baby goes down at 9:15, that's perfectly fine.

Many parents wonder how flexible they can be now that they've got a good sleeper. It's nice to have a newborn who will sleep anywhere so you can still have a life that doesn't revolve around sleep times. The reality is, many older babies won't sleep on the go anymore. With increased awareness and alertness comes more particularity about the sleep environment. Having a dark quiet room with a comfy crib, black-out curtains, and a sound machine is the best way to facilitate a quality nap. Some babies can sleep on the go for a few extra months, tuning out the excitement of the outside world when it's time to rest, and some simply can't.

My oldest was this way. If I didn't get the timing right and I put Maddie down late, she just missed sleep. My perfect, perpetually happy angel baby became cranky, and it just wasn't worth it. The short answer is, try occasionally to deviate from their perfect schedule and see how adaptable they are. In general, **aim for at least 85% of sleeps to be at their ideal time in their ideal place.** Leaving 10–15% wiggle room for a playdate or dinner out should still give you a good balance of having a life while maintaining their predictability.

The beauty is, when skills are built into their sleep system, they can adapt to changes. They're less prone to overtired meltdowns, and they bounce back more quickly after setbacks. Try your best to provide a predictable space and time to meet their sleep needs, but you'll be able to relax knowing that it's all going to work out and they'll be fine.

In fact, the structure that comes from having a sleep-trained baby brings a whole new level of freedom and ease. The predictability of your schedule allows you to plan activities with confidence, knowing you'll have a content baby and naps will happen when they should. It also gives you space to tackle chores or enjoy downtime at predictable intervals too. Even something as simple as scheduling a doctor's appointment is easier because you know exactly what time is ideal.

Sleep Anchors

Generally, the first components of a schedule to solidify consistently are **bedtime, morning wake time,** and the **first nap of the day.** When these are set, the rest of the day starts to unfold more predictably. Keep in mind that naps likely aren't fully buttoned up yet after just two weeks, but having these consistent anchor points will facilitate that process.

Babies 4–12 months old generally do best with a bedtime around 7 p.m. and a wake time, ideally, around 7. Usually a fairly consistent wake-up time will unfold if bedtime is consistent, but sometimes you'll need to jump in to help organize their sleep. Although I don't usually like to wake a sleeping baby, if a schedule is the goal, you may find it helpful to wake in the morning by a certain time, say

7:30 a.m. if they're sleeping in. More often, the intervention you're focused on is trying to get Baby to sleep in later.

Any time after 6 a.m. is an acceptable wake-up time, but if you're motivated to get that 7-7 schedule, you can allow them to hang out in the crib if they wake early. For example, if Baby wakes up at 6:30 a.m. and they're content, it's perfectly fine to let them chill in their crib until closer to 7 a.m. Let's say they wake at 6 a.m., but you'd really like to stretch them until 7 a.m., you can let them stay in the crib as long as they're content and then hold them in the nursery in the dark until 7 a.m. Once the clock strikes 7 a.m., they can "wake up."

You may feel silly since you've been up with your baby already, but try to make a show of it. Whereas just a few minutes ago the room was dark and anything you said was hushed, now it's time to throw open the curtains, put a big smile on your face and exclaim "Good morning!"

When morning wake-up time is regulated, the first nap of the day can easily start at a consistent time. If wake-up is around 7 a.m. and Baby usually has a two-hour awake window, the first nap will almost always be right around 9 a.m.

To keep bedtime at a consistent time, you may need to wake Baby from their last nap of the day by a certain time, let's say 5 p.m., to keep bedtime on track.

Bedtime

Most babies older than four months thrive with a 7 p.m. bedtime. However, that can feel early or unrealistic for some families. Maybe you or your partner work late or aren't ready to give up parts of your social routine. Some night owls hope that a later bedtime can offer a later wake-up time.

If you can make a later bedtime work for your baby, go for it. Some babies adapt really well and will fall into whatever schedule you assign to them. As long as their total sleep needs are accounted for and they're thriving, you can organize their schedule in whatever way works best for your family. This might look like sleeping from 9 p.m. to 9 a.m. overnight, for example, instead of the more typical 7 p.m. to 7 a.m. Or perhaps even 9 p.m. to 7 a.m., but they'll take longer day-time naps or an evening cat nap to make up for shorter overnight sleep.

Other babies are very particular.

A late bedtime pushes them into the wired and tired zone, and they have a harder time falling asleep. If you're doing everything else by the book but with a late bedtime and you're just not seeing the breakthroughs that you want, try moving bedtime earlier.

Dropping Naps

If you sleep trained at four months, Baby might still be taking four naps per day. Sometime over the course of the next month, that sleep will consolidate, and they start just needing three naps per day. There are two factors that combine to facilitate this process:

- Naps are lengthening, so they meet their total sleep needs in just three naps instead of four.

- Since they're getting good, restorative sleep, they can handle being awake for longer stretches.

Where a three-month-old might only be able to handle 90 minutes of awake time and some naps might be only 30–45 minutes, a sleep-trained 4.5-month-old might be consistently taking 1–2 hour naps. They're not necessarily needing less sleep; they're just getting more consolidated sleep.

Around six to seven months old, the third nap of the day becomes a shorter cat nap, and then around seven to nine months old, they'll drop to just two naps a day.

Around 12–16 months you'll drop to just one nap a day, and around age 3 most kids will drop naps completely.

When your baby is getting ready to drop a nap, it creates a bit of an awkward phase. You may notice that naps just aren't working like they used to. Baby doesn't seem tired yet, one of the naps is a fight, or when they *do* take all of the naps, it messes up bedtime. Those signals, in conjunction with their age, can let you know it might be time to drop one. If you are approaching the age where they'll drop soon but you know they aren't ready yet, you can intervene more to help that last cat nap happen. You can rock them or nurse them to sleep or go on a drive if it's a struggle. You might be in this cat-nap rescuing phase for a week or two as you warm up to dropping it.

Then, for another week or two, you might try lengthening those awake windows and having a reduced nap schedule. Some babies may benefit from having that extra nap offered once or twice a week as they are adjusting. For example, if Baby is seven months old and you're dropping from three naps to two, once or twice a week offer the three-nap schedule.

Awake Windows

If you're on a three-nap schedule, usually you'll have 90 minutes of awake time in the morning, then two hours between naps, and 2.5 hours before bed.

For a two-nap schedule, keep in mind the rule of thumb 2-3-4. This means approximately two hours of awake time before the first nap, three hours of awake time between naps, and four hours of awake time before bed.

For a single nap schedule, aim for about five hours of awake time before and after the nap.

Some babies do better with shorter awake windows in the morning and can stay awake for longer in the afternoon. Some babies are the inverse of this and do better with longer awake windows in the morning and shorter awake windows in the afternoon. None of it really matters as long as your baby's sleep needs are met and you're on a schedule that allows both of you to thrive.

Chapter 19

Sleep After Sleep Training

Now that you've sleep trained your baby, you may be wondering if it's smooth sailing from here. Unfortunately, no. There will be lots of hiccups along the way. Remember, perfection is not the goal. Even after your baby learns to take steps independently and well into toddlerhood, they'll still stumble and fall. It doesn't mean that this process doesn't work or isn't worth it. It just means your baby is human and development isn't linear. We learn and relearn things lots of times throughout life.

Several factors will disrupt your baby's sleep after they're fully sleep trained. The good news is that these natural upsets are temporary. Once they're sleep trained, it's pretty easy to get back into your rhythm if you know when and how to do it.

Things that might wake up a sleep-trained baby:

- Sickness

- Teething

- Overtiredness

- Poopy diaper (babies usually won't poop in the middle of the night, but if they do, they're likely uncomfortable)

- Leaking diaper

- Daylight savings

- Noises (neighbors, a dog barking, or a car alarm)

- Lost pacifier or comfort object
- Legs stuck in the bars of the crib
- Sleep regressions
- Developmental leap (learning a new skill such as sitting up or walking)
- Bad dream (not typically a cause of a wake-up until 18+ months)

After your baby has consistently been sleeping through the night, hunger will usually not be a *cause* of arousal. That's not to say you shouldn't feed them if they wake for a different reason, though. Feeding can be a great way of offering comfort and assistance to fall back to sleep.

One advantage of having a sleep-trained baby is that you can more easily discern when there's a real problem that needs your attention. If your baby wakes up in the middle of the night or is unusually upset after going down, you know it's worth checking out because it's out of the norm. Even if you did an accelerated approach with your baby during sleep training, you're fine to take a check-and-console approach in situations like these.

The question is whether they need support through this wake-up or if they just need some time to resettle on their own. Some disruptions warrant support, but some don't. Rely on your instinct, but I'll give you some questions to ask yourself as you discern whether to intervene or wait:

- First, how random is this? If they've been sleeping through the night for weeks or months with little to no disruption and suddenly they've woken up, I'm more inclined to go in right away. If, however, they've been slowly backsliding on sleep and this is the third night awakening this week with no other symptoms, I'd suggest giving them a few minutes to work it out before intervening.

- Next, do you have any guesses about what might be going on? If you were just around a toddler with a cold, you've spotted red swollen gums, or they were tugging on their ears all day, that gives you valuable information. If you suspect your baby is in pain, go comfort them. If, however, they had a weird nap today because of a conflict and you suspect it's some overtired wonkiness, it's perfectly fine to give them a few minutes to try to resettle. They're less likely to *need* you in a situation like that.

- How is their demeanor while crying? If your baby is sitting, standing, looking straight at the door, or even calling your name, they may want you. If they're rolling around with their eyes closed, they may just need a few minutes to sleep cycle transition or work through some mild discomfort.

- What does their cry sound like? A sudden, sharp cry may warrant a different response than dull, intermittent whining.

- Finally, have they woken repeatedly in one night? If you give your baby a few minutes to work it out and they fall back to sleep only to wake again an hour later and repeat the cycle, they may need more support as the night goes on. If it's a dull, uncomfortable whimper that happens repeatedly, they're more than likely getting sick or about to pop a tooth.

If you're unsure, wait for five minutes before deciding what is needed. After a few minutes of observation, you'll feel much more confident in knowing what to do. Often babies start with a sharp cry but quickly resettle, so rushing in could be unnecessary.

Unfortunately, sometimes babies become accustomed to night waking after illnesses or other reasons. Generally speaking, I give up to a week for an illness or teething to take its toll. After a week, you run the risk of enabling a bad habit when your baby usually isn't suffering at all anymore. If they are still sick or teething, then by all

203

Sleep After Sleep Training

means, keep going in at night. Tune into your baby and meet their needs. But then bounce back once they're ready to get back on track.

After the hiccup has passed, you really just need a night or two of returning to some timers before they'll bounce back to their regular routine. For a sleep-trained baby who has been out of their sleeping-through-the-night habit for only a week, one or two cycles of timers should do the trick.

Teething

Teething usually begins at around six months, and it can intermittently impact sleep for 12 months. This is one reason I recommend sleep training at four months, so we have a little more time to solidify sleep skills before teething gets in the way. Teething comes in waves, and we just deal with it when it comes up. Usually you'll notice more night awakenings though they barely eat anything, and you'll notice more fussiness overall.

You'll also notice more sensitivity when touching their mouths. Although babies generally like to chomp on anything, you may notice them crying or flinching away if you feel inside their mouths. You'll also notice red, swollen gums, or you may see a tooth bud popping through.

The worst of it is usually over in a few days, right when the tooth is about to erupt. Your main goal is pain management and helping them weather the storm. I like to give my kids frozen washcloths during the day, and I'll usually throw a teething toy in the crib with them at night so they can chomp on something. Make sure it's something crib safe like a large silicone or bamboo teething ring. Consult with your pediatrician, of course, and see if they have other suggestions for pain management.

Some babies barely react to teething, and others are thrown off for two weeks every time a tooth pops through. Just use your parental instinct to know how to respond and bounce back to sleeping through the night once the tooth has popped through.

Sleep Regressions

Aside from teething, the next most common wrench thrown into sleep is going to be sleep regressions. They can happen at any time but are usually associated with developmental leaps or the acquisition of new skills.

Crazy things happen to babies' sleep when they're on the cusp of some developmental milestone. Sometimes they'll have a huge sleep spurt, where they're taking three-hour naps and sleeping late into the morning. Or sometimes they'll have massive sleep regressions and fight sleep for a week or so.

This makes sense: when your brain is preoccupied with one project, some other things fall by the wayside temporarily. If you're focused on a big work deadline, for example, emails and texts might pile up. Similarly, if you're a baby and your brain is working hard on learning to talk or walk, your sleep skills might falter for a few days.

The solution is to be consistent and patient. If you've been on a schedule that has been working and it doesn't feel logical to drop a nap or adjust bedtime, it's most likely a regression.

Just stay the course, be consistent, and they'll bounce back. This may mean Baby starts protesting again before sleep times and takes longer to fall asleep. This may mean Baby starts waking in the middle of the night again or starts taking short naps. Go back to using 10-minute timers with soothing intervals. If they wake up early from a nap or try to skip the nap altogether, let them stay in the crib to finish out the hour.

Unfortunately, since babies are developing at astonishing rates, sleep regressions through these developmental bursts can be frequent. The most common ages to see sleep regressions are at 4 months, 8 months, 10 months, 15 months, and a longer regression, usually associated with more protesting and stubbornness, around 22–24 months.

Even the most perfectly sleep-trained babies will have setbacks from time to time. The skills you've built and their baseline of quality sleep will buffer these temporary disruptions. Many parents worry that these setbacks could "ruin everything," but rest assured, good habits aren't lost so easily. Just like skipping workouts on vacation won't erase your fitness, supporting your baby through their challenges won't undo their progress. Though it may feel clunky at first, getting back on track is always easier than starting from scratch. You've got the tools, and your baby has the skills. Together, you've got this.

Chapter 20

Nap Trapped: When Sacrifice Backfires

In this age where parents are hyper focused on doing everything right for their kids, I just want to take a quick moment before we wrap up to remind you that perfection isn't the goal. Not only is it impossible, but chasing it will rob your joy and will end up backfiring.

In my 15-year career as a therapist, I've walked alongside middle-aged women and teenaged girls in their most vulnerable moments. Through the Peaceful Sleeper, I've also had the privilege of supporting thousands of new parents navigating those raw, early years. Again and again, I've seen the same themes emerge. From the outside, many families look like they have it all together. On the inside though, burnout and resentment are quietly eroding their joy.

What strikes me most is that this struggle often shows up not in the "bad parents," but in the best ones—the ones willing to give everything for their kids and who routinely put themselves last. Ironically (and unfortunately), often their kids aren't thriving because of these sacrifices.

When I sit with teenage clients, I can see the ripple effects of these dynamics. Some are flourishing, but many are not. The most well-adjusted, well-behaved teens seem to have the happiest parents. As I try to connect the dots between the struggles of parents, the experiences of their kids, and the new parents starting out now, I wonder: What could have been different earlier? What can new parents do now to protect the future well-being of themselves and their children?

I would be remiss if I ended this book without sharing these insights. This book has always been about more than sleep training; it's about laying a foundation for you, your child, and your family to truly thrive.

The Sacrifice Trap

It's way too easy to wrap up your whole life and identity in your kids. When they're teeny tiny and they need so much, it feels like the obvious right answer. You feel like whatever your baby needs is your top priority, and you can focus on yourself and your relationship in a few years when the kids don't need so much. If Baby cries when you workout, leave for a brunch with girlfriends, or go on a date with your partner, these replenishing activities can get pushed off until "later." However, the kids will always "need so much." It changes and morphs over time, but in many ways it increases.

You have to work to find a balance now. Parents that sacrifice *everything* of themselves for the "well-being" of their child end up running out. The old saying "You can't pour from an empty cup" rings true. The cup dries up, patience *can* run out, and tension can grow. You may look at your precious babe in your arms and think "I love you so much, I will give everything for you, and I could never resent you," but you can and will if you're not diligent now.

I sat down with relationship expert Dr. Morgan Cutlip, PhD, who specializes in maternal burnout to get her perspective and advice. She identified this common pattern for mothers: "We put ourselves on the back burner for the people we love the most, and then we end up resenting them." That resentment builds slowly and silently when our needs go unmet for too long. The good news is, it doesn't have to be this way. You can take intentional steps now to prevent that slow slide into burnout and overwhelm. She cautions, "Do not become the victim in your own story. Do not become a martyr in motherhood. We have so much more agency than we think we do!"[1,2]

Of course, sacrifice is part of being a parent. It's the most beautiful part of how we stretch and grow as human beings. I imagine you'd give your life for your child's in an instant. Their needs can and do sometimes take precedence over yours. But finding the balance is key.

I recently posted on social media about striking this balance, and one mom lovingly responded, "I'm not thriving, but my baby is. And since the moment he was born, that's mattered more to me." Though a beautiful sentiment that is clearly rooted in love, this works only short term.

A Healthy Hierarchy

Losing yourself for the sake of your children is not sustainable. You can both thrive at the same time. A healthy hierarchy is simple: Meet their *needs* first, then your own, and only after that come their *preferences* and yours. If your child is safe, cared for, and their primary needs are met, it's okay for your *needs* to outweigh their *preferences*. If your child's perceived well-being consistently comes at the expense of your own, you risk getting out of balance. For example, don't skip a workout class you love because of a few minutes of protest at drop-off. Your health and energy matter too, and they can bounce back and adapt.

Sleep as the Keystone for Relationships

It's no secret that having a new baby changes your relationships. Take the pressure of being a good enough parent, how fragile and helpless they are, the fact that you likely feel like you have no idea what you're doing, and add to it massive hormone shifts and chronic sleep deprivation for the foreseeable future. It's no wonder relationship satisfaction dips after having children.[3] But it doesn't have to be this way! You can learn to be more connected than ever, and it all starts with optimizing sleep. Having a baby can be a beautiful adventure that expands your capacity to love. When you move through this stage with sleep and connection intact, it can be the new baby bliss you've dreamed of.

Pressure Points in Parenthood

Nevertheless, the transition to parenting can strain even the strongest relationships. The more proactively you recognize challenges and communicate through them, the more likely you are to build collaboration instead of disconnection. Common pain points for couples in this adjustment include division of labor, nighttime duty, keeping score, and intimacy.

Division of Labor

Suddenly your list of chores has dramatically *increased*, and your time to do them has dramatically *decreased*. Feedings take forever, and by the time you get baby fed, changed, and rocked to sleep, it's time to do it all over again.

For the first time in your relationship you may feel like the division of labor is not fair. This can lead to annoyance, bickering, and arguments over who should be taking on which new chores. If one parent works outside of the home and the other is at home, the majority of the new chores tend to fall on the at-home parent. If you have a baby who will only sleep in your arms, you can feel nap-trapped, overwhelmed, and wonder when on Earth you will find the time to get everything done.

One of the best ways to prevent bitterness is to sit down together, make a list of everything that needs to be done, and decide who does what. When the invisible becomes visible, couples are more likely to feel like teammates.

Nighttime Duty

There isn't one right or wrong way to do this, but just make sure you talk openly and give each other time to catch up on missed sleep. Typically a nighttime awakening in the first two months will last an hour by the time you get baby fed, changed, swaddled, burped, and back to sleep. Some couples will alternate feedings. Some nursing moms find it pointless to wake up Dad since she has to do the bulk of the work anyway. Regardless, the extended broken sleep takes a significant toll on the parent who wakes up. Try to catch up on sleep as much as possible by going to bed early, sleeping in, or taking naps when possible.

This goes without saying, but the quicker you can optimize sleep, the sooner those nighttime awakenings will drop off. It is possible to get six to eight hour stretches of sleep by six to eight weeks, and it is possible to get those nighttime awakenings to be closer to 20 minutes than 60. Life gets significantly easier when you're just woken up once at night and not five times.

Keeping Score

This is a game all couples play, and everyone loses. Dr. Morgan Cutlip, PhD, calls this the hardship Olympics. "Nobody wins the hardship Olympics. And even if you win, you're still losing!" Whether you're a stay-at-home parent, a working parent, a working-from-home parent, a working part-time parent. . .it's actually all hard. Parents who are out of the house while their partner is at home often feel immense guilt for not helping as much and missing family time. Parents who are at home solo with the baby feel an entirely different strain. They can feel a loss of self, loss of schedule, and sometimes boredom. Parents who are at home part-time and working part-time feel torn in a million directions, never able to do it all. It's all hard. Competing for who's got it the hardest creates division instead of unity.

I've played every single role, and I promise none of them are easier than another. Though I'll also admit whatever role I'm in I'm still tempted to think I've got it the hardest. At one point I remember saying "But at least you get to go to dental school and hang out with your friends all day long!" I do realize that being trapped in a basement classroom 10 hours a day wasn't exactly the party I envisioned.

Plain and simple, if you're getting more rest, you're not running on empty. You're way better equipped to sidestep this toxic debate and approach each other with gratitude instead.

Intimacy

Intimate connection can take a huge backseat once you have kids. Since it's one of the biggest sources of disconnection for couples, I'm going to spend some time breaking this down.

For one, there's a physical restriction on intercourse for at least six weeks after a vaginal birth. Then, for women: You're sleep deprived, touched out, your body looks different, your boobs hurt, and you're covered in spit-up. Being a new mom doesn't feel "sexy" in the slightest. Not to mention, from an evolutionary perspective, you just fulfilled your biological urge to have offspring and aren't looking to get pregnant again, so a sex drive serves no "purpose." Thus, it typically disappears. Don't worry—you'll get it back; it just might look different.

For the partner, you logically understand all of this, but you likely still crave your partner on a deep level. You long for that connection but are trying to be sensitive to the fact that she is taking care of someone else right now. Despite your logical awareness of all of this, you may still feel distant, disconnected, and lonely. They call it "sexual frustration" for a reason. Don't get mad at me; I don't make the rules. The reality is that often when men haven't had the sexual release they crave, they can be grumpier and more on edge. And when women sense that their partners are edgy because they haven't had sex, they can get more resentful.

Despite all of the challenges that make sex more complicated, it's actually more important than ever to carve out that time for each other to get the brain chemical boost that sex provides.

One of the most powerful chemical reactions in the sexual response cycle is the release of the hormone oxytocin, often referred to as the cuddle hormone. What you may not know is that oxytocin is responsible for birthing contractions,[4] which I believe is one of the most fascinating processes in our human evolution. Let me explain.

I don't know about you, but my pregnancies were brutal: months of nausea, vomiting, and pain. Labor and delivery weren't much better: hours of cramps, a baby ripping their way out, and you know they're about to wreck your nipples and your sleep. They're not even objectively cute at that point; they're purple, cone-headed, and crying.

Even so, when that goopy little blob is placed on your chest, you're instantly in love. You'd give your life for them without a second thought. That, my friends, is the miracle of oxytocin. There's no logical reason to feel so much love after all that turmoil, except that your body floods you with this powerful love chemical.

If you can get even a shred of that "unconditional love despite everything" feeling for your partner on a regular basis, your relationship is going to benefit.

To be clear, you also get oxytocin from snuggles, deep conversations that feel validating and supportive, laughing together, eye contact, handholding, and more, but you get the most from sex. If you want a salve to mend some of the day-to-day disconnections, sex is a powerful tool.

Nap Trapped: When Sacrifice Backfires

Of course, I understand the limitations that are present with a new baby, so it's normal if it's less than it used to be, but just don't brush it off completely. Nurturing your relationship after Baby comes looks different but is still just as important.

Don't forget that there can be other types of intimate and sexual connection even if intercourse is restricted. Sex isn't just about fulfilling your partner either. Sexual connection can be a powerful way a partner can tend to the intimate, tender needs of a woman when she's doing everything for everyone else all day long.

Other powerful chemicals in the sexual response cycle that are going to benefit your life:

- **Testosterone** makes us feel powerful, confident, and competent. At a time when we likely feel overwhelmed, testosterone can give us an extra boost.

- **Serotonin** is the happy chemical that makes us feel content and at peace. It's one of the best anxiety-relieving chemicals.

- **Dopamine** is the happy chemical that makes us feel energized and excited. It gives us a boost to do more activities that will increase dopamine, like exercising, and also contributes to a confident feeling.

- **Norepinephrine** is the chemical responsible for the "runners high." It's a happy boost chemical that makes us feel accomplished and energized.[5]

I know, I know. If you just had a baby, there are a million things to feel pressured about. Don't let this be a source of pressure but just a gentle reminder that sex is really good for you and good for your relationship as long as other dynamics with your intimacy are healthy. The better you sleep, the more energy you'll have for sex and other aspects of pouring into your relationship.

Maintaining Friendship

The truth is, it's a whole lot easier to love someone you genuinely like. Though it may seem obvious, nearly every couple that I've worked with says a version of the same thing: *I love my partner deeply; I just don't like them that much.*

Your partner should be your most important best friend, which means treating them with the same kindness, respect, and generosity you'd offer to your closest friends. It's surprisingly easy to slip into giving our best selves to acquaintances while our partners get the leftovers. When you consistently show up as a good friend, you'll usually see that warmth reflected back.

The happiest relationships honor each other and have fun together. Prioritize laughter and fun. Life is serious enough as it is with jobs and the new pressure of parenthood. Be silly, and let loose with each other more than you would with anyone else. After all, laughter truly is the best medicine. Create inside jokes, share experiences, and find things you like to do together. Remember why you fell for each other in the first place and nurture those parts.

Marriage Insurance

A friend of mine once pointed out that we pay money every month to insure our most valuable assets. Things like homeowners insurance, life insurance, car insurance, health insurance, and more are non-negotiable. Why then, wouldn't we diligently set aside resources every month for "marriage insurance"?

Invest in things like date nights, couples therapy, trips away together, or even shared books or podcasts. Keep in mind that your most valuable premium is your time and energy, and pouring into your relationship doesn't have to cost money, though it can.

The strength of your relationship is one of your most important assets, not only financially but because the health of your relationship impacts your happiness, your well-being, and even your health and your children's future romantic relationships.[6] Much like a retirement account, if you invest little amounts early and often, you'll find a wealth of love as you go through life. Too often, couples forget to invest early on assuming it'll come later, only to find they've run empty by the time later comes.

I recommend you carve out time for one date night per month, one overnight every six months, and at least one weekend away every year without the kids.

You started off as lovers and need to maintain that thread even though you're parents now. As amazing as my husband is, I'm shocked at how much more I remember my love for him when we're away together. The truth is, your kids will benefit far more from having deeply connected parents than the relative discomfort of you being away. I hate to break it to you, but they probably won't miss you nearly as much as you think.

The most common pushback I hear is: *We don't have childcare that we trust.* I've got great news: This is a solvable problem. If you don't have family close by or the means for a babysitter, find good friends and date swap. When we got married, we were both still in school and lived away from family. I worked part-time, but Tom didn't have a real income until we'd been married for seven years and had two kids. I assure you, if you get creative, you can have meaningful quality time for less than $20.

Self-Care

Taking care of yourself is a gift to the whole family. Self-care can be relatively quick and easy, but it shouldn't be neglected. You function better when you've taken care of yourself, and your family benefits from parents and partners who are thriving. Similarly, supporting your partner's self-care is a powerful way to show love, collaboration, and support. When both of you feel seen and rejuvenated, the whole family thrives.

Surfing the Internet is an easy distraction, but it rarely fills your cup. Worse, it can put you in a downward spiral of comparisons, divisiveness, or fear, which is far from the restorative break you were hoping for.

Instead, put your phone down and find joy and peace in the little things. Self-care doesn't have to mean a spa day. Sometimes you can add meaning to really simple, accessible experiences. When I first started my career, I had an insanely stressful job. I realized that simply eating a grapefruit in a bubble bath with a show (*Gossip Girl*, to be exact) was the perfect way to unwind.

Meaningful self-care doesn't have to cost much time or money. You and your partner deserve an opportunity to unwind. Sit down and brainstorm ways to recharge in 10 minutes or less, and then create a plan to carve out that time in your day. Meditate, go on a walk, stretch, go to bed early, or call a friend.

Delegate and Let Go

In her book *A Better Share*, Dr. Cutlip explores the emotional and invisible labor of motherhood and how couples can more equitably share the mental load.[7] She notes that the research is clear: Early and meaningful partner involvement leads to smoother maternal adjustment and reduced postpartum depression and anxiety. If you have a partner, ask for help. Let them jump in and figure things out, even if they do things differently than you or you think you can meet Baby's needs better. We call this "maternal gatekeeping." It's driven by anxiety, perfectionism, and social conditioning, and it happens subtly and unconsciously. But when moms (unintentionally) limit or control

Nap Trapped: When Sacrifice Backfires

their partner's involvement, their partner ends up doing less of the work that she desperately craves help with.

You must practice communicating this. Often, the biggest source of disappointment, resentment, and eventual burnout in both partners is unmet expectations. The problem is, often these unmet expectations go unspoken. Dr. Cutlip says, "We go into parenthood with all these visions of what it's going to be like...and a lot of times, we never talk about them. By the time Baby is born, we're already managing unmet expectations." These unmet expectations can be communicated and repaired. "If you develop hurts after kids and never repair them, it becomes a pattern. It's not that love fades, it's that reconnection never happens."

A favorite tool of mine in therapy is to make a list of everything in your life that needs to get done. Then, on a separate page, make three columns and sort your tasks where they belong:

- I do it.
- Someone else does it.
- It doesn't get done.

These are the only three options we truly have.

What usually happens is the "I do it" column is overflowing and unrealistic. This leads to overwhelm and burnout. The "Someone else does it" column becomes rife with frustration because we either hate asking for help or feel let down. And the "It doesn't get done" column carries unnecessary guilt.

I challenge you to set more realistic expectations for yourself. Accept your limitations and make peace with the fact that you can't do it all. Look to your community. Let others help you. Powerfully choose to put more things in the "it doesn't get done" column and move on.

Sometimes you'll serve Cheerios for dinner. Sometimes "cleaning" your house means frantically throwing stuff in the hall closet.

Sometimes your kid shows up at play group with dirty feet and pizza sauce on their shirt. It's fine. It's all fine.

Though it will stretch you in more ways than you can imagine, the journey to becoming a parent can and should be incredible. Your relationships can flourish even with these challenges. As you dig in, protest, and grow, you'll come out the other side stronger and more resilient.

Nap Trapped: When Sacrifice Backfires

Conclusion

Congratulations! You now have a fundamental understanding of baby sleep. You know the theory behind why sleep is so important, and you know how to optimize your baby's sleep in a way that is effective, efficient, and protects secure attachment. Parenting isn't easy, and your little one's sleep habits will throw you for a loop from time to time. But you won't be thrown off your game, because you know how to bounce right back to your regular routine.

You know that your number-one tool for good sleep is establishing a solid sleep foundation. You understand that allowing room for growth and development is not only supportive but necessary for their optimal outcomes. And most importantly, you now understand the various methods to achieve optimal sleep in a way that works for your family system.

Your next step is to get to work. Figure out your plan and go for it. Remember to use a sleep log to track your progress and pivot as needed. In no time at all, your baby will be sleeping blissfully, and you'll feel a renewed energy that you didn't even realize you'd lost. It's such a good feeling when something that was previously stressful no longer is.

Please keep in touch! Follow me on Instagram @the.peaceful. sleeper and share this book with your friends. I post sleep tips constantly and love to connect with you. If you need individualized help, don't hesitate to schedule a consultation. We have an incredible team of compassionate consultants as well as courses and a plethora of resources to help every aspect of sleep.

Go be a light to others. Be kind. Uplift and support. Spread goodness. Parenting is really freaking hard sometimes, and none of us can do it alone. Show up each day doing your best, looking for the good in yourself and in others. Strive to be the most grounded, fulfilled version of yourself, and give others the grace to do the same. Tell your friends all about what you've learned, and send them my way.

Above all, happy sleeping!

xoxo,

Chrissy

How to Choose Your Approach to Sleep Training

If you are unsure which approach is best to start with, the following quiz can be a helpful resource. This quiz is meant to help you determine what approach to sleep learning is the best fit for *you*.

When you choose an approach to sleep training, keep in mind this is a starting point. Once you begin your chosen approach, you will either *see progress* or *gather data*. You will continue to tune in, adapt, and modify the approach as you go, based on the information you are gathering through the process.

Remember, just because an approach feels right for you doesn't guarantee it will be the perfect fit for your baby. Every child is unique, and what works beautifully for one may not work for another. Success comes from finding the overlap between your teaching style and your baby's learning needs—what researchers call the *zone of proximal development*. While it's true that many babies respond more quickly when given space to protest, that's only an average. The most efficient path for your baby will always be the approach that best matches their individual readiness and temperament.

Quiz

To help you assess the right starting point for you and your little one, please answer the following questions. At the end, you'll tally up your "score" and find the approach that may fit best. If you're feeling stuck or need more support figuring out a learning path for your baby, consider reaching out to a sleep consultant for support.

1) The thought of giving my baby room to protest while they learn independent sleep makes me feel:

    a) Very anxious. I can't imagine doing that right now.

    b) Overwhelmed, but I'm open to try it in a gentle way.

    c) Nervous in the moment, but I see the value in giving them some space.

    d) Calm. I know babies cry for lots of reasons, and it feels worth it.

2) What best describes your thoughts on a sleep training timeline?

    a) I have no timeline. It can take as long as it takes.

    b) I'm okay if it takes a few weeks to a few months.

    c) I'd love quick results, but I'm okay with it taking a few weeks.

    d) I really need results ASAP.

3) Using sleep timers feels:

    a) Not right for me—I don't want to use timers.

    b) Stressful—I'd prefer only very short timers.

    c) Okay—10 minutes feels manageable and helpful as a guide.

    d) Totally fine—I'd be comfortable with 20–60 minutes if my baby was actively working on self-soothing.

4) The statement that best aligns with my parenting philosophy is:

    a) I don't expect my baby to learn without me. I want to support them fully and don't feel a need for independent sleep right now.

b) My baby might learn a little on their own, but they learn best when I am physically present with them.

c) Some protest is okay—it's a normal part of learning and development. I believe my baby is capable, and pushing through protest can build confidence and resilience.

a) = 0 points

b) = 1 point

c) = 2 points

d) = 3 points

Score:

0–2 = Gradual Approach

3–5 = Modified-Modified Approach

6–10 = Modified-Accelerated (10-Minute Method)

11–12 = Accelerated

Creating a Sleep Log

Whichever method you choose for sleep training, it's helpful to keep a detailed sleep log for the first two weeks rather than relying on your own subjective experiences. Facts are helpful to track progress, see improvements, discern patterns, keep your motivation, and maintain your sanity.

What Is a Sleep Log?

A *sleep log* is a detailed chart you can use to visually represent and track patterns in your process and your baby's progress while sleep training. This log can be as simple or as granular as you'd like it to be, but having clear data to refer to is incredibly helpful.

I personally think it has to be in a chart form so it's easier to see patterns. If you just have written notes with details from the day, it's difficult to discern information and patterns that you're looking for.

There are lots of apps that provide charting similar to this, so use whatever is most natural for you. I find that paper and pencil are still easier for me, so feel free to use my sleep log as a guide or create your own.

I like to know when my baby is sleeping, eating, playing (out of crib), happy in their crib, fussing off and on, mildly crying, moderately crying, and screaming. This helps me picture how the day went. I don't track every meal throughout the day, but I do measure when I feed them around sleep times. It's helpful for me to know how many times

I fed them in the night and whether they went right back to sleep afterward.

I also need to know how the crying went—whether they were just rolling around in their crib calling out every few minutes or actually crying really hard. You'll notice that I document every hour in the day, which may seem like overkill. But it doesn't take long, and documenting every hour helps me to discern patterns and see that my baby really is happy most of the time.

If you're doing a modified-cry version, you can also track when you went to soothe and for how long. This is important because your subjective memory sucks when you're sleep training. Listening to your baby cry for 10 minutes can feel like an hour. Plus, you can look back over a few days' data to see patterns and improvement.

Even if you're doing a no-cry option or you're not wanting to fully start sleep training yet, a sleep log is helpful to track your baby's natural patterns. You will be able to see roughly when they go down for each nap and about how long they sleep. You'll be better able to learn about optimal awake windows and play detective when your baby randomly protests for a longer time. And it makes it much easier to move to a clock-based schedule because you can see some of those patterns unfold too. I can't tell you how much freedom you'll feel knowing exactly what times your baby needs to sleep and being able to plan your schedule predictably. For instance, if you need to schedule a doctor's appointment next Thursday, it's so nice to know what time to aim for.

Here's a blank version for you to use and a copy of my sleep logs from when I trained my first and third babies. I sleep trained my first two children right at five months, and my third and fourth I sleep trained at four months. Keep in mind, with my first, I was totally winging it, and I realize now I made some big scheduling mistakes.

Creating a Sleep Log

the peaceful
sleeper

sleep log

	Day 1	Day 2	Day 3	Day 4	Day 5	Day 6	Day 7	Day 8	Day 9	Day 10	Day 11	Day 12	Day 13	Day 14
12 a.m.														
11														
10														
9														
8														
7														
6														
5														
4														
3														
2														
1														
12 p.m.														
11														
10														
9														
8														
7														
6														
5														
4														
3														
2														
1														
12 a.m.														

Legend:
- Sleeping
- Eating
- Playing (Out of Crib)
- Set in Crib
- Happy in Crib
- Fussing (On/Off)
- Mild Cry
- Crying
- Screaming

Creating a Sleep Log

the peaceful sleeper

Maddie's Sleep Log

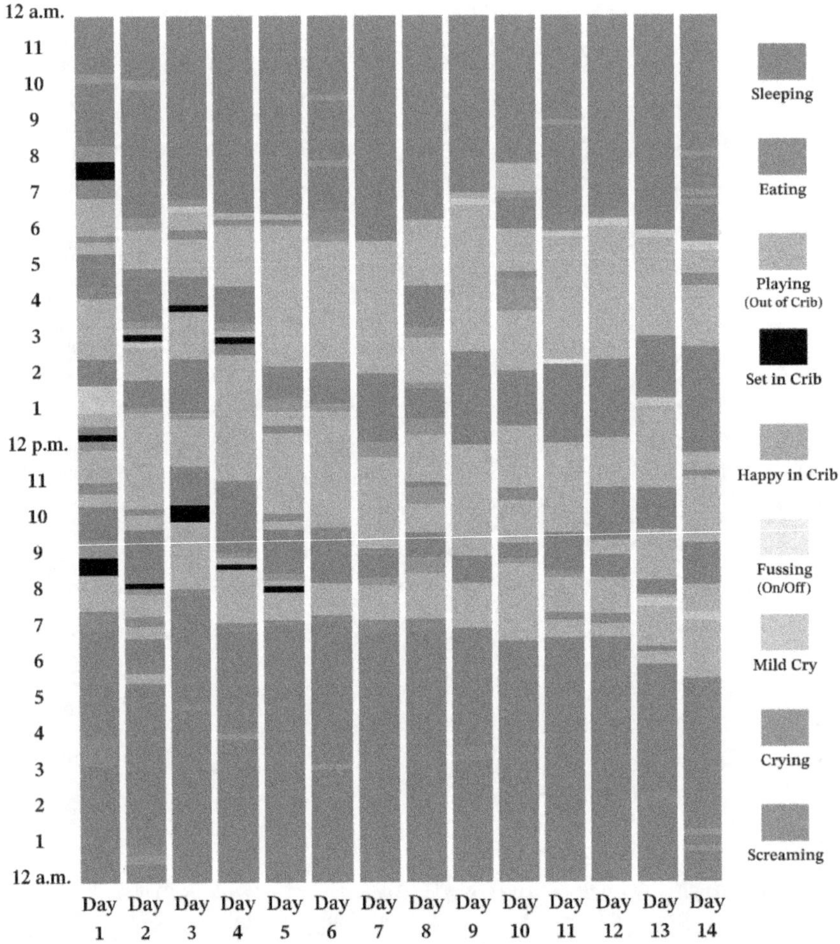
12 a.m.
11
10
9
8
7
6
5
4
3
2
1
12 p.m.
11
10
9
8
7
6
5
4
3
2
1
12 a.m.
Day 1
Day 2
Day 3
Day 4
Day 5
Day 6
Day 7
Day 8
Day 9
Day 10
Day 11
Day 12
Day 13
Day 14
Sleeping
Eating
Playing (Out of Crib)
Set in Crib
Happy in Crib
Fussing (On/Off)
Mild Cry
Crying
Screaming

*If you're reading the paperback version of this book, it may be nearly impossible to discern these charts. Hop on my Instagram highlights to see them in color @the.peaceful.sleeper.

Observations:

- Sleep training started on day 1 at the first nap. What I know now is that I put her down for that first nap too late (two hours after she woke up). She would have been happier if I'd put her down 30 minutes earlier.

- You'll notice that the first nap stabilizes rather quickly about 90 minutes after she woke up for the day from there on out.

- The second nap that day was also a little rough, with about 30–40 minutes of crying before she fell asleep.

- At bedtime she cried for about 30 minutes before she fell asleep that night too. (It's funny because until I pulled this out, I would have told you she cried for longer than an hour that first night. See, this is why charting is important!)

- She woke up again a little after 10 p.m. and cried, but I didn't get her, and she fell back asleep after a few minutes.

- On day 2 there was a significant drop in crying. She still woke up and cried around 10 p.m., but that was short-lived.

- On day 3, she didn't wake up at 10 p.m. and almost never did again after that. You'll notice that her nap times really developed and solidified.

- On day 13, she had a rough night going to sleep. She cried for about 10 minutes four different times before really going to sleep for the night. It wasn't even that bad—but when you're in the moment, 10 minutes of listening to her cry feels like an eternity. It felt like a huge regression, but this rough night was totally an exception. Expect to have an outlier rough night here and there. We have to allow room for imperfection or else we'll overwhelm ourselves unnecessarily. Had it not been for this log and seeing how many good days we'd had, I could have easily concluded that this wasn't working. But I had proof that her crying time was diminishing and her schedule was solidifying. After these two weeks, we shifted bedtime even earlier, to about 6:15 p.m., and also had a consistent early-morning feeding at about 5 a.m. Smooth sailing.

On the next page, you'll find my chart from when I sleep trained London.

London's Sleep Log

the peaceful sleeper

Legend:
- Sleeping
- Eating
- Playing (Out of Crib)
- Set in Crib
- Happy in Crib
- Fussing (On/Off)
- Mild Cry
- Crying
- Screaming

Creating a Sleep Log

Observations:

- The first thing I notice when I see this chart again is that I clearly knew what I was doing this time. I did a way better job scheduling right off the bat, and she caught on with very minimal crying.

- The next thing that stands out is that she did great the first two days and then night 3 was really rough. Don't be dismayed if everything seems to go to crap around day 3–5. Just stay the course, and it will get better again.

- Notice since she was four months old, she had very short awake times and not super long naps. You can see her schedule solidifying though, so after about a week, I could have created a schedule based off the clock instead of only following her cues. This is where the sweet spot happens: when you can map out a schedule that looks the same every day.

- Since London was my third, I had bigger kids with set schedules, carpools, and activities. I made a separate log of my schedule conflicts, compared that to my sleep log, and created an optimal schedule for her that allowed for consistent, uninterrupted naps. It didn't always unfold perfectly, and sometimes I had to stretch her awake time or wake her up early, but it was a great backbone to our already hectic schedules. It may feel impossible to prioritize baby's naps, but with some creativity and motivation it can be easier than you think.

Sleep Training Twins

With twins, some things will be a little different, but most of the process will be the same. Part of the trickiness with twins lies in getting them onto the same schedule. Often, you will have one baby that's just a little bit better of a sleeper than the other baby, or one baby that has more or less sleep needs. After all, they are individuals.

This was the case for Savvy and Ziggy, twin sister and brother. Savvy needed about 90 minutes more sleep in a 24-hour period than her brother did. Where she was calm and content and loved to sleep, he was amped and energetic and wanted to be everywhere all the time. In the first two weeks of sleep training, we're trying to learn as much about each baby as possible. It's important to keep a separate sleep log for each twin so that you can better discern their individual patterns. We want to meet each baby's individual needs while also trying to get their schedules to line up as well as possible.

Let's say baby A sleeps for 90 minutes during a nap and baby B sleeps for only 60 minutes. Technically both naps are sufficient. Baby B might just be a 60-minute napper. But if both babies need 90 minutes of awake time, it won't take long for their schedules to become totally out of sync, which can be really overwhelming for parents. The goal is to figure out how to line schedules up best to make sure they both get the most sleep possible without being interrupted by their sibling. In this instance, we'd put baby B down 15 minutes later than baby A, and he might wake up 15 minutes earlier. We'll stretch his awake window slightly so that he's ready to go down for the next nap around the same time as his twin.

But for your first week or so of sleep training, let it be okay if their schedules get off from each other. Aim for the same bedtime, same wake-up time, and probably the same naptime for nap 1, but then follow their leads. The more accurately we can assess each twin's natural rhythm, the easier it will be to create a clock-based schedule that works for both babies.

The question I'm asked the most about sleep training twins is: Should we separate them and put them in different sleep spaces, or keep them together?

Most often twins do great sharing space. If you're not sure, I'd say default to keeping them in the same space and pivot if needed. They've been sharing space since conception, so they are usually remarkably good at learning to ignore each other's protest. Though sometimes they can ramp each other up, more often than not they can calm each other down.

Additionally, being in the same space can help them sync their schedules eventually. They can learn to fall asleep around the same time, and one twin's sounds will start to gently rouse their sibling that's still sleeping. If your babies have about the same sleep needs and about the same schedule, keep them together. If they have drastically different sleep needs and temperaments, you may consider putting them in separate spaces during naptime or even bedtime for the first week or two of sleep training.

They can and will learn to sleep through each other's sounds though. It's amazing the number of times I've seen one twin super agitated and angry while the other peacefully drifts off to sleep. When their best friend and womb-mate isn't upset that they're upset, it's kind of a reminder to you that they really are just fine. Protest is just protest.

The 10-minute approach will look slightly different while you're sleep training twins. Here are a few things to note:

- If your partner or alternate caregiver can help you these first few days, that would be great. But you may find yourself solo with both babies doing timers. When you go in to soothe, whoever is the most escalated gets picked up. The baby who is a little more calm can be soothed while they're still laying in the crib. You'll have one baby in your arms soothing and the other you're shushing and patting in the crib.

- If the twin in the crib isn't having it, you may need to soothe one in your arms, put them down, and then grab the other to soothe. Start your timer again when you're done soothing both and back out of the room.

- If baby A has fallen asleep but baby B hasn't yet, you can still allow for 20 more minutes of protest but then go rock to sleep. Though they can learn to sleep through each other's sounds, we don't want to risk baby A getting woken up in a sleep cycle transition and feeling like it was a cat nap.

- I hate to wake a sleeping baby, but we do want to wake baby A when baby B wakes up in the morning. Often leaving them in the room together will solve this, and baby A will naturally start to stir when they hear their sibling.

- Now you'll pay attention to sleepy cues. Try to keep them on the same schedule, but you may notice that one twin has higher sleep needs than the other. We don't want to hold the higher sleep needs baby back to be on pace with the one who doesn't need as much sleep. So, keep charting as naps start to unfold and see if you have one baby who seems to always nap longer than the other.

Sleep Training Twins

- If baby A wakes from a short nap but the other is still sleeping, see if you can intervene to help baby A back to sleep. Try for 10–15 minutes, but if not, just take them out and try again at the next nap. You can let baby B keep sleeping for now. Again, nap schedules might get skewed in the first two weeks, but we want to give each a chance to nap lengthen when they will. Pay attention to the clock and see how to time it so that both babies will be ready for bed at the same time. It may mean that one baby has four naps and the other has three or that we wake someone from an evening cat nap to keep bedtime together on track.

- At night, feed each baby when they wake for these first two weeks. Don't worry about waking the other to feed. They may start dropping night feeds on their own.

After your first two weeks, dive into your sleep logs. For the sake of your sanity, you can move a little more quickly to a clock-based schedule and see how the babies do with it.

What to look for in each baby:

- General levels of protest before falling asleep
- Optimal awake windows
- Total sleep time in a 24-hour period
- Synchronization with the other twin
- Intervals between night feeds
- Nap lengthening

The priority the first two weeks was to teach each of them to initiate sleep independently and see how they do once we have some of these skills buttoned up. Now the priority is getting their schedules aligned.

If you have one or both babies who are really struggling with nap lengthening, I might separate them for naps for just a week while you work on it. You can put a portable crib in your room, a well-ventilated walk-in closet, or a spare bedroom or home office. That'll make it easier to allow for some protest so they'll go back to sleep without running the risk of waking up their sibling.

You'll also want to figure out your plan for night awakenings. If both twins wake every three hours for feedings, but they're staggered, go back to feeding them both at the same time. When one wakes up to feed, try to dream feed the other. If, however, one twin wakes every three hours and the other wakes every five or six hours, you may want to give it a little more time feeding them on their own schedules so those night awakenings can continue to drop on their own.

With regard to dropping night awakenings, if CIO is needed once you get to that stage, trust your instinct as to whether or not they'll do better in the same space or separated. My usual instinct is to keep them together since they can sleep through each other's sounds and usually serve to calm and comfort each other, but there are definitely pros and cons of each. What you know of your babies will help make that decision for you.

Twins may come with extra variables, but the same principles apply: consistency, observation, and flexibility. Keep tuning in, making adjustments, and trusting your instincts. Even parents of multiples can get great sleep!

Notes

Introduction

1. Elisa Delvecchio et al., "Parenting Styles and Child's Well-being: The Mediating Role of the Perceived Parental Stress," *Europe's Journal of Psychology* 16, no. 3 (August 28, 2020): 514–31, https://doi.org/10.5964/ejop.v16i3.2013.

2. Sofie Kuppens and Eva Ceulemans, "Parenting Styles: A Closer Look at a Well-Known Concept," *Journal of Child and Family Studies* 28, no. 1 (September 18, 2018): 168–81, https://doi.org/10.1007/s10826-018-1242-x.

3. Ariana Awiszus, Melissa Koenig, and Julie Vaisarova, "Parenting Styles and Their Effect on Child Development and Outcome," *Journal of Student Research* 11, no. 3 (August 31, 2022), https://doi.org/10.47611/jsrhs.v11i3.3679.

Chapter 1: What Exactly Is Sleep Training?

1. Michael L. Perlis et al., *Cognitive Behavioral Treatment of Insomnia: A Session-by-Session Guide* (Springer, 2008).

2. Mathew Ednick et al., "A Review of the Effects of Sleep During the First Year of Life on Cognitive, Psychomotor, and Temperament Development," *SLEEP* 32, no. 11 (November 1, 2009): 1449–58, https://doi.org/10.1093/sleep/32.11.1449.

3. Michal Kahn et al., "Behavioral Interventions for Infant Sleep Problems: The Role of Parental Cry Tolerance and Sleep-related Cognitions," *Journal of Clinical Sleep Medicine* 16, no. 8 (April 13, 2020): 1275–83, https://doi.org/10.5664/jcsm.8488.

4. Sonia Marie Lenehan et al., "The Architecture of Early Childhood Sleep Over the First Two Years," *Maternal and Child Health Journal* 27, no. 2 (December 31, 2022): 226–50, https://doi.org/10.1007/s10995-022-03545-9.

5. Bronwyn M. Sweeney, T. Leigh Signal, and Duncan R. Babbage, "Effect of a Behavioral-educational Sleep Intervention for First-time Mothers and Their Infants: Pilot of a Controlled Trial," *Journal of Clinical Sleep Medicine* 16, no. 8 (April 10, 2020): 1265–74, https://doi.org/10.5664/jcsm.8484.

6. Nina Quin et al., "Preventing Postpartum Insomnia: Findings From a Three-arm Randomized-controlled Trial of Cognitive Behavioral Therapy for Insomnia, a Responsive Bassinet, and Sleep Hygiene," *SLEEP* 47, no. 8 (May 13, 2024), https://doi.org/10.1093/sleep/zsae106.

7. Helene Werner et al., "The Zurich 3-Step Concept for the Management of Behavioral Sleep Disorders in Children: A Before-and-After Study," *Journal of Clinical Sleep Medicine* 11, no. 03 (March 13, 2015): 241–49, https://doi.org/10.5664/jcsm.4536.

8. Oliviero Bruni et al., "Longitudinal Study of Sleep Behavior in Normal Infants During the First Year of Life," *Journal of Clinical Sleep Medicine* 10, no. 10 (October 14, 2014): 1119–27, https://doi.org/10.5664/jcsm.4114.

9. Michael Gradisar et al., "Behavioral Interventions for Infant Sleep Problems: A Randomized Controlled Trial," *PEDIATRICS* 137, no. 6 (May 24, 2016), https://doi.org/10.1542/peds.2015-1486.

10. Filip Drozd et al., "An Overview of Reviews for Preventing and Treating Sleep Problems in Infants," *Acta Paediatrica* 111, no. 11 (July 2, 2022): 2071–76, https://doi.org/10.1111/apa.16475.

11. Michal Kahn et al., "Behavioral Interventions for Pediatric Insomnia: One Treatment May Not Fit All," *SLEEP* 43, no. 4 (November 2, 2019), https://doi.org/10.1093/sleep/zsz268.

Chapter 2: Everyone Is an Expert (and Everything Is on Fire!)

1. Office of the Surgeon General, "Parents Under Pressure," NCBI Bookshelf, 2024, https://www.ncbi.nlm.nih.gov/books/NBK606667/.

2. Matthew Walker, *Why We Sleep: Unlocking the Power of Sleep and Dreams* (Simon and Schuster, 2017).

3. Soroush Vosoughi, Deb Roy, and Sinan Aral, "The Spread of True and False News Online," *Science* 359, no. 6380 (March 8, 2018): 1146–51, https://doi.org/10.1126/science.aap9559.

4. "Utah Vs Franke/Hildebrandt | Washington County of Utah," n.d., https://www.washco.utah.gov/departments/attorney/case-highlights-media/utah-vs-franke-hildebrandt/.

Chapter 3: Debunking the Myths

1. "Instagram," n.d., https://www.instagram.com/reel/C1ims-LuFUK/?igsh=MWU0MmtjbmlxNjM0dg%3D%3D.

2. Pudding. "Is Sleep Training Harmful?" The Pudding, n.d. https://pudding.cool/2024/07/sleep-training.

3. Pudding, "Is Sleep Training Harmful?"

4. Ayten Bilgin and Dieter Wolke, "Parental Use of 'Cry It Out' in Infants: No Adverse Effects on Attachment and Behavioural Development at 18 Months," *Journal of Child Psychology and Psychiatry* 61, no. 11 (March 10, 2020): 1184–93, https://doi.org/10.1111/jcpp.13223.

5. Bill Sears, "The Effects of Excessive Crying," Ask Dr Sears, September 28, 2023, https://www.askdrsears.com/topics/health-concerns/fussy-baby/science-excessive-crying-harmful/.

6. Mark D. Seery, E. Alison Holman, and Roxane Cohen Silver, "Whatever Does Not Kill Us: Cumulative Lifetime Adversity, Vulnerability, and Resilience.," *Journal of Personality and Social Psychology* 99, no. 6 (October 12, 2010): 1025–41, https://doi.org/10.1037/a0021344.

7. Sears, "The Effects of Excessive Crying."

8. Bruce D. Perry, "Incubated in Terror: Neurodevelopmental Factors in the 'Cycle of Violence,'" in *Children in a Violent Society*, ed. Joy D. Osofsky (New York: Guilford Press, 1997), 124–149.

9. Stephen R. Butler, Mark R. Suskind, and Saul M. Schanberg, "Maternal Behavior as a Regulator of Polyamine Biosynthesis in Brain and Heart of the Developing Rat Pup," *Science* 199, no. 4327 (January 27, 1978): 445–47, https://doi.org/10.1126/science.202031.

10. Daphne Blunt Bugental, Gabriela A Martorell, and Veronica Barraza, "The Hormonal Costs of Subtle Forms of Infant Maltreatment," *Hormones and Behavior* 43, no. 1 (January 1, 2003): 237–44, https://doi.org/10.1016/s0018-506x(02)00008-9.

11. Martin H. Teicher et al., "The Neurobiological Consequences of Early Stress and Childhood Maltreatment," *Neuroscience & Biobehavioral Reviews* 27, no. 1–2 (January 1, 2003): 33–44, https://doi.org/10.1016/s0149-7634(03)00007-1.

12. Jeffrey Kluger, "The Science Behind Dr. Sears: Does It Stand up? | TIME.com," TIME.com, May 10, 2012, https://ideas.time.com/2012/05/10/the-science-behind-dr-sears-does-it-stand-up/.

13. Kluger, "The Science Behind Dr. Sears: Does It Stand up? | TIME.Com."

14. Sears, "The Effects of Excessive Crying."

15. C. M. Kuhn, None Butler, and S. M. Schanberg, "Selective Depression of Serum Growth Hormone During Maternal Deprivation in Rat Pups," *Science* 201, no. 4360 (September 15, 1978): 1034–36, https://doi.org/10.1126/science.684424.

16. Sears, "The Effects of Excessive Crying."

17. M R Rao, "Long Term Cognitive Development in Children With Prolonged Crying," *Archives of Disease in Childhood* 89, no. 11 (October 21, 2004): 989–92, https://doi.org/10.1136/adc.2003.039198.

18. Dieter Wolke, Patrizia Rizzo, and Sarah Woods, "Persistent Infant Crying and Hyperactivity Problems in Middle Childhood," *PEDIATRICS* 109, no. 6 (June 1, 2002): 1054–60, https://doi.org/10.1542/peds.109.6.1054.

19. Cynthia A. Stifter and Tracy L. Spinrad, "The Effect of Excessive Crying on the Development of Emotion Regulation," *Infancy* 3, no. 2 (April 1, 2002): 133–52, https://doi.org/10.1207/s15327078in0302_2.

20. Stephanie Hollington-Sawyer, "Gabor Maté Parenting Ferberization," *Dr. Gabor Maté* (blog), May 15, 2014, https://drgabormate.com/no-longer-believe-babies-cry-sleep/.

21. Darcia F. Narvaez PhD, "The Practice Comes From a Misunderstanding of Child Development.," *Psychology Today*, May 17, 2024, https://www.psychologytoday.com/us/blog/moral-landscapes/201112/dangers-of-crying-it-out.

22. Charles A. Nelson et al., "Cognitive Recovery in Socially Deprived Young Children: The Bucharest Early Intervention Project," *Science* 318, no. 5858 (December 21, 2007): 1937–40, https://doi.org/10.1126/science.1143921.

23. Charles A. Nelson, *Romania's Abandoned Children: Deprivation, Brain Development, and the Struggle for Recovery,* 2014, http://ci.nii.ac.jp/ncid/BB14970888.

24. Charles A. Nelson, Nathan A. Fox, and Charles H. Zeanah, "Romania's Abandoned Children: The Effects of Early Profound Psychosocial Deprivation on the Course of Human Development," *Current Directions in Psychological Science* 32, no. 6 (October 27, 2023): 515–21, https://doi.org/10.1177/09637214231201079.

25. Nelson, Fox, and Zeanah, *Romania's Abandoned Children: Deprivation, Brain Development, and the Struggle for Recovery.*

26. Kirsten Weir, "*The Lasting Impact of Neglect,*" American Psychological Association, June 2014, https://www.apa.org/monitor/2014/06/neglect.

27. Buried Signals, "Is Sleep Training Harmful? What Science Really Shows," February 27, 2025, https://www.youtube.com/watch?v=JB6uIyrQ2iQ.

28. C. L. Coe et al., "Endocrine and Immune Responses to Separation and Maternal Loss in Non-Human Primates," in *The Psychology of Attachment and Separation,* ed. M. Reite and T. Fields (New York: Academic Press, 1985), 165.

29. Buried Signals, "Is Sleep Training Harmful? What Science Really Shows."

30. Buried Signals, "Is Sleep Training Harmful? What Science Really Shows."

31. Allan N. Schore, "The Effects of Early Relational Trauma on Right Brain Development, Affect Regulation, and Infant Mental Health," by Michigan Association for Infant Mental Health, *Infant Mental Health Journal,* vol. 22–22 (Michigan Association for Infant Mental Health, 2001), https://www.allanschore.com/pdf/SchoreIMHJTrauma01.pdf.

32. Allan N. Schore, "The Experience-Dependent Maturation of a Regulatory System in the Orbital Prefrontal Cortex and the Origin of Developmental Psychopathology," *Development and Psychopathology* 8 (1996): 59–87.

33. Joan Kaufman and Dennis Charney, "Effects of Early Stress on Brain Structure and Function: Implications for Understanding the Relationship Between Child Maltreatment and Depression," *Development and*

Psychopathology 13, no. 3 (September 1, 2001): 451–71, https://doi
.org/10.1017/s0954579401003030.

34. Anna M.H. Price et al., "Five-Year Follow-up of Harms and Benefits of
    Behavioral Infant Sleep Intervention: Randomized Trial," PEDIATRICS
    130, no. 4 (September 11, 2012): 643–51, https://doi.org/10.1542/
    peds.2011-3467.

35. Wendy A. Hall et al., "A Randomized Controlled Trial of an Intervention
    for Infants' Behavioral Sleep Problems," BMC Pediatrics 15, no. 1
    (November 12, 2015), https://doi.org/10.1186/s12887-015-0492-7.

36. Michael Gradisar et al., "Behavioral Interventions for Infant Sleep
    Problems: A Randomized Controlled Trial," PEDIATRICS 137, no. 6
    (May 24, 2016), https://doi.org/10.1542/peds.2015-1486.

37. Anna M.H. Price et al., "Five-Year Follow-up of Harms and Benefits of
    Behavioral Infant Sleep Intervention: Randomized Trial," PEDIATRICS
    130, no. 4 (September 11, 2012): 643–51, https://doi.org/10.1542/
    peds.2011-3467.

38. Avi Sadeh et al., "Sleep and Sleep Ecology in the First 3 Years: A Web-
    based Study," Journal of Sleep Research 18, no. 1 (October 16, 2008):
    60–73, https://doi.org/10.1111/j.1365-2869.2008.00699.x.

Chapter 4: Why Quality Sleep Matters for Baby

1. Katharina Pittner et al., "Sleep Across the First Year of Life Is Prospectively
   Associated With Brain Volume in 12-months Old Infants," Neurobiology
   of Sleep and Circadian Rhythms 14 (March 8, 2023): 100091, https://
   doi.org/10.1016/j.nbscr.2023.100091.

2. Mark Lawrence Wong et al., "The Interplay Between Sleep and Mood in
   Predicting Academic Functioning, Physical Health and Psychological
   Health: A Longitudinal Study," Journal of Psychosomatic Research 74, no. 4
   (September 25, 2012): 271–77, https://doi.org/10.1016/j.jpsychores
   .2012.08.014.

3. Ednick et al., "A Review of the Effects of Sleep During the First Year of
   Life on Cognitive, Psychomotor, and Temperament Development."

4. Marc Weissbluth, *Healthy Sleep Habits, Happy Child* (Fawcett, 1999).

5. Eline R. De Groot, Jeroen Dudink, and Topun Austin, "Sleep as a Driver of Pre- and Postnatal Brain Development," *Pediatric Research*, July 3, 2024, https://doi.org/10.1038/s41390-024-03371-5.

6. Liat Tikotzky et al., "Sleep and Physical Growth in Infants During the First 6 Months," *Journal of Sleep Research* 19, no. 1-Part-I (October 14, 2009): 103–10, https://doi.org/10.1111/j.1365-2869.2009.00772.x.

7. Heather Turgeon Mft et al., *The Happy Sleeper: The Science-Backed Guide to Helping Your Baby Get a Good Night's Sleep-Newborn to School Age* (TarcherPerigee, 2014).

8. Michelle Lampl and Michael L. Johnson, "Infant Growth in Length Follows Prolonged Sleep and Increased Naps," *SLEEP* 34, no. 5 (May 1, 2011): 641–50, https://doi.org/10.1093/sleep/34.5.641.

9. Camila Dos Santos El Halal and Magda Lahorgue Nunes, "Sleep and Weight-height Development," *Jornal De Pediatria* 95 (December 7, 2018): 2–9, https://doi.org/10.1016/j.jped.2018.10.009.

10. Violeta Clement-Carbonell et al., "Sleep Quality, Mental and Physical Health: A Differential Relationship," *International Journal of Environmental Research and Public Health* 18, no. 2 (January 8, 2021): 460, https://doi.org/10.3390/ijerph18020460.

11. Pranshu A. Adavadkar et al., "Association Between Sleep Disorders and Health Care Utilization in Children With Chronic Medical Conditions: A Medicaid Claims Data Analysis," *Journal of Clinical Sleep Medicine* 20, no. 4 (January 17, 2024): 595–601, https://doi.org/10.5664/jcsm.10936.

12. Tikotzky et al., "Sleep and Physical Growth in Infants During the First 6 Months."

13. Jiaxiao Yu et al., "Insufficient Sleep During Infancy Is Correlated With Excessive Weight Gain in Childhood: A Longitudinal Twin Cohort Study," *Journal of Clinical Sleep Medicine* 17, no. 11 (May 17, 2021): 2147–54, https://doi.org/10.5664/jcsm.9350.

14. Halal and Nunes, "Sleep and Weight-Height Development."

15. Seung-Schik Yoo et al., "The Human Emotional Brain Without Sleep — a Prefrontal Amygdala Disconnect," *Current Biology* 17, no. 20 (October 1, 2007): R877–78, https://doi.org/10.1016/j.cub.2007.08.007.

16. Mft et al., *The Happy Sleeper: The Science-Backed Guide to Helping Your Baby Get a Good Night's Sleep-Newborn to School Age.*

17. Fan Jiang, "Sleep and Early Brain Development," *Annals of Nutrition and Metabolism* 75, no. Suppl. 1 (January 1, 2019): 44–54, https://doi.org/10.1159/000508055.

18. Perlis et al., *Cognitive Behavioral Treatment of Insomnia: A Session-by-Session Guide.*

19. Jianghong Liu et al., "Childhood Sleep: Physical, Cognitive, and Behavioral Consequences and Implications," *World Journal of Pediatrics* 20, no. 2 (November 23, 2022): 122–32, https://doi.org/10.1007/s12519-022-00647-w.

20. Karen Spruyt, "A Review of Developmental Consequences of Poor Sleep in Childhood," *Sleep Medicine* 60 (December 15, 2018): 3–12, https://doi.org/10.1016/j.sleep.2018.11.021.

21. Jiang, "Sleep and Early Brain Development."

22. Weissbluth, *Healthy Sleep Habits, Happy Child.*

23. Alexandre Faisal-Cury et al., "The Impact of Postpartum Depression and Bonding Impairment on Child Development at 12 to 15 Months After Delivery," *Journal of Affective Disorders Reports* 4 (February 25, 2021): 100125, https://doi.org/10.1016/j.jadr.2021.100125.

24. Misty C. Richards et al., "The Impact of Postpartum Depression on the Early Mother-Infant Relationship During the COVID-19 Pandemic: Perception Versus Reality," *International Journal of Environmental Research and Public Health* 21, no. 2 (January 31, 2024): 164, https://doi.org/10.3390/ijerph21020164.

25. Sue Bhati and Kathy Richards, "A Systematic Review of the Relationship Between Postpartum Sleep Disturbance and Postpartum Depression," *JOGN Nursing* 44, no. 3 (March 29, 2015): 350–57, https://doi.org/10.1111/1552-6909.12562.

26. Andrea Lawson et al., "The Relationship Between Sleep and Postpartum Mental Disorders: A Systematic Review," *Journal of Affective Disorders* 176 (January 30, 2015): 65–77, https://doi.org/10.1016/j.jad.2015.01.017.

27. Zain Khan-Afridi et al., "Impact of Sleep on Postpartum Health Outcomes: A Systematic Review and Meta-analysis," *British Journal of Sports Medicine*, February 26, 2025, bjsports-109604, https://doi.org/10.1136/bjsports-2024-109604.

28. Nancy Eisenberg et al., "The Role of Emotionality and Regulation in Children's Social Functioning: A Longitudinal Study," *Child Development* 66, no. 5 (October 1, 1995): 1360–84, https://doi.org/10.1111/j.1467-8624.1995.tb00940.x.

29. Helen Demetriou and Dale F. Hay, "Toddlers' Reactions to the Distress of Familiar Peers: The Importance of Context," *Infancy* 6, no. 2 (September 1, 2004): 299–318, https://doi.org/10.1207/s15327078in0602_9.

30. Oliviero Bruni et al., "Executive Functions in Preschool Children With Chronic Insomnia," *Journal of Clinical Sleep Medicine* 16, no. 2 (January 16, 2020): 231–41, https://doi.org/10.5664/jcsm.8172.

31. Jiang, "Sleep and Early Brain Development," January 1, 2019.

32. Wanqi Sun et al., "A Community-Based Study of Sleep and Cognitive Development in Infants and Toddlers," *Journal of Clinical Sleep Medicine* 14, no. 06 (June 14, 2018): 977–84, https://doi.org/10.5664/jcsm.7164.

33. Liu et al., "Childhood Sleep: Physical, Cognitive, and Behavioral Consequences and Implications."

34. Ednick et al., "A Review of the Effects of Sleep During the First Year of Life on Cognitive, Psychomotor, and Temperament Development."

35. Tham, Elaine, Nora Schneider, and Birit Broekman. "Infant Sleep and Its Relation With Cognition and Growth: A Narrative Review." *Nature and Science of Sleep* Volume 9 (May 1, 2017): 135–49. https://doi.org/10.2147/nss.s125992.

36. Sanna Lokhandwala and Rebecca M.C. Spencer, "Relations Between Sleep Patterns Early in Life and Brain Development: A Review," *Developmental Cognitive Neuroscience* 56 (June 26, 2022): 101130, https://doi.org/10.1016/j.dcn.2022.101130.

37. Lenehan et al., "The Architecture of Early Childhood Sleep Over the First Two Years," December 31, 2022.

38. Bruni et al., "Executive Functions in Preschool Children With Chronic Insomnia."

39. Jiang, "Sleep and Early Brain Development," January 1, 2019.

40. Wanqi Sun et al., "A Community-Based Study of Sleep and Cognitive Development in Infants and Toddlers," *Journal of Clinical Sleep Medicine* 14, no. 06 (June 14, 2018): 977–84, https://doi.org/10.5664/jcsm.7164.

Chapter 5: Why Quality Sleep Matters for Parents

1. Walker, Why We Sleep: Unlocking the Power of Sleep and Dreams.

2. Xiaoying Li et al., "Sleep Characteristics and Cancer-Related Outcomes: An Umbrella Review of Systematic Reviews and Meta-Analyses of Observational Studies," *Journal of Clinical Medicine* 11, no. 24 (December 8, 2022): 7289, https://doi.org/10.3390/jcm11247289.

3. W. Li et al., "Self-reported Sleep Disorders and the Risk of All Cancer Types: Evidence From the Kailuan Cohort Study," *Public Health* 223 (September 5, 2023): 209–16, https://doi.org/10.1016/j.puhe.2023.08.007.

4. Shichan Wang et al., "Sleep Characteristics and Risk of Alzheimer's Disease: A Systematic Review and Meta-analysis of Longitudinal Studies," *Journal of Neurology* 271, no. 7 (April 24, 2024): 3782–93, https://doi.org/10.1007/s00415-024-12380-7.

5. Mingxian Meng et al., "Insomnia and Risk of All-cause Dementia: A Systematic Review and Meta-analysis," *PLoS ONE* 20, no. 4 (April 9, 2025): e0318814, https://doi.org/10.1371/journal.pone.0318814.

6. Zhilei Shan et al., "Sleep Duration and Risk of Type 2 Diabetes: A Meta-analysis of Prospective Studies," *Diabetes Care* 38, no. 3 (February 12, 2015): 529–37, https://doi.org/10.2337/dc14-2073.

7. Hongyi Liu et al., "Sleep Features and the Risk of Type 2 Diabetes Mellitus: A Systematic Review and Meta-analysis," *Annals of Medicine* 57, no. 1 (January 2, 2025), https://doi.org/10.1080/07853890.2024.2447422.

8. Shanshan Wang et al., "Associations Between Sleep Duration and Cardiovascular Diseases: A Meta-review and Meta-analysis of Observational

Notes

and Mendelian Randomization Studies," *Frontiers in Cardiovascular Medicine* 9 (August 11, 2022), https://doi.org/10.3389/fcvm.2022.930000.

9. Nicole Lovato and Michael Gradisar, "A Meta-analysis and Model of the Relationship Between Sleep and Depression in Adolescents: Recommendations for Future Research and Clinical Practice," *Sleep Medicine Reviews* 18, no. 6 (April 12, 2014): 521–29, https://doi.org/10.1016/j.smrv.2014.03.006.

10. Anna Marie Medina, Crystal L. Lederhos, and Teresa A. Lillis, "Sleep Disruption and Decline in Marital Satisfaction Across the Transition to Parenthood," *Families Systems & Health* 27, no. 2 (January 1, 2009): 153–60, https://doi.org/10.1037/a0015762.

11. Wendy M. Troxel et al., "Marital Quality and the Marital Bed: Examining the Covariation Between Relationship Quality and Sleep," *Sleep Medicine Reviews* 11, no. 5 (September 12, 2007): 389–404, https://doi.org/10.1016/j.smrv.2007.05.002.

12. Walker, Why We Sleep: Unlocking the Power of Sleep and Dreams.

13. Walker, Why We Sleep: Unlocking the Power of Sleep and Dreams.

14. A. Wilder-Smith et al., "Impact of Partial Sleep Deprivation on Immune Markers," *Sleep Medicine* 14, no. 10 (August 28, 2013): 1031–34, https://doi.org/10.1016/j.sleep.2013.07.001.

15. M. G. Poluektov, "Sleep and Immunity," *Neuroscience and Behavioral Physiology* 51, no. 5 (June 1, 2021): 609–15, https://doi.org/10.1007/s11055-021-01113-2.

16. Orfeu M. Buxton and Enrico Marcelli, "Short and Long Sleep Are Positively Associated With Obesity, Diabetes, Hypertension, and Cardiovascular Disease Among Adults in the United States," *Social Science & Medicine* 71, no. 5 (June 17, 2010): 1027–36, https://doi.org/10.1016/j.socscimed.2010.05.041.

17. Walker, Why We Sleep: Unlocking the Power of Sleep and Dreams.

18. Larissa C. Engert and Luciana Besedovsky, "Sleep and Inflammation: A Bidirectional Relationship," *Somnologie - Schlafforschung Und Schlafmedizin*, January 27, 2025, https://doi.org/10.1007/s11818-025-00495-6.

251

Notes

19. Jonathan Charest and Michael A. Grandner, "Sleep and Athletic Performance," *Sleep Medicine Clinics* 15, no. 1 (January 29, 2020): 41–57, https://doi.org/10.1016/j.jsmc.2019.11.005.

20. Damien Leger, Virginie Bayon, and Alice De Sanctis, "The Role of Sleep in the Regulation of Body Weight," *Molecular and Cellular Endocrinology* 418 (June 30, 2015): 101–7, https://doi.org/10.1016/j.mce.2015.06.030.

21. Kathryn R. Hesketh et al., "Activity Levels in Mothers and Their Preschool Children," *PEDIATRICS* 133, no. 4 (March 25, 2014): e973–80, https://doi.org/10.1542/peds.2013-3153.

22. Marco Fabbri, "The Mechanisms of Sleep Function and Regulation for Health and Cognitive Performance," *Brain Sciences* 13, no. 12 (December 6, 2023): 1680, https://doi.org/10.3390/brainsci13121680.

23. Faisal-Cury et al., "The Impact of Postpartum Depression and Bonding Impairment on Child Development at 12 to 15 Months After Delivery."

24. Alanna E. F. Rudzik et al., "Relationships Between Postpartum Depression, Sleep, and Infant Feeding in the Early Postpartum: An Exploratory Analysis," *Frontiers in Psychiatry* 14 (March 24, 2023), https://doi.org/10.3389/fpsyt.2023.1133386.

25. Laurent and Ablow, "The Missing Link: Mothers' Neural Response to Infant Cry Related to Infant Attachment Behaviors."

26. Sarah Oldbury and Karen Adams, "The Impact of Infant Crying on the Parent-infant Relationship," *Journal of Reproductive and Infant Psychology* (March 1, 2015), https://pubmed.ncbi.nlm.nih.gov/25812239/.

27. Laurent and Ablow, "The Missing Link: Mothers' Neural Response to Infant Cry Related to Infant Attachment Behaviors."

28. Jiarui Li et al., "Mother-child Autonomic Nervous System Interaction as an Indication of Parental Stress: 24-hour Cross Recurrence Plot Analysis.," *PubMed* 20, no. 9 (January 1, 2025): e0320175, https://doi.org/10.1371/journal.pone.0320175.

29. Laurent and Ablow, "The Missing Link: Mothers' Neural Response to Infant Cry Related to Infant Attachment Behaviors."

30. Amie M. Gordon, Belinda Carrillo, and Christopher M. Barnes, "Sleep and Social Relationships in Healthy Populations: A Systematic Review," *Sleep Medicine Reviews* 57 (January 26, 2021): 101428, https://doi.org/10.1016/j.smrv.2021.101428.

31. Brian D. Doss et al., "The Effect of the Transition to Parenthood on Relationship Quality: An 8-year Prospective Study.," *Journal of Personality and Social Psychology* 96, no. 3 (March 1, 2009): 601–19, https://doi.org/10.1037/a0013969.

32. Yoo et al., "The Human Emotional Brain Without Sleep — a Prefrontal Amygdala Disconnect."

33. Jillian Dorrian et al., "Self-regulation and Social Behavior During Sleep Deprivation," *Progress in Brain Research*, January 1, 2019, 73–110, https://doi.org/10.1016/bs.pbr.2019.03.010.

34. Bruni et al., "Executive Functions in Preschool Children With Chronic Insomnia."

35. Kannan Ramar et al., "Sleep Is Essential to Health: An American Academy of Sleep Medicine Position Statement," *Journal of Clinical Sleep Medicine* 17, no. 10 (June 21, 2021): 2115–19, https://doi.org/10.5664/jcsm.9476.

36. Mohammad A. Khan and Hamdan Al-Jahdali, "The Consequences of Sleep Deprivation on Cognitive Performance," *Neurosciences* 28, no. 2 (April 1, 2023): 91–99, https://doi.org/10.17712/nsj.2023.2.20220108.

37. JB Pritzker and Michael D. Kleinik, "Workplace Fatigue Is Nothing to Yawn At," press-release (Illinois Department of Labor, June 20, 2019), https://labor.illinois.gov/content/dam/soi/en/web/idol/news/documents/national-safety-month-fatigue-press-release.pdf.

38. Government of Canada, Canadian Centre for Occupational Health and Safety. "Fatigue," August 28, 2025. https://www.ccohs.ca/oshanswers/psychosocial/fatigue.html.

39. Michal Kahn et al., "Sleepless on the Road: Are Mothers of Infants With Insomnia at Risk for Impaired Driving?," *Journal of Sleep Research* 33, no. 4 (October 30, 2023), https://doi.org/10.1111/jsr.14083.

Chapter 6: Why Quality Baby Sleep Matters for the Rest of the Family

1. Dorrian et al., "Self-Regulation and Social Behavior During Sleep Deprivation."
2. Markus Paulus et al., "The Impact of Mother-child Interaction Quality and Cognitive Abilities on Children's Self-concept and Self-esteem," *Cognitive Development* 48 (July 31, 2018): 42–51, https://doi.org/10.1016/j.cogdev.2018.07.001.
3. Maud Edvoll et al., "The Relations Between Parent and Toddler Emotion Regulation," *Mental Health & Prevention* 30 (March 13, 2023): 200266, https://doi.org/10.1016/j.mhp.2023.200266.
4. Catrinel A. Ştefan and Ingrid Dănilă, "Pathways From Parenting Emotion Regulation, Emotion Socialization and Parenting Practices to Preschoolers' Emotion Regulation," *Early Childhood Research Quarterly* 72 (January 1, 2025): 273–83, https://doi.org/10.1016/j.ecresq.2025.04.006.
5. Walker, *Why We Sleep: Unlocking the Power of Sleep and Dreams.*

Chapter 7: Secure Attachment

1. Laura Bozicevic et al., "The Role of Maternal Sensitivity, Infant Temperament, and Emotional Context in the Development of Emotion Regulation," *Scientific Reports* 15, no. 1 (May 19, 2025), https://doi.org/10.1038/s41598-025-01714-8.
2. Vaishali Raval et al., "Maternal Attachment, Maternal Responsiveness and Infant Attachment," *Infant Behavior and Development* 24, no. 3 (March 1, 2001): 281–304, https://doi.org/10.1016/s0163-6383(01)00082-0.
3. National Institute for Health and Care Excellence (NICE), "Children's Attachment," NCBI Bookshelf, November 1, 2015, https://www.ncbi.nlm.nih.gov/books/NBK338143/.
4. R. Pasco Fearon et al., "The Significance of Insecure Attachment and Disorganization in the Development of Children's Externalizing Behavior: A Meta-Analytic Study," *Child Development* 81, no. 2 (March 1, 2010): 435–56, https://doi.org/10.1111/j.1467-8624.2009.01405.x.

5. Ashley M. Groh et al., "The Significance of Attachment Security for Children's Social Competence With Peers: A Meta-analytic Study," *Attachment & Human Development* 16, no. 2 (February 18, 2014): 103–36, https://doi.org/10.1080/14616734.2014.883636.

6. John Bowlby, *Attachment: Second Edition*, 1982.

7. Mary D. S. Ainsworth, Mary C. Blehar, Everett Waters, and Sally Wall, Patterns of Attachment: A Psychological Study of the Strange Situation (Hillsdale, NJ: Erlbaum, 1978).

8. Na Hu et al., "Associations Between Overparenting and Offspring's Mental Health: A Meta-Analysis of Multiple Moderators," *Behavioral Sciences* 15, no. 9 (September 11, 2025): 1235, https://doi.org/10.3390/bs15091235.

9. Dawei Wang et al., "The Relationship Between Overparenting and Adolescent Anxiety: The Mediating Role of Cognitive Avoidance," *International Journal of Mental Health Promotion* 26, no. 8 (January 1, 2024): 643–50, https://doi.org/10.32604/ijmhp.2024.052885.

10. Heidemarie K. Laurent and Jennifer C. Ablow, "The Missing Link: Mothers' Neural Response to Infant Cry Related to Infant Attachment Behaviors," *Infant Behavior and Development* 35, no. 4 (September 13, 2012): 761–72, https://doi.org/10.1016/j.infbeh.2012.07.007.

11. Bowlby, *Attachment: Second Edition*.

12. Laura J. Sherman, Katherine Rice, and Jude Cassidy, "Infant Capacities Related to Building Internal Working Models of Attachment Figures: A Theoretical and Empirical Review," *Developmental Review* 37 (July 13, 2015): 109–41, https://doi.org/10.1016/j.dr.2015.06.001.

13. Theodore E A Waters, Victoria L Zhu, and Glenn I Roisman, "A Secure Base Script Perspective on Attachment: Progress, Promise, and Prospects," *Advances in Child Development and Behavior*, January 1, 2025, https://doi.org/10.1016/bs.acdb.2025.07.002.

14. Dylan G. Gee and Emily M. Cohodes, "Leveraging the Developmental Neuroscience of Caregiving to Promote Resilience Among Youth Exposed to Adversity," *Development and Psychopathology* 35, no. 5 (November 6, 2023): 2168–85, https://doi.org/10.1017/s0954579423001128.

255

Notes

15. Ana Berástegui and Carlos Pitillas, "What Does It Take for Early Relationships to Remain Secure in the Face of Adversity?," *in Oxford University Press eBooks*, 2021, 271–90, https://doi.org/10.1093/oso/9780190095888.003.0016.

16. Ainsworth et al., *PATTERNS OF ATTACHMENT*.

17. A Montell, *The Age of Magical Overthinking: Notes on Modern Irrationality* Atria/One Signal Publishers, 2024).

18. Elena Bodrova and Deborah Leong, *Tools of the Mind: The Vygotskian Approach to Early Childhood Education* Pearson, 2007).

19. Kahn et al., "Behavioral Interventions for Infant Sleep Problems: The Role of Parental Cry Tolerance and Sleep-Related Cognitions."

20. Gradisar et al., "Behavioral Interventions for Infant Sleep Problems: A Randomized Controlled Trial."

21. Jodi A Mindell et al., "Behavioral Treatment of Bedtime Problems and Night Wakings in Infants and Young Children," *SLEEP*, October 1, 2006, https://doi.org/10.1093/sleep/29.10.1263.

22. Pudding, "Is Sleep Training Harmful?"

23. Gerald F. Giesbrecht et al., "Parental Use of 'Cry Out' in a Community Sample During the First Year of Infant Life," *Journal of Developmental & Behavioral Pediatrics* 41, no. 5 (February 24, 2020): 379–87, https://doi.org/10.1097/dbp.0000000000000791.

24. Grazyna Kochanska and Danming An, "The Parent's and the Child's Internal Working Models of Each Other Moderate Cascades From Child Difficulty to Socialization Outcomes: Preliminary Evidence for Dual Moderation?," *Development and Psychopathology*, February 8, 2023, 1–14, https://doi.org/10.1017/s0954579422001365.

25. Danming An, Lilly C. Bendel-Stenzel, and Grazyna Kochanska, "Negative Internal Working Models as Mechanisms That Link Mothers' and Fathers' Personality With Their Parenting: A Short-term Longitudinal Study," *Journal of Personality* 90, no. 6 (February 25, 2022): 1004–20, https://doi.org/10.1111/jopy.12711.

Chapter 8: The Gifts of Independence, Resilience, and Self-Soothing

1. Kay Donahue Jennings and Amy J Abrew, "Self-efficacy in 18-month-old Toddlers of Depressed and Nondepressed Mothers," *Journal of Applied Developmental Psychology* 25, no. 2 (March 1, 2004): 133–47, https://doi.org/10.1016/j.appdev.2004.02.001.
2. Martin E.P. Seligman, *Learned Optimism: How to Change Your Mind and Your Life* (Vintage, 2006).
3. Martin E. P. Seligman et al., "Positive Education: Positive Psychology and Classroom Interventions," *Oxford Review of Education* 35, no. 3 (May 29, 2009): 293–311, https://doi.org/10.1080/03054980902934563.
4. Carol S. Dweck, *Mindset: The New Psychology of Success* (Ballantine Books, 2007).
5. Jonathan Haidt, *The Anxious Generation: How the Great Rewiring of Childhood Is Causing an Epidemic of Mental Illness*, (Penguin Press, 2024).
6. Gradisar et al., "Behavioral Interventions for Infant Sleep Problems: A Randomized Controlled Trial," May 24, 2016.
7. Haidt, The Anxious Generation: How the Great Rewiring of Childhood Is Causing an Epidemic of Mental Illness.

Chapter 9: The Zone of Proximal Development

1. L. S. Vygotsky, *Mind in Society*, 1980, https://doi.org/10.2307/j.ctvjf9vz4.
2. Reut Shachnai et al., "Pointing Out Learning Opportunities Reduces Overparenting," *Child Development*, November 21, 2024, https://doi.org/10.1111/cdev.14198.
3. Hu et al., "Associations Between Overparenting and Offspring's Mental Health: A Meta-Analysis of Multiple Moderators."
4. Qi Zhang and Wongeun Ji, "Overparenting and Offspring Depression, Anxiety, and Internalizing Symptoms: A Meta-analysis," *Development and Psychopathology* 36, no. 3 (May 30, 2023): 1307–22, https://doi.org/10.1017/s095457942300055x.

5. J. M. Armitage, S. Collishaw, and R. Sellers, "Explaining Long-term Trends in Adolescent Emotional Problems: What We Know From Population-based Studies," *Discover Social Science and Health* 4, no. 1 (March 25, 2024), https://doi.org/10.1007/s44155-024-00076-2.

Chapter 10: Understanding Newborn Sleep

1. Alexander Thomas and Stella Chess, *Temperament and Development* (Brunner/Mazel, 1977).

2. Thomas and Chess, *Temperament and Development*.

3. Thomas and Chess, *Temperament and Development*.

4. Max Hirshkowitz et al., "National Sleep Foundation's Sleep Time Duration Recommendations: Methodology and Results Summary," *Sleep Health* 1, no. 1 (March 1, 2015): 40–43, https://doi.org/10.1016/j.sleh.2014.12.010.

5. Karp, *The Happiest Baby on the Block: The New Way to Calm Crying and Help Your Baby Sleep Longer*.

6. Hirshkowitz et al., "National Sleep Foundation's Sleep Time Duration Recommendations: Methodology and Results Summary."

7. Wong SD, Wright KP Jr, Spencer RL, Vetter C, Hicks LM, Jenni OG, LeBourgeois MK. Development of the circadian system in early life: maternal and environmental factors. *Journal of Physiological Anthropology* 2022;41(1):22. https://doi.org/10.1186/s40101-022-00294-0. PMID: 35578354; PMCID: PMC9109407.

8. Wong et al. "Development of the circadian system in early life: maternal and environmental factors."

9. Melissa M. Burnham et al., "Nighttime Sleep-wake Patterns and Self-soothing From Birth to One Year of Age: A Longitudinal Intervention Study," *Journal of Child Psychology and Psychiatry* 43, no. 6 (July 29, 2002): 713–25, https://doi.org/10.1111/1469-7610.00076.

10. "Nutrition in Infancy," in *American Academy of PediatricsItasca, IL eBooks*, 2023, https://doi.org/10.1542/9781610026628-ch16.

11. Anastasis Georgoulas et al., "Sleep–wake Regulation in Preterm and Term Infants," *SLEEP* 44, no. 1 (August 8, 2020), https://doi.org/10.1093/sleep/zsaa148.

Chapter 11: Feeding and Timing

1. Tuck Seng Cheng et al., "Predominantly Nighttime Feeding and Weight Outcomes in Infants," *American Journal of Clinical Nutrition* 104, no. 2 (July 7, 2016): 380–88, https://doi.org/10.3945/ajcn.116.130765.
2. Xiaoxi Fu et al., "Type of Milk Feeding and Introduction to Complementary Foods in Relation to Infant Sleep: A Systematic Review," *Nutrients* 13, no. 11 (November 16, 2021): 4105, https://doi.org/10.3390/nu13114105.
3. "How Often and How Much Should Your Baby Eat?," HealthyChildren.org, n.d., https://www.healthychildren.org/English/ages-stages/baby/feeding-nutrition/Pages/how-often-and-how-much-should-your-baby-eat.aspx.
4. Harvey Karp, *The Happiest Baby on the Block: The New Way to Calm Crying and Help Your Baby Sleep Longer*, 2002, http://ci.nii.ac.jp/ncid/BA85015633.
5. Natalie V. Scime et al., "Breastfeeding Difficulties in the First 6 Weeks Postpartum Among Mothers With Chronic Conditions: A Latent Class Analysis," *BMC Pregnancy and Childbirth* 23, no. 1 (February 2, 2023): 90, https://doi.org/10.1186/s12884-023-05407-w.
6. Georgoulas et al., "Sleep–Wake Regulation in Preterm and Term Infants."
7. Weissbluth, *Healthy Sleep Habits, Happy Child.*

Chapter 12: Calming Strategies and Treating Discomfort

1. Karp, The Happiest Baby on the Block: The New Way to Calm Crying and Help Your Baby Sleep Longer.
2. J Pinelli and A Symington, "Non-nutritive Sucking for Promoting Physiologic Stability and Nutrition in Preterm Infants," *Cochrane Database of Systematic Reviews*, July 23, 2001, https://doi.org/10.1002/14651858.cd001071.
3. Rita H. Pickler et al., "Effects of Nonnutritive Sucking on Behavioral Organization and Feeding Performance in Preterm Infants," *Nursing Research* 45, no. 3 (May 1, 1996): 132–35, https://doi.org/10.1097/00006199-199605000-00002.

4. S Fucile, Eg Gisel, and C Lau, "Effect of an Oral Stimulation Program on Sucking Skill Maturation of Preterm Infants," *Developmental Medicine & Child Neurology* 47, no. 3 (February 18, 2005): 158–62, https://doi.org/10.1017/s0012162205000290.

5. Thomas and Chess, Temperament and Development.

6. Tu Mai et al., "Infantile Colic," *Gastroenterology Clinics of North America* 47, no. 4 (September 28, 2018): 829–44, https://doi.org/10.1016/j.gtc.2018.07.008.

7. Judith Zeevenhooven et al., "Infant Colic: Mechanisms and Management," *Nature Reviews Gastroenterology & Hepatology* 15, no. 8 (May 14, 2018): 479–96, https://doi.org/10.1038/s41575-018-0008-7.

8. Jeaneth Indira Gonzalez Ayerbe et al., "Diagnosis and Management of Gastroesophageal Reflux Disease in Infants and Children: From Guidelines to Clinical Practice," *Pediatric Gastroenterology Hepatology & Nutrition* 22, no. 2 (January 1, 2019): 107, https://doi.org/10.5223/pghn.2019.22.2.107.

9. Jennifer Thomas et al., "Identification and Management of Ankyloglossia and Its Effect on Breastfeeding in Infants: Clinical Report," *PEDIATRICS* 154, no. 2 (July 29, 2024), https://doi.org/10.1542/peds.2024-067605.

Chapter 13: The Importance of Four Months and Teaching Independent Sleep

1. Sujay Kansagra, MD Pediatric Neurology and Sleep Medicine Interview, June 18, 2025.

2. Wong et al. "Development of the circadian system in early life: maternal and environmental factors."

3. Burnham et al., "Nighttime Sleep-wake Patterns and Self-soothing From Birth to One Year of Age: A Longitudinal Intervention Study."

Chapter 14: The 10-Minute Method

1. Michelle Zimmer et al., "Sensory Integration Therapies for Children With Developmental and Behavioral Disorders," *PEDIATRICS* 129, no. 6 (May 29, 2012): 1186–89, https://doi.org/10.1542/peds.2012-0876.
2. Bruni et al Longitudinal Study of Sleep Behavior in Normal Infants During the First Year of Life

Chapter 20: Nap Trapped: When Sacrifice Backfires

1. Morgan Cutlip, PhD, Maternal Burnout Interview, July 31, 2025.
2. Morgan Cutlip, *A Better Share: How Couples Can Tackle the Mental Load for More Fun, Less Resentment, and Great Sex* (Thomas Nelson, 2026).
3. Doss et al., "The Effect of the Transition to Parenthood on Relationship Quality: An 8-Year Prospective Study."
4. Michael H. Walter, Harald Abele, and Claudia F. Plappert, "The Role of Oxytocin and the Effect of Stress During Childbirth: Neurobiological Basics and Implications for Mother and Child," Frontiers in Endocrinology 12 (October 27, 2021), https://doi.org/10.3389/fendo.2021.742236.
5. C M Meston and P F Frohlich, "The Neurobiology of Sexual Function," *Archives of General Psychiatry* 57, no. 11 (November 1, 2000): 1012, https://doi.org/10.1001/archpsyc.57.11.1012.
6. Mengya Xia et al., "A Developmental Perspective on Young Adult Romantic Relationships: Examining Family and Individual Factors in Adolescence," *Journal of Youth and Adolescence* 47, no. 7 (February 13, 2018): 1499–1516, https://doi.org/10.1007/s10964-018-0815-8.
7. Cutlip, *A Better Share: How Couples Can Tackle the Mental Load for More Fun, Less Resentment, and Great Sex.*

Index

Numerics

1 nap schedule (14 months old), 195
2 nap schedule (7 months old), 194
3 nap schedule (5 months old), 194
4 nap schedule (4 months old), 194
4 months and teaching independent sleep,
  127–134
10-minute approach, 180–182, 237
10-minute timers, 138
  self-soothing behaviors, 140–141
  soothing baby between timers,
    141–143
  variability in crying, 138
18 hours of sleep, newborns, 86

A

AAP. See American Association of
  Pediatrics (AAP)
accelerated approach, sleep
  training, 178–180
acid reflux, 119–121
adequate sleep, 33–34
Advanced Behavioral Sleep Medicine, 7
Ainsworth, Mary, 58
American Association of Pediatrics
  (AAP), 94
amygdala, 45
anti-CIO voices, 24
anti-sleep training, 42
anxiety-relieving chemicals, 214
anxious attachment, 59
The Anxious Generation (Haidt), 72
anxious mothers, 46, 47
arching back, head and neck, 120
asleep
  "at least one hour asleep", 104
  fall/falling asleep. See fall/falling asleep
A+ sleeper, 134

"at least one hour asleep", 104
attachment, 58
  anxious, 59
  bond, 52, 61
  secure, 59–61
    and sleep training, 65–67
attachment theory, 58–59
authoritative parenting, xvi
awake
  "drowsy but awake", 106
  middle-of-the-night, 134
  nighttime, 33, 38, 128, 131, 163, 167, 168,
    204, 211, 239
  "one hour awake", 104
  overnight, 150
awake windows, 78, 90, 103, 104, 107, 113,
  158, 187, 199–200

B

baby down drowsy, 89
"baby sleep consultants", 14
baby sleep patterns shift, 127
bad parenting, 10, 13
bad rap, sleep training, 17–19, 66, 149
baths, 21, 60, 137
Bayley Scales of Infant Development, 38
bedtime, 197–198
  newborns, 104
  routine, 136–137
  snapshot for, 136
behaviors
  antisocial, 23
  everyday, 58
  overparenting, 79, 80
  self-soothing, 140–141, 148
  toddler, 51–52
A Better Share (Cutlip), 217
bias, conformity, 13

blissful sleep, 101
bond/bonding
    attachment, 52, 61
    mother-infant, 46–47
    parent-child, 35
Booty pat, 113
Bowlby, John, Dr., 58
brain
    balance, 45
    development, 38
    emotional "survival brain", 171
    emotion centers, 33, 35
    emotion systems, 33–34
    maturation and plasticity, 37
breastfeeding, 97, 117
breastmilk, 89, 98, 99
burping, 117, 120

C
calming
    newborn sleep, 90
    strategies, 109–113
caloric intake, 33, 89, 165
caregivers, 35
    soothing with, 141–143
chart, feeding, 94
chiropractic care, 121, 122
chronic stress, 22
CIO. See cry it out (CIO)
circadian rhythm, 41, 87, 103
cognitive effects, of sleep deprivation, 50
cognitive functioning, job performance
    and, 49–50
cognitive performance, and mental
    development, 38
conformity bias, 13
co-regulation, 47
    emotional, 36
cortisol (stress hormone), 22, 24, 27–28,
    45, 74, 101, 137
co-sleeping, 185, 189
cottage cheese consistency, acid reflux, 120
craniosacral therapy, 121, 122
crib, as developmental playground, 161
crying, 20–22
    burps followed by, 120
    "The Effects of Excessive Crying", 20
    excessive, 20, 23
    persistent, 23
    variability in, 138

cry it out (CIO), 18, 24, 27, 28, 95,
    176, 185, 239
    anti-CIO voices, 24
    cortisol as raised during periods of, 74
    criticism of, 172–173
Cutlip, Morgan, Dr., 208, 218

D
dark quiet room, 195
day/night confusion, 87
daytime sleep, 87–88
deep sleep, 32–33
depressed mothers, 46, 47
depression
    maternal overwhelm and, 36
    report, postpartum, 35–36
deprivation, sleep, 33
developmental psychology, 3
discomfort
    food intolerances, 123–124
    gas, 116–119
    oral ties, 121–122
    sources of, 115–116
    stress and, 21
    treating, 114–116
        newborn sleep, 90
    while feeding, 120
disrupt sleep, 38
    factors for, 201–202
dopamine, 45, 214
dozy feeds, prevent, 94–95
dropping naps, 198–199
"drowsy but awake", 106

E
easy temperament, 85, 89
"The Effects of Excessive Crying", 20
emotional co-regulation, 36
emotional damage, sleep training
    causes, 23–24
emotional development, 33–35
"emotional implications of excessive
    crying", 23
emotionally regulated toddler, 53–54
emotional "survival brain", 171
emotion centers, brain, 33, 35
emotion system, brain, 33–34
empathetic responding, 35
empathy, social relations and, 36
esophageal sphincter, 119, 121

excessive crying, 20, 23
executive function development, 37–38
exhausted mothers, 46

F
fall/falling asleep, 18, 66, 73, 75, 76, 81, 97,
    103, 129, 131, 134–136, 143–144,
    147, 154–157, 160, 161, 163, 179,
    185, 198, 205, 236
  cry before, 25, 28, 185
  improvement in, 160
  independently, 4, 76, 81, 106, 128, 131,
    132, 140, 149, 163, 170
    for bedtime and naptime, 148, 163
  with minimal intervention, 89
  protest, 65
  during that last feeding, 137
fatigue
  effects of, 49
  feeding, 98, 122
feeding, 93–94
  chart, 94
  discomfort while, 120
  dropping last, 171–172
  ensure a good latch, 97–98
  falls asleep during that last, 137
  fatigue, 98, 122
  foremilk vs hindmilk, 99
  full, 89, 93, 98, 110, 122, 124,
    132, 168, 178
  Kary recommend, 99
  middle-of-the-night, 165
  newborn sleep, 89
  prevent dozy feeds, 94–95
  recognize the signs, 95–97
  Solid Starts, 95–96, 99
  swallowing air, 99–100
feeds, decrease, 167
FOMO babies, 54, 102, 160
food intolerances, 123–124
foremilk, 99
  vs hindmilk, 99
fostering independence, 69
"four-month sleep regression", 127
fourth trimester, 94
Franke, Ruby, 14–15
friendship, maintaining, 215
full feeding, 89, 93, 98, 110, 122, 124,
    132, 168, 178
full-hand clockwise massage, 118

"functional health coaches", 14
fussiness, 99

G
gassiness, 99
gas, treating discomfort, 116–119
"gentle" no-cry approach, 169
ghrelin, 33
"giving up" phenomenon, 24
'good-enough' parenting, 22, 48
good sleep, 11, 17, 38, 41–43, 50, 66, 143,
    146, 186, 195, 221
  foundation, 34, 85, 89, 178
  impacts babies cognitive
    development, 37
  language development, 37
  physical health, 43–44
gradual/"no-cry" approach, sleep training,
    184–189
gradual step-down approach, 188
great sleep, xvi, xvii, 3–4, 35, 38, 41, 49, 54,
    85, 91, 93, 184
green stools, 99
grounding criteria, 26
growth stagnation, overparenting, 79

H
Haidt, Jonathan, 72, 74
The Happiest Baby on the Block
    (Karp), 110
"happy spitters", 119
health, metabolic, 33
healthy hierarchy, 209
hindmilk, 99
  vs foremilk, 99
hormone
  balance, 45
  sleep affects, 33
  stress, 21, 22, 24, 27–28, 45, 74,
    101, 137
hunger, 33, 43, 93, 94, 96, 131, 134,
    141, 150, 202

I
"I love you" massage, 118
immune function
  physical health and, 32–33
  sleep and, 32–33
immune system, 33, 43, 62, 72–73
independence in babies, 69–72

independent sleep, 129–134
    initiation, 176–178
        accelerated approach, 178–180
        gradual/"no-cry" approach, 184–189
        modified-accelerated (10-minute
            method), 180–182
        modified-modified approach, 182–184
infant chiropractic care, 121
infant soothing, sixth S for, 110
    shushing, 112
    side positioning, 112
    stroking, 113
    sucking, 110–111
    swaddling, 111–112
    swinging, 112–113
inherently selfish, 42
insufficient sleep, 38, 43
insurance, marriage, 215–216
intellectual development, 37–39
intense sleep pressure, 95
internal working model, 60
intimacy, parenthood, 214

J
job performance, and cognitive
        functioning, 49–50

K
Kansagra, Sujay, Dr., 31–32, 127, 128
Kapoor, Radhika, Dr., 122–123
Karp, Harvey, Dr., 110
Kary recommend feeding, 99

L
lactation consultant, 97, 100, 122, 123
language development, 37
last feeding, dropping, 171–172
learning
    framework for, 145–146
    opportunity, overparenting, 79
leptin, decreased levels of, 33
living room, 87, 137, 154
London's sleep log, 232

M
Maddie's sleep log, 230
magic burp, 117
marriage insurance, 215–216
massage, 114
    belly, 118

full-hand clockwise, 118
"I love you" massage, 118
quick, 137
"maternal gatekeeping", 217–218
maternal overwhelm, and depression, 36
melatonin, 101
memory consolidation, 37
mental development, 38
    cognitive performance and, 38
mental health, 6, 34
    quality of sleep affects, 44–46
metabolic health, and weight
        management, 33
middle-of-the-night awakenings, 134
middle-of-the-night feeding, 165
middle-of-the-night timers, 171
Mindell, Jodi A., Dr., 26–27
    grounding criteria, 26
    relevance criteria, 26
modified-accelerated (10-minute method)
        approach, sleep training,
        180–182
modified-cry version, 228
modified-modified approach, sleep
        training, 182–184
moralization, in parenting, 10
mother-infant bonding, quality of sleep
        affects, 46–47
mothers
    anxious, 46, 47
    depressed, 46, 47
    exhausted, 46
    sleep-deprived, 50

N
nap
    1 nap schedule (14 months old), 195
    2 nap schedule (7 months old), 194
    3 nap schedule (5 months old), 194
    4 nap schedule (4 months old), 194
    dropping, 198–199
    lengthening, 155–160
    training, 160
naptime
    routine, 154
    snapshot for, 153–154
    timers and soothing, 154
Narvaez, Darcia, Dr., 26
neglect, sleep training as form of, 24–28
neurodivergence, 185
neurotransmitters, 45

newborns
    18 hours of sleep, 86
    Achilles' heel, 101–102
    bedtime, 104
    brand-new, 86
newborn sleep, 85–91
    calming, 90
    feeding, 89
    orienting day and night, 87–88
    self-soothing, 88–91
    sleep needs, 86–87
    timing, 90
    treating discomfort, 90
night awakenings, 33, 38, 128, 131, 163,
        167–168, 188, 189, 203,
        204, 211, 239
nighttime duty, 211
nighttime sleep, 88, 163–173
"no-cry" approach, 169, 182, 184–189, 228
non-sleep-trained babies, 74
norepinephrine, 214

O
"one hour awake", 104
optimal sleep, 50
    foundation, 133
optimal well-being, 41
oral ties, 121–122
orphanage, Romanian, 25
overnight, 149–151
overparenting, 59, 79–81
    "buy-in", 79
    behaviors, 79, 80
    growth stagnation, 79
    learning opportunity, 79
overstimulation, 101–102, 115, 137
overtiredness, preventing, 101–103

P
parental stress, 10
parent-child bond, 35
parenthood, pressure points in, 210
    division of labor, 210–211
    intimacy, 214
    keeping score, 211–212
    nighttime duty, 211
parenting, 9–10, 14, 28
    authoritative, xiv
    bad, 10, 13
    'good-cnough', 22, 48
    moralization in, 10

philosophy, 224–225
    snowplow, 59
    with social media, 12–13
parents' relationship, 47–49
Pediatric Neurology Sleep Medicine
        Program, 31–32
peer-reviewed studies, 11
persistent crying, 23
physical development, 32
physical health
    and immune function, 32–33
    quality of sleep affects, 43–44
plasticity, brain maturation and, 37
poor sleep, 23, 33–35
    cumulative effects of, 43
    quality, 34
    trickle-down effect of, 44
postpartum depression report, 35–36
"postpartum fitness trainers", 14
potty-trained children, 70
pressure points in parenthood, 210
    division of labor, 210–211
    intimacy, 214
    keeping score, 211–212
    nighttime duty, 211
productive stress, 21
prolonged periods, stress hormones for, 21
"proprietary recipe", 14
proximal development, zone of, 77–81
psychology, developmental, 3

Q
quality of sleep, 42–43, 49
    affects
        mental health, 44–46
        mother-infant bonding, 46–47
        physical health, 43–44
quality sleep, 3, 6, 14, 17, 31, 34, 38, 39,
        41–43, 54, 80, 81, 89, 173
    impacts hormone balance and weight
        control, 43
quick massage, 137
quiet room, dark, 195

R
Rappaport, Kary, 95–97, 123
    recommend feeding, 99
reflux
    acid, 119–121
    silent, 120
relationships, sleep as keystone for, 209–210

relevance criteria, 26
REM sleep, 44, 45, 113
resilience in babies, 72–73
resting tongue position matters, 122
restorative sleep, 35, 66, 81, 127,
        128, 198
rhythm, circadian, 41, 87, 103
Romanian orphanage, 25
room
    dark quiet, 195
    living, 87, 137, 154
    wiggle, 195, 196

S
schedule
    consistent, 195–196
    nap. See nap
    sample, 193–195
    timing, 103–108
Sears, Bill, Dr., 20–23, 26
secure attachment, 60–61
    and sleep training, 65–67
Seery, Mark, Dr., 21
self-care, 129–130, 216–217
self-efficacy, 70, 73
self-esteem, 6, 52, 70, 73
selfish
    inherently, 42
    of parent, 17
self-soothing, 24, 74–76, 88–91
    in babies, 74–76
    behaviors, 140–141
    not capable of, 185
sensory needs, 123–124
serotonin (happy chemicals), 45, 214
sexual response cycle, 214
shushing, 112
side positioning, 112
silent reflux, 120
skim milk, 99
sleep anchors, 196–197
sleep architecture, 4–6
"Sleep begets sleep", 101
sleep consultant, 224
sleep cycle, 4, 5, 106, 113, 129, 131, 135,
        155, 163, 170
    transition, 4, 6, 66, 128, 131, 149, 150,
        153, 172, 203, 237
sleep deprivation, 33–34, 41, 49
    cognitive effects of, 50
sleep-deprived mothers, 50

sleep initiation, independent, 176–178
    accelerated approach, 178–180
    gradual/"no-cry" approach,
        184–189
    modified-accelerated (10-minute
        method), 180–182
    modified-modified approach, 182–184
sleep log, 227–233
sleep needs, 31, 86–87
sleep pressure, intense, 95
sleep quality. See quality of sleep;
        quality sleep
sleep regressions, 205–206
sleep resets, 35
sleep timers, 224
sleep times, syncing, 101
sleep-trained babies, 67, 74, 146,
        172, 205–206
sleep training, 3–4, 14, 17–19, 54, 57,
        62, 73, 132
    approach selection, 223–225
    bad rap, 17–19, 66, 149
    causes emotional damage, 23–24
    on childhood outcomes, 28
    criticism of, 172
    as form of neglect, 24–28
    long-term implications, 28
    myths about
        crying and/or stress is harmful to
            babies, 20–22
        separation from parents is
            harmful, 22–23
        sleep training causes emotional
            damage, 23–24
        sleep training is a form of
            neglect, 24–28
    pillars of, 132–133
    secure attachment and, 65–67
    setting timers during, 146
        allow for struggle, 146
        ensure calm and safety, 146–147
        intervene mindfully, 147
        try again, 147–149
    sleep after, 201–206
    timeline, 224
    twins, 235–239
sleep well, xiii, xiv, 7, 38, 124
sleepy cues, 107–108
    vs tired cues, 108
snowplow parenting, 59
social development, 35–36

social media, 11, 18
    parenting with, 12–13
social relations and empathy, 36
societal pressures, 10
Solid Starts feeding, 95–96, 99
soothing
    with caregiver support, 141–143
    self-soothing, 24, 74–76, 88–91
        behaviors, 140–141
        not capable of, 185
    sixth S for infant, 110
        shushing, 112
        side positioning, 112
        stroking, 113
        sucking, 110–111
        swaddling, 111–112
        swinging, 112–113
stinky breath and sour spit up, acid
        reflux, 120
stools, green, 99
"The Strange Situation" experiment,
        58, 61–62
stress
    chronic, 22
    and discomfort, 21
    parental, 10
    productive and nonproductive, 21
stress hormone (cortisol), 21, 22, 24,
        27–28, 45, 74, 101, 137
stroking, 113
sufficient sleep, 43, 47
"survival brain", emotional, 171
swaddling, 111–112
swallowing air, feeding, 99–100
swinging, 112–113
syncing sleep times, 101

T
teething, 204
testosterone, 214
timers
    adjust, 167
    middle-of-the-night, 171
    set during sleep training, 146
        allow for struggle, 146
        ensure calm and safety, 146–147
        intervene mindfully, 147
        try again, 147–149
    and soothing, naptime, 154

timing, 100
    newborn sleep, 90
    preventing overtiredness, 101–103
    schedule, 103–108
tired cues, 107–108
    vs sleepy cues, 108
toddlers
    attachment bond, 52
    behavior, 51–52
    emotionally regulated, 53–54
    FOMO, 54
    social relations and empathy, 36
    well-rested babies and, 36
tongue position matters, 122
"too much sleep", 87
transition, sleep cycle, 4, 6, 66, 128,
        131, 149, 150, 153, 172,
        203, 237
tricky babies, 169–171
twins, sleep training, 235–239

U
United States Surgeon General, parental
        stress, 10

V
vagus nerve, tongue position, 122
Valliant, Tom, 19
voices, anti-CIO, 24
Vygotsky, Lev, 77

W
wake-up time, 236
    acceptable, 197
    consistent, 103, 196
    later, 197
    morning, 197
weight management, metabolic
        health and, 33
Weissbluth, Marc, Dr., 101
well-being
    optimal, 41
    sleep as cornerstone of, 6–8
well-rested babies, 35–37, 67
wiggle room, 195, 196

Z
zone of proximal development, 77–81

Index

Ready for better sleep?
More rest. More confidence.
More connection.

Find the sleep resources that help your family thrive.

Visit ThePeacefulSleeper.com for access to:

-courses
-assessments
-consultations
-community
-live coaching
-articles
-media

Your family's well-being is well worth it.
Let us help.

ThePeacefulSleeper.com